SOAR: A COGNITIVE ARCHITECTURE IN PERSPECTIVE

STUDIES IN COGNITIVE SYSTEMS

VOLUME 10

The titles published in this series are listed at the end of this volume.

SOAR: A COGNITIVE ARCHITECTURE IN PERSPECTIVE

A Tribute to Allen Newell

Edited by

JOHN A. MICHON

and

ALADIN AKYÜREK

Department of Psychology,
University of Groningen, Groningen, The Netherlands

SPRINGER SCIENCE+BUSINESS MEDIA, B.V.

ISBN 978-94-010-5070-8 ISBN 978-94-011-2426-3 (eBook)
DOI 10.1007/978-94-011-2426-3

ALLEN NEWELL

SERIES PREFACE

This series will include monographs and collections of studies devoted to the investigation and exploration of knowledge, information, and data-processing systems of all kinds, no matter whether human, (other) animal, or machine. Its scope is intended to span the full range of interest from classical problems in the philosophy of mind and philosophical psychology through issues in cognitive psychology and sociobiology (concerning the mental powers of other species) to ideas related to artificial intelligence and computer science. While primary emphasis will be placed upon theoretical, conceptual, and epistemological aspects of these problems and domains, empirical, experimental, and methodological studies will also appear from time to time.

The present volume counts both as a tribute to Allen Newell, one of the most important theoreticians in AI today, and as a contribution toward the development of SOAR, one of the most promising cognitive architectures AI has produced. SOAR incorporates and elaborates several of the fundamental themes that have characterized Newell's work, including the symbol system conception and the problem space hypothesis. In Newell's view, a cognitive architecture such as SOAR affords the foundation for a unified theory of cognition by supplying the hardware capability essential to the success of various software programs intended to simulate cognitive abilities. The studies collected here offer persuasive evidence of the brilliance of this endeavor.

J. H. F.

CONTENTS

ACKNOWLEDGEMENTS

The Study Contract with IBM Nederland NV provided the necessary and much appreciated support without which we would never have succeeded in bootstrapping our Soar work. Under this contract two RT 6150 workstations were made available to the Groningen Soar Research Group, and to a large extent the present book reflects the way we fulfilled our part of the contract. We regret that circumstances have made it impossible to continue the cooperation beyond the terms of the original contract.

We particularly like to acknowledge the efforts and support of Janet L. Jackson and Corine Claveaux. Finally, we wish to express our gratitude to Simon Ross, Editor Cognitive Sciences at Kluwer Academic Publishers for his support, and to the reviewer whose suggestions and criticism were indispensable in improving the contributions in this book.

"Knowledge Level and Inductive Uses of Chunking (EBL)," by Paul S. Rosenbloom and Jans Aasman, was first published in *Proceedings of the Eight National Conference on Artificial Intelligence*, pp. 821-827. Copyright © 1990 American Association for Artificial Intelligence. It is reprinted here by kind permission of the American Association for Artificial Intelligence.

"Basic References for Soar," contains a reading list compiled by the Soar Group at Carnegie Mellon University. It is reproduced here by kind permission of the Soar Group.

The activities of the Soar Research Group are incorporated in the program of the Groningen Center for Behavioral, Cognitive, and Neurosciences (BCN).

INTRODUCTION

JOHN A. MICHON, ALADIN AKYÜREK
AND THE GRONINGEN SOAR RESEARCH GROUP
University of Groningen, Groningen, The Netherlands

The contributions to this book present our perspective on Soar, and as such they are our tribute to Allen Newell on the occasion of his 65th birthday. Except for the one by Newell, the various papers derive, directly or indirectly, from the work of the Soar Research Group which was established at the University of Groningen in The Netherlands in the fall of 1987.

Soar in Groningen

The involvement of the University of Groningen in Soar had started the year before. During the year 1986-1987 the senior author had been able to spend a sabbatical leave as visiting professor of psychology at Carnegie Mellon University. This visit served two purposes in particular. The first was to develop a production-based model of the road user, more specifically the automobile driver (Michon, 1985a, 1987; Michon & McLoughlin, 1991) and, second, to establish a comprehensive model for the representation of temporal relations in cognition and behavior (Michon, 1985b, 1990). The idea was initially to use ACT* (Anderson, 1983) as the vehicle for implementing these two models, but almost immediately upon arrival in Pittsburgh it became evident that the thing to really take a close look at was Soar. Like ACT* Soar could pass more or less for a general theory of human cognition, but unlike ACT* Soar had reached the level of integrated implementation; Soar was up and working and actually did some of the things that ACT* had only stimulated one to think about.

Allen Newell, at the time, did not feel traffic to be a "sufficiently well-defined task." Of course Michon had to agree, but on the other hand he felt that, if Newell claimed that Soar was a sufficiently well-defined model archi-

J. A. Michon and A. Akyürek (eds.), Soar: A Cognitive Architecture in Perspective, 1–10.

tecture, rethinking road user behavior in the context of Soar might in fact provide just the level of definition that Newell demanded.

Thus Michon had an opportunity to get acquainted with Soar in sufficient depth to, subsequently, introduce it in Groningen, but he wishes to emphasize that he would not have succeeded but for the indispensable and much appreciated cooperation of Jans Aasman who, on leave from the Traffic Research Center, joined him at CMU in the spring of 1987 and who picked up the essence of Soar programming in an incredibly short time span.

Soar: A Cognitive Architecture in Perspective reflects the research efforts of the Groningen Soar Research Group over the past three years. Understandably it deals with the two topics—road user behavior and temporal organization of behavior—that precipitated our interest in Soar in the first place. It should transpire to the reader, however, that we have gone beyond using Soar as just a convenient medium for modeling human cognitive activity. Of course, as a natural consequence of good applied research, it did not take us long to become engaged in some rather more fundamental issues that guide (and frequently bother) the Soar research community. These issues have confronted us with the very nature and consistency of Soar as an intelligent architecture. As a result the reader will learn about the operator implementation problem, chunking, multitasking, the need to constrain the depth of the goal stack, and induction. These are fundamental issues that we subjected to close scrutiny in the past three years.

The Soar Community in Perspective

Until 1986 the development of Soar took place in the relative privacy of the offices of the architecture's *auctores intellectuales,* Allen Newell, John E. Laird, and Paul S. Rosenbloom. It came out in the open particularly through a seminal paper by Laird, Newell, and Rosenbloom in *Artificial Intelligence* (Laird, Newell, Rosenbloom, 1987) and two reports by Waldrop (1988a, b) in *Science.* Since then the interest in Soar has been growing at a moderate but persistent rate. In the United States there are presently about 20 different locations working with Soar, in Europe perhaps half that number, mostly still on a comparatively small scale. A list compiled about a year ago shows major research sites:

United States

Carnegie Mellon University
University of Michigan
University of Southern California
Ohio State University

Europe

University of Groningen
MRC Applied Psychology Unit
University of Nottingham

The Groningen Soar Research Group constitutes a comparatively large center of Soar activities in Europe—together with the groups in Cambridge and Nottingham. The group has built a substantial international position both in size and quality of research, a position that is reflected by this volume.

Given the state of flux that is characteristic of Soar in its present stage of development, this picture may change quickly and drastically. In late August 1991 Soar as a software system was transferred to the public domain, allowing many more research groups all over the world unrestrained access to the architecture. This will, no doubt, accelerate the further spreading of Soar, as will a future release (i.e., Soar6) that will be C-based and that also promises a much improved interface with the researcher.

The Significance of Soar

Soar is still in a relatively early stage of development. We should realize, however, that it does constitute an important breakthrough in the area of computer architectures for general intelligence. Soar will guide the direction that future efforts to build intelligent systems must take towards a comprehensive, psychologically meaningful, theory of cognition. This is argued in a powerful way by Newell in his contribution to this volume. For this reason, the Soar system will probably play an important, integrative role within cognitive science in bringing together important subdomains of psychology, computer science, linguistics, and the neurosciences. Although Soar is not the only architecture for intelligence, it is one of the most advanced and theoretically best motivated architectures presently available.

Those who have been involved in Soar before will recognize that in the Soar context there is a constant unifying pressure towards putting it all together. Allen Newell first used this expression as the title of a paper at a symposium in honor of Herbert Simon (Newell, 1989a), then added a poetic postscript under the title "How it all got put together" (Newell, 1989b), and one of the papers at the Tutorial Workshop organized by the Groningen Soar Research Group in 1989 was again entitled "Putting it all together." One might therefore begin to suspect that, perhaps, this pretentious title is hiding the fact that we are unable to put it all together. Despite such doubts it appears to us that the significance of Soar as a *unified theory of cognition* resides in its capability of putting together a lot of features, such as the following five, that are particularly significant from the psychological perspective. If those concerned with Soar as an intelligent architecture would abandon this perspective, Soar would become just another achievement of artificial intelligence: still impressive but hardly exciting. This, in a nutshell, reflects our perspective on Soar as a cognitive architecture.

(1) Soar appears to cover the full range of behavior from the communication between single neuron (in the millisecond range) to the symbolic interaction between civilizations (in the century range). These two extremes are separated by a number of levels, or bands, including the cognitive band and the rational band. The ways in which processes at one level are related to the processes at another are well specified. So is the process of symbol access and reference that defines the way in which components at one level communicate with the other components at the same level. Particularly interesting in this context, is Newell's claim that there is not enough room to insert an extra system level between the neural and the cognitive band: there appears to be simply no place for the connectionist's subsymbolic level.

(2) Some of the most interesting issues in modern philosophy of mind pertain to the distinction between levels of description. In recent years we have had a number of proposals, including the well known three stances proposed by Dennett, the four levels proposed by Pylyshyn, and the six levels proposed earlier by Newell. Much as one tends to become fascinated by the arguments that various authors have put forward in favor of such levels, it appears that only Soar is explicit about what is actually going on at each level, and about the ways in which they relate.

(3) A third interesting point is the potential that Soar seems to have for dealing with the problem of intentionality, and more specifically the propensity for rapid shifts in semantic context (also known as set or *Einstellungseffekt* and as *Aha-Erlebnis*). One of the strongest features of human intelligence, it seems, is our ability to vacillate between our points of view instantly, if that helps us to solve a particular problem (Goodman, 1984). It turns

paper weights into hammers and match boxes into candelabras. Soar, it seems, has just this flexibility of mind: if one problem representation does not work Soar will find itself another problem space to work in. The power to deal autonomously with multiple problem spaces is certainly one of the greatest assets of Soar.

(4) Fourth, one should welcome the explicit presentation of Soar as an approximate theory, especially if one happens to be a psychologist. The conventional paradigm of experimental psychology was already been attacked by Newell in a famous paper entitled "You can't play twenty questions with nature and win" (Newell, 1973), but at last Soar allows us to take his criticism in a positive way: a theory, such as Soar, that gives a reasonable account of a large number of known facts, is imposing more constraints on the class of candidate general models of cognition than would even a very large number of conventional experiments. This reflects the important distinction between top-down and bottom-up theory building, one that has created Copernican revolutions in science more than once.

(5) Finally Soar takes a quite explicit stance with respect to the issue of the macro-structure of the human mind. On the scale that runs from extreme modularity to extreme uniformity Soar definitely sides with the uniformists. Yet modularity, understood in a special sense of the word—namely as the prevalence of well established default problem spaces, that deal with certain fundamental, say innate, functions—is not beyond the inherent potential of Soar. Similarly, on the scale that runs from extreme connectionism to extreme computationalism Soar definitely sides with those who prefer to take a reasonable position. Soar's liberal treatment of the implementation issue, plus its intrinsic parallelism, seem to put some of the more extravagant claims of connectionists into perspective.

The Contents of the Book

We will now introduce each of the following papers by putting it into the perspective just outlined. Authors and editors have made a genuine effort to make their contributions as self-contained as possible. Soar, however, is a fairly recent addition to the repertoire of intelligent architectures. Discussions with a variety of—highly intelligent and perceptive—colleagues have made it clear to us that, to date, the accessibility of Soar leaves something to be desired. We wish to point out, therefore, that there is now an authorized list of recommended readings which are considered to be the required basis for those who want to become informed about Soar. To assist the reader we have added this list at the end of this book as it will help readers to find their way into the ramifications of Soar.

Allen Newell: A Portrait, by John A. Michon, is essentially an artist's impression of the man and the scientist to whom this book is a tribute. It sketches some facts of life, and some of the main themes in Newell's work as they have developed in the course of the past 35 years. The paper was originally written as a kudos for Newell when, on 16 June 1989, he received a doctorate *honoris causa* in the Behavioral and Social Sciences from the University of Groningen.

Then follows a major background paper by Allen Newell: Unified Theories of Cognition: The Role of Soar. This is essentially an expanded version of the lecture presented by the young doctor upon the acceptance of the honorary degree in Groningen. It presents a wide-angle perspective on Soar, thus setting the stage for a good many of the issues that return in the later papers of the book, and putting them in the context of the overarching concept of *unified theories of cognition.* Specifically Newell's contribution succeeds in showing how 30 years of cognitive science seem now to be converging on the pressing need for a theory that is capable of integrating the 3000 or so 'robust facts' about human behavior and that, at the same time, succeeds in generating high-novelty predictions. Whilst Newell argues that Soar is not the only, or even the first contender for the status of unified theory of cognition, he does in fact claim that Soar has set a qualifying threshold of theoretical competence that contenders must clear before they can compete with Soar in a meaningful way.

The first of two papers by Aladin Akyürek is called On a Computational Model of Human Planning. Planning is presented as a predominantly adaptive, situation-controlled activity. Plans are retrieved on the basis of episodic information and adapted to the required use. This process of retrieving and adapting is similar to Schank's reminding and tweaking procedures. The way in which it can be mapped onto the Soar architecture is considered. This analysis brings out several quite important issues that need to be solved if Soar is to deal with planning over time in a 'natural' way. That is, without a need for ad hoc additional mechanisms.

The second paper by Aladin Akyürek under the title Means-Ends Planning: An Example Soar System, is related to the preceding paper. Soar responds to impasses that naturally arise during problem solving by universal subgoaling.

That is, subgoals are created automatically by the architecture itself in a task-independent manner. Whereas there are several reasons why such impasses can occur, one of them, the so-called 'operator no-change' impasse, is of particular interest. It leads to a strategy known as operator subgoaling, an important weak method which is intimately related to means-ends analysis. Although the Soar architecture is intended to cover the full range of problem solving methods, earlier attempts to add the heuristic of means-ends analysis to its repertoire of methods have not been particularly successful or convincing. The paper presents a Soar system that successfully integrates a difference reduction scheme with operator subgoaling to jointly embody the means-ends heuristic. The system provides a general scheme that can be used in modeling task performance in dynamic environments requiring interaction such as text editing or file manipulation on computers. In the course of building the system, two major results are obtained. First, Soar is shown to acquire novel procedures, called macrochunks, which are posited to be involved in routine behavior such as driving. Second, a nasty problem has been discovered that points to an 'error' in the architecture. It is shown that the mechanism involved here causes Soar to generate unintended actions, which are undesirable both for internal problem solving and for interacting with external world. Whilst the author's system effectively catches this error, a proposal is also made to modify the architecture itself to solve the problem. A special feature of this paper is its Appendix, which contains the complete listing of the planner system that will allow a robot to deal with a box-moving task. The Groningen Soar Research Group will supply readers with the program upon request.

Multitasking in Driving is the title of a paper by Aasman and Michon. It reflects what is perhaps the original motivation behind the efforts of the Groningen Soar Research Group: the construction of a general model of the automobile driver. The paper stipulates the multifarious nature of the driving task which requires drivers to keep track of several cognitive activities at the same time. This is illustrative of the special interaction humans have with the dynamic world around them: people are capable of engaging in more than one task simultaneously. Soar, in its current implementation, has great difficulty in dealing with 'multitasking,' especially in dynamic environments. This is the so-called 'real time' or 'interrupt' problem. For example, when an immediate action is required while in a subgoal trying to resolve some impasse, the current goal stack will be interrupted and, as a result, lost. After the interruption is over, that goal stack will have to be rebuilt. Compared to people in similar situations, Soar needs more time to return to where it was before the interruption. The proposed solution makes use of a process manager space, a special, high level, problem space that allows the agent to time-switch between tasks requiring attention. This functions by generating frames that will admit any suitable context in which it is possible to perform a required action. Switching may be controlled internally or externally and a series of rather basic issues pertinent to the Soar architecture result from the analysis of the required interrupt-handling procedures. A point of interest to note is that the notion of multitasking as advanced here seems to be relevant to the long-term structure that Newell posits, in his paper, to hold "content goals."

More or less related is the following contribution by Aasman and Akyürek entitled Flattening Goal Hierarchies. The problem they tackle is the psychologically rather unconvincing property of Soar to increase the depth of its goal stack indefinitely if the task environment creates one impasse after the other. In its present form, therefore, Soar appears too powerful as an approximation of human cognition, an outcome of Soar's default rules that arrange for uninformed or heuristic search, such as generate-and-test. These rules become active whenever the architecture sets up a subgoal for resolving a 'tie impasse.' Their behavior reveals traits that are clearly at variance with what is known about human cognition. It may induce, for instance, an unbounded goal stack, the equivalent of an infinite working memory—a distinctly unrealistic assumption given the known limits of human working memory. Effortless backtracking and duplicate state detection may be an efficient way of dealing with complex decision trees, but human beings often have great difficulty in noticing cycles in their thinking and in returning to a previous problem state from which to try something else after an unsuccessful attempt at solving a problem. Human problem solving apparently is based on much more constrained goal hierarchies. It is not enough, however, to point out that the physiological limitations of working memory prevent indefinite subgoaling. Even though this may be the case, the question remains how the human organism succeeds in dealing with such limitations. The claim of the authors is that the cognitive architecture itself be structured so as to avoid unbounded subgoaling, and in this context they consider three ways in which goal hierarchies might plausibly be 'flattened.' These alternatives are shown to solve the problems mentioned above although, unfortunately, they also raise new clusters of problems. One of the proposed solutions, however, whilst altogether avoiding the 'selection space' into which Soar conventionally enters when attempting to deal with a tie impasse, appears to retain Newell's 'single state principle,' and at the same time remains close to known constraints on the depth of human memory.

The last paper is Knowledge level and inductive uses of chunking (EBL) by Rosenbloom and Aasman. It deals with some aspects of explanation-based learning (EBL), particularly its role at the knowledge level and the symbol level respectively. It is frequently maintained that EBL is in fact a form of partial evaluation of a domain theory: it would only appear to deal with the part of the domain that is instantiated by the example. It is argued by the authors that EBL relies fundamentally on the availability of training instances that exemplify a domain theory. This requires the assumption that not everything in such an instance, or in the exemplified domain theory, needs to be believed a priori. The paper proposes that learning may in fact proceed in two steps. The first stage involves explanation—or rationalization—of instances via a low-belief domain theory, which then is followed by a second, confirmatory, stage in which EBL is used to acquire a high-belief rule from this base explanation. This, importantly, permits the use of un-believed knowledge for the purpose of induction (knowledge acquisition) in the domain theory itself.

NOTES

[1]At present (1 October 1991), the Groningen Soar Research Group consists of the following persons, apart from the senior editor: Aladin Akyürek, Corine Claveaux, Niels Taatgen (all of the Institute for Experimental and Occupational Psychology), and Jans Aasman, Wiebo H. Brouwer, Ep H. Piersma, and Marcel Wierda (all of the Traffic Research Center).

REFERENCES

Anderson, J. R. (1983). *The architecture of cognition.* Cambridge, MA: Harvard University Press.

Goodman, N. (1984). *Of mind and other matters.* Cambridge, MA: Harvard University Press.

Laird, J. E., Newell, A., & Rosenbloom, P. S. (1987). SOAR: An architecture for general intelligence. *Artificial Intelligence, 33,* 1-64.

Michon, J. A. (1985a). A critical review of driver behavior models: What do we know, what should we do? In L. A. Evans & R. C. Schwing (Eds.), *Human behavior and traffic safety* (pp. 487-525). New York: Plenum Press.

Michon, J. A. (1985b). The compleat time experiencer. In J. A. Michon & J. L. Jackson (Eds.), *Time, mind, and behavior* (pp. 20-52). Berlin: Springer-Verlag.

Michon, J. A. (1987, September 2). Twenty-five years of road safety research. *Staatscourant, 168,* 4-6. (Opening address to the Second International Road Safety Conference, Groningen, 1-4 September 1987.)

Michon, J. A. (1990). Implicit and explicit representations of time. In R. A. Block (Ed.), *Cognitive models of psychological time* (pp. 37-58). Hillsdale, NJ: Erlbaum.

Michon, J. A., & McLoughlin, H. (1991). The intelligence of GIDS. In Commision of the European Communities (Ed.), *Advanced telematics in road transport* [Proceedings of the DRIVE Conference Brussels, 4-6 February 1991] (Vol. 1, pp. 371-376). Amsterdam: Elsevier.

Newell, A. (1973). You can't play twenty questions with nature and win. In W. G. Chase (Ed.), *Visual information processing* (pp. 283-308). New York: Academic Press.

Newell, A. (1989a). Putting it all together. In D. Klahr & K. Kotovsky (Eds.), *Complex information processing: The impact of Herbert A. Simon* (pp. 399-440). Hillsdale, NJ: Erlbaum.

Newell, A. (1989b). How it all got put together: A story. In D. Klahr & K. Kotovsky (Eds.), *Complex information processing: The impact of Herbert A. Simon* (pp. 443-445). Hillsdale, NJ: Erlbaum.

Waldrop, M. M. (1988a). Towards the unified theory of cognition. *Science, 241,* 27-29.

Waldrop, M. M. (1988b). SOAR: A unified theory of cognition? *Science, 241,* 296-298.

ALLEN NEWELL: A PORTRAIT

JOHN A. MICHON
Department of Psychology and Traffic Research Center
University of Groningen, Groningen, The Netherlands

Introduction

In the summer of 1989 Allen Newell received an honorary doctorate in the Behavioral and Social Sciences at the University of Groningen for the very special role he has played in the development of cognitive science during the last 35 years. As a matter of fact Newell's impact is felt, not just in cognitive science, but also in management science, ergonomics and the philosophy of science. He has shown how the choice of a rather simple assumption about reality—known as the problem space hypothesis—may eventually lead to a *unified theory of cognition,* if only such a simple thesis can be incorporated in an abstract, computational theory that allows the formalization of extremely general concepts such as symbol systems, recursion, representation, and universal subgoaling.

The history of psychology as an independent field of scientific study spans a period of approximately a century and a half. In this period it gradually evolved from a speculative doctrine into an empirical, experimental science with a substantial cumulative body of knowledge and a methodological canon of its own (see, for instance, Boff, Kaufman, & Thomas, 1986, or Atkinson, Herrnstein, Lindzey, & Luce, 1988). Although there are still prominent differences of opinion that keep theorists apart, such differences are increasingly becoming empirically decidable. This is largely due to the degree of formalization within psychology that took place in the course of the past 35 years.

This trend towards greater exactness has also resulted in a remarkable strengthening of the philosophical and logical foundations of psychological theory. During the past 15 years considerable attention has been devoted to these foundations. This development was one of a series that took place in a relatively short time, roughly between 1955 and 1960, within the framework

J. A. Michon and A. Akyürek (eds.), Soar: A Cognitive Architecture in Perspective, 11–23.

of several scientific disciplines. Thus in linguistics we saw the onset of the theory of grammar and computational linguistics. We could also witness the first applications of the 'early' digital computer to tasks that had been, until then, the exclusive domain of human intelligence: proving theorems, solving puzzles, playing games, especially chess. Among those who did contribute to this development right from the beginning are Allen Newell and Herbert A. Simon.[1]

The impact of these developments on American psychology was dramatic. North-American psychology was, then, still dominated by behaviorism, but within a period of hardly more than four or five years many of the underlying assumptions of behaviorism were found to be wrong or irrelevant, or both. In the course of the sixties we see behaviorism as the dominant school of psychology gradually being replaced by the cognitive approach.

In Europe, where behaviorism had never acquired such an exclusive, prominent position, the cognitive paradigm was found to fit more or less smoothly into accepted patterns of psychological thought. European psychology —particularly in Great Britain, The Netherlands, and Sweden—has therefore been in the forefront of the cognitive approach. The strong position of The Netherlands has persisted and continues to be surprising, in view of the size of the country.

Take Off

Allen Newell was born in San Francisco on the 19th of March, 1927, to grow up in a typical American upper middle class family. His father was a professor of radiology at Stanford Medical School. Newell remains somewhat silent on his childhood. The most outspoken self-qualification I have been able to find is that in school Allen Newell was an "indifferent pupil, though some people seemed to think he was bright" (American Psychological Association, 1986, p. 347). He went to a high school that was generally considered to be excellent, but the best thing that seems to have happened to him at this school was that it allowed him to get acquainted with the girl of his dreams, Noël McKenna. They married when he was just 20 years of age. They have one son, Paul, who has developed a career in computer graphics.

Newell was just old enough to get actively involved in the Second World War. Soon after he had been conscripted into the US Navy, peace broke out, but he was just in time to witness, free of charge and courtesy of the US Naval Command, the atomic bomb tests in the Bikini atoll.

Soon afterward Newell registered at Stanford University where he obtained a B.A. in physics. Subsequently he went to Princeton with the intention of working towards a Ph.D. in mathematics. There, however, he became convinced that he might actually end up suffering from lack of breath in the thin air of pure mathematics, a reason for young Newell to quit and to join RAND Corporation in Santa Monica, California, as a research scientist in a more down-to-earth setting. It was here and then that he became involved in the experimental study of human behavior in organizations. Since then he considers himself a psychologist, and indeed, his membership in the American Psychological Association dates from 1952.

Newell's career began with the idea that it must be possible to use digital computers for the simulation of task environments and thereby to study, in detail, the information processing by the human component in a system. This idea, quite new at the time, has become one of the pillars of contemporary ergonomic wisdom.

His views on this matter were closely related to what Simon had said about the human rational decision maker in his classic *Administrative Behavior* (Simon, 1947). In the summer of 1954 Simon, then already prominent, spent some time at RAND as a consultant. It was there that he met Newell, and already this first encounter established what would turn out to be one of the closest scientific cooperative efforts of the century (Simon, 1980, p. 460). Newell decided to resume his academic career and to obtain a Ph.D., in industrial administration under Simon, at Carnegie Institute of Technology[2] in Pittsburgh, Pennsylvania.

In that same memorable summer of 1954 at the same RAND Corporation in California, Oliver Selfridge of Lincoln Laboratories presented his ideas about an adaptive, learning system for visual pattern recognition, which would become known as *Pandemonium.* For Newell this lecture is the single most important event that was to give direction to all his scientific work ever since. "It was instantly clear ... that intelligent adaptive systems could be built that were far more complex than anything yet done, and that they would be programmed on digital computers. Imprinting had occurred and Newell has been working ever since on discovering the mechanisms that constitute mind" (American Psychological Association, 1986, p. 348).

Newell obtained his Ph.D. in 1957 and subsequently accepted a position at Carnegie Tech. In 1961 he decided to stay there, a decision so definitive that he has remained in town even during his sabbaticals! Presently he holds the prestigious "U. A. and Helen Whitaker University Chair of Computer Science."

Flight

With Newell's Ph.D. work out of the way, Simon and Newell embarked on a unique and extraordinarily close cooperation. They deployed in an inimitable and highly focused—some would say singleminded—way their program for cognitive science. In doing so they have had a tremendous influence on the development of cognitive science, which persists till the present day. Few approaches to human cognition can boast a similar impact.

The basic idea is simple enough to be summarized in a few sentences. According to Newell and Simon human beings, like computers, are physical embodiments or instantiations of symbol processing or computational systems. It is therefore possible, in principle, to derive a formal theory that can describe and explain the (intelligent) behavior of both natural and artificial computational systems.

The close ties between Newell and Simon make it fairly difficult at times to specify the core contribution of each. Yet it is possible in a number of cases to outline who should be considered the *auctor intellectualis*. Simon, for instance, has consistently emphasized the intrinsically bounded nature of rationality, while Newell has concentrated on the formalization of problem solving and complex task performance. In any case, the following issues are among the ones that have been central to Newell's work in the past 35 years.

THE COMPUTER AS SYMBOL PROCESSOR

Initially the programmable digital computer was almost exclusively seen as a fast and efficient calculator, a number cruncher. Newell was one of the first to implement non-numerical applications, specifically the use of the computer as a medium for simulation complex task environments. The insight that computers are generic symbol processing systems, rather than just calculators, lies at the root of Artificial Intelligence. For this early work Newell and Simon received the 1975 Turing Award.

COMPUTER LANGUAGES FOR COGNITIVE SCIENCE

For many years the standard 'list processing' programming language of artificial intelligence and cognitive psychology has been *Lisp*. Lisp was preceded by other list processors, however, and Allen Newell was the first to develop such a language. Actually his *Information Processing Language* (IPL) may even be considered the first high level programming language. IPL went through five versions, most recently in 1964 (Newell, Tonge, Feigenbaum, Green, & Mealy, 1964). Already it incorporated most of the principles that would later be applied in other, more recent attempts at creating a special medium for formal symbol processing applications. The unsurmountable weakness of IPL was its extremely unfriendly input-output organization combined with a pernicious lack of readability for human users; even Newell himself was unable to program in IPL without the help of a Quick Reference Guide. In 1965 Lisp, newly developed by John McCarthy at MIT, gained the upper hand. One should keep in mind though that Newell and Simon's ground-breaking work on heuristic problem solving (embodied in Logic Theorist and General Problem Solver) has been carried out by means of IPL.

RECURSION

Recursion is a general procedure to perform a mathematical or, more generally, a symbolic operation by means of that operation itself.[3] Recursion is an extremely important and generally used mathematical principle. The insight that recursion is also an essential feature of higher programming languages and that it plays an important role in human cognition as well, is largely due to Newell. General Problem Solver, for example, executed copies of itself on subgoals that it created.

THE THEORY OF HUMAN PROBLEM SOLVING

In 1972 Newell and Simon's—now classic—book on human problem solving appeared (Newell & Simon, 1972). In this weighty volume, actually more a progress report than a text, the authors presented their comprehensive views on problem solving as a general form of human behavior. Thus they were able to place a central domain of cognitive activity into a coherent and consistent theoretical frame of reference. Their theory of human problem solving is based on the *problem space hypothesis,* the idea that all problem solving activity can eventually be described in terms of a systematic (exhaustive or heuristic) search through a problem space.

Starting from a given current state the problem solver will try applying an operator which transforms the current state into a next state within the domain of all possible, legitimate states that the problem solver can represent internally: this domain is called the problem space. The condition for applying an operator is that it ultimately leads to a state that is closer to the desired goal. It has proved to be possible to formally describe if not all, then at least a very large class of problems.

The development of this theory is undoubtedly the fruit of the continuing and close cooperation between Newell and Simon. Within this symbiotic frame of reference one of Newell's characteristic contributions has been the theory's formulation in terms of production systems. Around 1943 the American logician Post showed that an important class of formal problems can be described by means of sets of so-called production rules, rules that have the following general format:

If $\{condition_1, condition_2, \dots condition_k\}$
Then $\{action_1, action_2, \dots action_m\}$

Such rules specify one or more actions or consequences that follow if a set of conditions is satisfied. One of Newell's achievements is to have introduced production rules into psychology. The relevance of this formalism for psychological theory became clear later, for instance, in John R. Anderson's work on the adaptive control of thought (Anderson, 1983). The influence on the field of artificial intelligence is commensurate: the construction of expert systems would be practically unthinkable without production systems.

A psychologically important aspect of Newell and Simon's work is the rehabilitation of introspective data, that is, the systematic use in psychological studies of verbatim think-aloud protocols as valid data. Newell and Simon have argued that although thinking aloud does not provide insight in the structure of consciousness—which had been the received view among the early introspectionists a century ago—a verbatim protocol does give indications about the course of the process of problem solving in which the subject is engaged. In other words, a think-aloud protocol provides information about the position of the problem solver within the problem space in which he or she is operating. Newell's contribution to this revision of the role of verbal protocols entails, among other things, the translation of these protocols into formal problem behavior graphs illustrating the course of the problem solving process (see Figure 1).

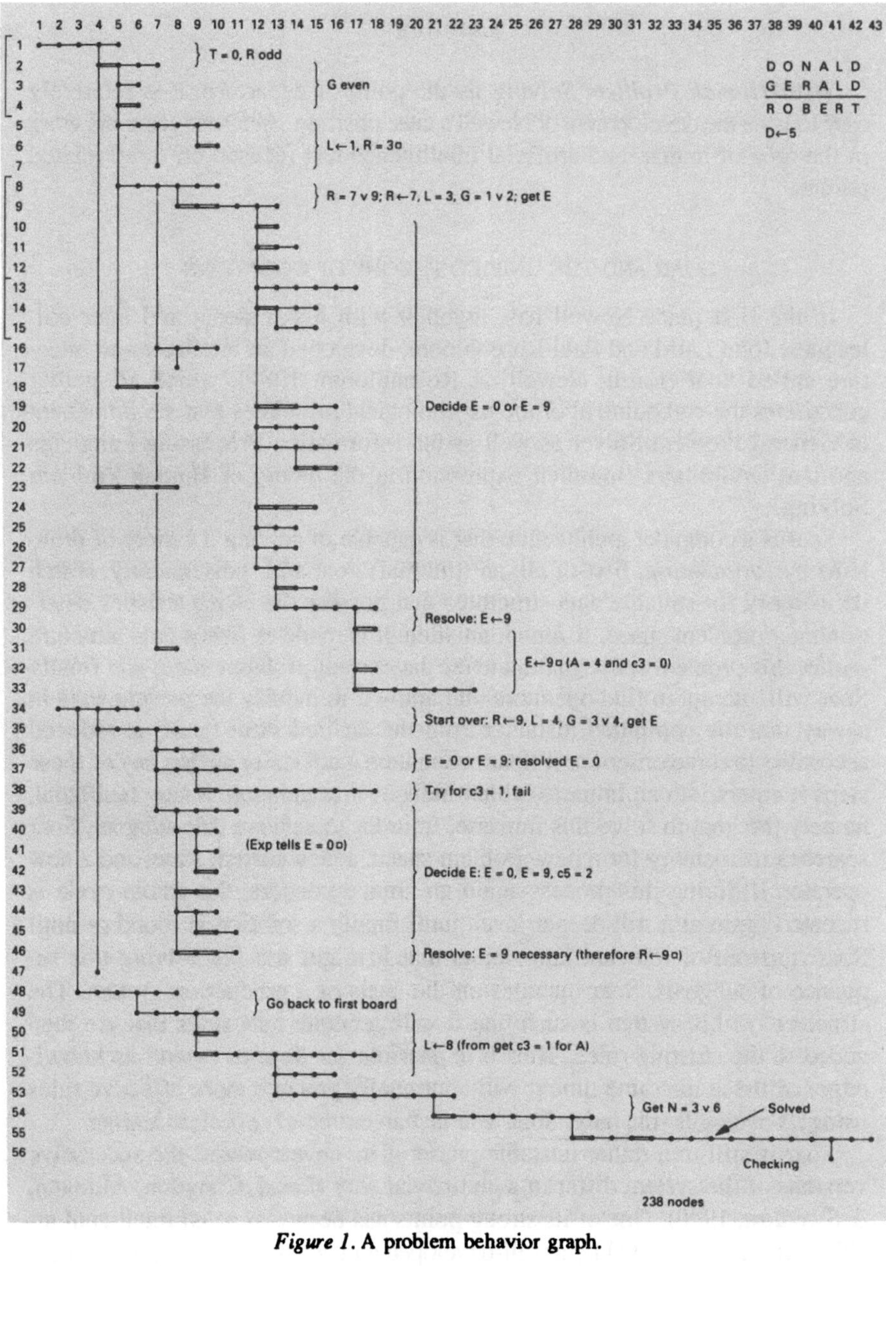

Figure 1. **A problem behavior graph.**

Landing

With *Human Problem Solving* as the point of departure, it is relatively easy to trace the development of Newell's later position. In recent years his work in the area of human and artificial intelligence has focused on three related points.

SOAR AND THE UNIFIED THEORY OF COGNITION

In the first place Newell has, together with his students and later colleagues, John Laird and Paul Rosenbloom, developed an intelligent architecture called Soar (Laird, Newell, & Rosenbloom, 1987), which altogether constitutes the embodiment of the psychological principles that are immanent in General Problem Solver as well as the Information Processing Language and that would later find their expression in the theory of Human Problem Solving.

Soar is a computer architecture that is capable of solving a variety of problems by formulating, first of all, an (internal) goal and, subsequently, search its memory for suitable data structures that possess the characteristics determining a problem space. If found, an attempt is made to find a data structure within this problem space that matches the current problem state, and finally Soar will attempt to find operators that allow it to modify the present state in a way that the computed distance from the desired state (goal) is reduced according to some criterion. If Soar encounters a difficulty during any of these steps it enters into an impasse which induces it to generate a new (sub)goal, namely the goal to solve this impasse. In order to achieve this subgoal, Soar searches its memory for a new problem space, a new current state, and a new operator. If during this process again an impasse occurs, the whole cycle is repeated again at a still deeper level, until finally a solution is found or until Soar runs out of relevant knowledge that it might use for solving this sequence of subgoals. Soar operates on the basis of a production system. The structure of this system is such that it will generate new rules that are then added to the existing rules. Thus it is possible for Soar to extend its knowledge, whilst at the same time it will continually produce more effective rules using its available rule base: Soar is in fact an extremely efficient learner.

Soar is still in a rather unstable phase of its development: the successive versions of the system differ in a non-trivial way (Laird, Congdon, Altmann, & Swedlow, 1990). One of its strong points has been that as an intelligent architecture it is supported by a well-developed and coherent psychological theory. This would qualify Soar as a suitable instrument for connecting several lines of thought in cognitive psychology and in artificial intelligence or, in other words, as an important step on the way to a unifying theory covering all aspects of cognition.

THE TIMELINESS OF A UNIFIED THEORY OF COGNITION

Recently Newell has adopted a quite radical position. In his William James Lectures—held at Harvard in the spring of 1987 and now available in final form—he has claimed that it is time for a unified theory of cognition (Newell, 1990). In his view psychology has progressed far enough to allow the construction of a general theoretical framework within which the discipline should evolve—rather than being born again and again every time a new theory is proposed. His argument is largely based on a generalization of the problem space hypothesis: all problem solving can be characterized as search in problem spaces. But Newell now extends this position to include all forms of intelligent behavior: all intelligent behavior is a form of problem solving and it too can, therefore, be characterized in terms of search through problem spaces. The William James Lectures—the most prestigious *oratio ex cathedra* in scientific psychology—constitute Newell's truly herculean attempt to provide the fundaments for this claim over a very wide range of psychological topics. Even if this claim will turn out to be premature the Lectures emphasize Newell's lasting importance for the advancement of psychological theory.

THEORETICAL FOUNDATIONS OF COGNITIVE SCIENCE

Newell's activities over the past ten years are characterized by an increasing weight of epistemological arguments in support of his, by and large, relatively technical work. In a series of influential papers he has reviewed important issues of experimental methodology. In his paper "You can't play twenty questions with nature and win" the conventional paradigms of hypothesis testing are critically reviewed (Newell, 1973). In addition he has made a serious effort to provide the necessary philosophical underpinnings for his theoretical position (Newell, 1982, 1990). Not many empirically inclined behavioral scientists have dissected their assumption so concisely. It has led Newell to distinguish between the knowledge level and the symbol level, a distinction similar, in many but not all, respects to Dennett's distinction between intentional and functional (Dennett, 1978), or to Marr's distinction between computational and algorithmic (Marr, 1982). Although many implications of Newell's position still remain untraced, it appears at least consistent with his conception of the human being as exemplar of the species *physical symbol system.*

HUMAN-COMPUTER INTERACTION (COGNITIVE ERGONOMICS)

In spite of a strong emphasis on theoretical and modeling aspects, Newell's work retains a distinctly practical flavor; it is replete with applied studies in a variety of ergonomic issues, particularly in the field of human-computer interaction. Like his efforts towards a Unified Theory of Cognition, his applied work bear the signs of an integrative mind at work. As an important exercise in system identification he has, in cooperation with Card and Moran, revived and extended a paradigm—now known as the Model Human Processor (Card, Moran, & Newell, 1983)—that derives from the once popular field of time and motion studies. The basic idea is deceptively simple: every elementary action—perceptual, cognitive, or motor—requires a certain more or less constant time. Thus a perceptual input requires approximately 150 ms processing time, whilst an elementary cognitive decision takes on average some 50 ms. Complex behaviors are optimized concatenations of these simple elementary actions and an appropriate analysis of a complex task allows specific predictions about the quality, the bottlenecks, and the errors of performance.

Although Newell perceives his work as a fairly arbitrary mixture of psychology and computer science—"as chance would have it"—he is quick in emphasizing that throughout the past 35 years he has worked in an extremely straight and straightforward way towards the goal that Selfridge had pointed out to him in that important summer of 1954. He has been actively involved in various administrative and advisory capacities, but he has never considered them important aspects of his academic work; neither have they proved particularly relevant for the recognition Newell has won in the world of learning, recognition that is illustrated by the following selection from the honors he has received thus far.

In 1972 Newell was elected to the National Academy of Science and to the American Academy of Arts and Sciences. In 1975 he received, with Herbert Simon, the Turing Award. In 1980 followed his election to the National Academy of Engineering. In the same year he became the first President of the American Association for Artificial Intelligence. In 1985 he received the American Psychological Association's Award for Distinguished Scientific Contributions. In 1989 he received an honorary doctorate in the Behavioral and Social Sciences at the University of Groningen, and later in the same year he was presented with the Research Excellence Award of the International Joint Conferences on Artificial Intelligence.

Newell and The Netherlands

Allen Newell established a relation with Dutch psychology already early in his career. His first contacts were actually established in 1955 through active exchange of ideas with Adriaan de Groot and Nico Frijda at the University of Amsterdam. De Groot, in particular, has served as an important *trait d'union* between Newell and Simon and the European tradition in the period between 1955 and 1965.[4]

A memorable extension of the connections between Newell and Europe took place in 1964. During the summer of that year he took part in the first NUFFIC Summer School for Experimental and Mathematical Psychology. The perspective on cognition represented by Newell was, at that time, not yet well known among European students and Newell's teaching did indeed have considerable impact. Many of the students who took part in this memorable Summer School do in fact remember three things about Newell's contribution: his intensely personal intellectual commitment, the unbelievable rate at which he is able to verbalize his thoughts and finally and, perhaps not in the last place, the remarkable agility with which he succeeded to simulate, despite his heavy stature, the stream of information in a computer.

Since these early days there has remained a regular, intensive contact between Newell and Dutch cognitive scientists. The approach advocated by Simon and Newell has drawn many from The Netherlands to Pittsburgh, PA. Among them are, apart from De Groot and Frijda, roughly in chronological order: John Michon, David Brée, Maan Leeuwenberg, Leo Noordman, Wietske Vonk, Hans Buffart, Alma Schaafstal, Jan Maarten Schraagen, Jans Aasman, and Aladin Akyürek. Although not all of them have been involved with Newell's work on a day-to-day basis, this has been the case for those who are presently based at the University of Groningen. Here a considerable research effort involving Soar is concentrated in a joint program of the Department of Psychology and the Traffic Research Center (VSC), under the aegis of the Groningen Center for Behavioral, Cognitive, and Neurosciences (BCN). The size of this program makes it, presently, the third largest Soar research unit in the world. The activities of this Soar Research Group have been supported, among others, by IBM Nederland (as part of a study contract), the European Commission, and the Netherlands Ministry of Transport. When Newell received his honorary degree at the University of Groningen in 1989, the Soar Research Group organized a Symposium on "Soar and Unified Theories of Cognition." The lecture presented by Allen Newell on this occasion appears as the next paper in the present volume. At the same time, a Tutorial Workshop took place, the first ever attempt to teach Soar from first principles to students with varying, but by and large limited background knowledge in AI programming. Although successful, this workshop also revealed some of the intrinsic difficulties of formally teaching concepts and procedures that are developmentally still in full swing. In spite of the ambiguities involved, Soar has progressed both in the USA and in Europe where the EuroSoar Research Network is now meeting regularly to discuss the ins and outs of the Soar architecture and related issues of Unified Theories of Cognition.

NOTES

[1] The date 11 september 1956 is usually regarded as the start of cognitive science, for it was the date of a conference held at the Massachusetts Institute of Technology where, along with Newell and H. A. Simon, also Noam Chomsky, George A. Miller, John McCarthy, Marvin Minsky, and others launched—at the same time—their ground-breaking ideas (Gardner, 1985).

[2] Since 1969 Carnegie Mellon University.

[3] A simple example of a recursive function is the expression $N! = N(N-1)!$, which says that the factorial of a number N, that is, the product of $1 \times 2 \times ... \times N$, can be obtained by multiplying N with the factorial of N−1, that is, the product of $1 \times 2 \times ... \times (N-1)$.

[4] In an interview G. Mandler relates the following: "There's another influence, and that was the Simon and Newell direction, partly out of the cybernetic and the computational field, and partly out of European work. If you read the first Simon and Newell papers in the '50s, they paid their respects to a German psychologist named Selz. Otto Selz was a psychologist who influenced the Dutch psychologist De Groot, who did research on the cognitive abilities of chess players. (...) Selz talked about operators (...) functions that operate on concepts. That was 1911 to 1913. De Groot applied this work to chess problems, and Newell and Simon incorporated those ideas in their work on problem solving. So Newell and Simon used a European tradition, and came up with a cognitive psychology that, again, was totally uninfluenced by behaviorism. It developed not 'in response to' but 'independently of' behaviorism" (Baars, 1986, p. 262).

REFERENCES

American Psychological Association. (1986). Awards for distinguished scientific contributions: 1985. *American Psychologist, 41,* 337-353.

Anderson, J. R. (1983). *The architecture of cognition.* Cambridge, MA: Harvard University Press.

Atkinson, R. C., Herrnstein, R. J., Lindzey, G., & Luce, R. D. (Eds.). (1988). *Stevens' handbook of experimental psychology* (Vols. 1 & 2). New York: Wiley.

Baars, B. J. (1986). *The cognitive revolution in psychology.* New York: Guilford Press.

Boff, K. R., Kaufman, L., & Thomas, J. P. (Eds.). (1986). *Handbook of perception and human performance* (Vols. 1 & 2). New York: Wiley.

Card, S. K., Moran, T. P., & Newell, A. (1983). *The psychology of human-computer interaction.* Hillsdale, NJ: Erlbaum.

Dennett, D. C. (1978). *Brainstorms: Philosophical essays on mind and psychology.* Hassocks, UK: Harvester Press.

Gardner, H. (1985). *The mind's new science: A history of the cognitive revolution.* New York: Basic Books.

Laird, J. E., Congdon, C. B., Altmann, E., & Swedlow, K. (1990). *Soar user's manual: Version 5.2* (Tech. Rep. CMU-CS-90-179). Pittsburgh, PA: Carnegie Mellon University, School of Computer Science.

Laird, J. E., Newell, A., & Rosenbloom, P. S. (1987). SOAR: An architecture for general intelligence. *Artificial Intelligence, 33,* 1-64.

Marr, D. (1982). *Vision: A computational investigation into the human representation and processing of visual information.* New York: Freeman.

Newell, A. (1973). You can't play twenty questions with nature and win. In W. G. Chase (Ed.), *Visual information processing* (pp. 283-308). New York: Academic Press.

Newell, A. (1982). The knowledge level. *Artificial Intelligence, 18,* 81-132.

Newell, A. (1990). *Unified theories of cognition.* Cambridge, MA: Harvard University Press.

Newell, A., & Simon, H. A. (1972). *Human problem solving.* Englewood Cliffs, NJ: Prentice-Hall.

Newell, A., Tonge, F. M., Feigenbaum, E. A., Green, B., & Mealy, G. (1964). *Information processing language V manual* (2nd ed.). Englewood Cliffs, NJ: Prentice-Hall.

Simon, H. A. (1947). *Administrative behavior.* New York: Macmillan.

Simon, H. A. (1980). Herbert A. Simon. In G. Lindzey (Ed.), *A history of psychology in autobiography* (Vol. 3, pp. 435- 472). San Francisco, CA: Freeman.

UNIFIED THEORIES OF COGNITION AND THE ROLE OF SOAR

ALLEN NEWELL
Computer Science and Psychology
Carnegie Mellon University
Pittsburgh, Pennsylvania

I start this paper by focusing on unified theories of human cognition —what they are and what their general status is in the current scene of cognitive science. Then I consider an exemplar of a unified theory of cognition, namely, the Soar theory and system, which has been developed by my colleagues and myself over almost a decade. I will provide some historical context for Soar and then treat the Soar theory of cognition in somewhat greater detail, selecting several specific topics that should help to appreciate the nature of unified theories of cognition. At the end I will raise a number of general issues that apply concretely to Soar, but in fact apply in analogous form to any candidate unified theory of cognition. As will become apparent, the considerations stated here flow largely from my 1987 William James Lectures on *Unified Theories of Cognition* (Newell, 1990), but several new issues and results are incorporated.

The Current Situation in Cognitive Science

Let us reflect on the present situation in cognitive science. The cognitive revolution has been around for some time. Actually, it is well over thirty years old. Those of us who know about 'being over thirty' should think a little about what it means for cognitive science. It means that cognitive science should begin dealing seriously with the rest of its career. It should grow up, make a living, settle down. It is no longer a young science—as so many have called it for so long. But, you protest, cognitive science still *feels* so young. Then you need to realize that behaviorism, this most established of psycholo-

J. A. Michon and A. Akyürek (eds.), Soar: A Cognitive Architecture in Perspective, 25–79.

gical movements, was itself in the saddle only for thirty years, from Watson's manifesto in 1913 (Watson, 1913) to Clark Hull's *Principles of Behavior* in 1943 (Hull, 1943). It is true that it took another ten years and a World War before the cognitive revolution stirred. But in 1943, at thirty, behaviorism was mature.

We can, then, no longer think of cognitive science as a revolution against behaviorism, or as an effort that is still gathering itself together. Cognitive science is now pervasive in the heartland of individual psychology. It has penetrated perception, cognition, memory, learning, language, motor behavior, and it has crossed the boundaries with neuroscience. We must also recognize that cognitive science is much less pervasive if the entire universe of psychology is considered, with such ramifications as developmental, social, clinical, and animal psychology. Cognitive science has made some inroads, but it is still not the only relevant formulation or even the dominant one. So cognitive science has not yet spread, as behaviorism did, to every nook and cranny of psychology. But it does already occupy the heartland and its destiny lies entirely with its ability to become an integrated scientific theory.

During the thirty years of cognitive science a deep understanding of computational mechanisms has emerged. This is not a matter of cognitive science alone—cognitive science is embedded in artificial intelligence and more generally computer science. But, whatever its attachments thus far, by now we really do have a rich theory of the mechanisms out of which cognition is built. From quite a different quarter we appear also to be moving towards a coming-together of neuroscience and cognition: within a stretched decade broad connections will be established between these two domains. Connectionism is one current expression of this trend, one that is more theoretically than empirically motivated, but nonetheless an important harbinger of where we are heading.

An aspect of this thirty-year growth that I particularly wish to emphasize is that psychology has developed an immense number of robust regularities —repeatable, quantitative and often parametric regularities. Elsewhere (e.g., see Newell, 1990) I have estimated that there are of the order of three thousand good, quantitative regularities waiting to fuel the attempt to understand the nature of human cognition. This number is growing rapidly—about three or four hundred regularities a year, I reckon. Such an ample pool of regularities has consequences for us all, but especially for experimentalists. It takes about ten good experiments to establish a regularity. Hence each good experiment an experimentalist performs provides about one tenth of the three thousandth and first addition to the body of knowledge now available. Remember that, however out of fashion they may become, the old regularities do not wither in value—and that new regularities do not gain value by being this year's new crop. The point is not to discourage good experimentation—I would never do such a thing. The point is that we need to attend to how these regularities will be integrated into some sort of theory. Again, it is not that we are totally without theory. Cognitive science positively encourages theory, and many of the three thousand regularities are covered by good microtheories. But as the thirty years have shown us, these microtheories do not seem to accumulate into an integrated theory. The fate of short-term memory, from a heralded beginning (Miller, 1956), through being one of the major achievements of cognitive science (Crowder, 1976), to its apparent demise (Crowder, 1982), provides ample testimony of how difficult is the struggle for theoretical cumulation and integration working bottom up from microtheories.

If we go on as we have in the past—if we do not find some way of putting it all together—then we will soon face ten thousand regularities, then twenty thousand, then... Even the microtheories will then begin approach a thousand. We face the prospect of being overwhelmed, of having such a huge data base of regularities that we can never work our way through it. It does not do to note that other sciences have hundreds of thousands or even millions of regularities. They have unified theories that provide the frameworks that keep these regularities tamed and useful. Perhaps, I sound alarmist, but the situation actually appears decidedly serious to me.

UNIFIED THEORIES OF COGNITION

These considerations have been on my mind for a long time (Newell, 1973). Thus, when I was invited to give the William James lectures at Harvard University in 1987, I took as my theme the notion of unified theories of cognition. Admittedly, unified theories were a fantasy for the future. But my point was not just that we need them. My point was that the current scene of cognitive science enables us to move towards getting them. We do indeed have thirty years of solid growth behind us.

Cognitive science has one result of extreme generality and general acceptance. In the present context it can be expressed as: *unified theories take the form of architectures*. An architecture is a fixed set of mechanisms that enable the acquisition and use of content in a memory to guide behavior in the pursuit of goals. In effect, this is the hardware-software distinction: the architecture is the hardware that is supporting the software and the software is the collection of data structures that encode the content. This is the essence of the computational theory of mind.

Problem solving, decision making, routine action
Memory, learning, skill
Perception, motor behavior
Language
Motivation, emotion
Imagining, dreaming, daydreaming

Figure 1. Areas to be covered by a unified theory of cognition (Newell, 1990).

Thus a unified theory is given by specifying the architecture of human cognition.[1] However, behavior is determined by much more than the architecture, namely, by the content in the memories of the system, by the tasks the environment effectively sets the system, and by the goals the system has for itself. All these comprise what is called the *knowledge-level structure*. Indeed, the architecture is the mechanism that makes it possible for a human being to behave as a function of its goals and its knowledge. If a system were a perfect intelligence, its behavior could be described entirely in terms of the knowledge level—meaning that with *this* knowledge and *these* goals, the system behaves so as to attain its goals using the full extent of its knowledge. In this case the architecture would never be noticed. But humans are not perfectly intelligent and the architecture shows through in their behavior in many ways. The specifically psychological character of humans derives from the organic nature of the human architecture and from the special ways in which this architecture fails to make the human a pure knowledge-level system.

With the accretion of more and more insight in the human cognitive architecture we should expect a unified theory of cognition to move towards covering all the phenomena listed in Figure 1. Ultimately, one theory should cover them all. We should want this because all sciences should want unification. But there are much more important reasons too. Perhaps most important is that unification allows us to bring many constraints to bear on specific phenomena—knowledge about problem solving and concept formation brought to bear on linguistics, and conversely, knowledge of linguistics brought to bear on reasoning. Such mutual constraints help to discover and identify the nature of the whole cognitive architecture. Indeed, as will become clear later, the great plague for psychological theory is that theory is seriously underdetermined by the data, at least by the data locally assembled. We can hope that a unified theory will let us bring enough additional knowledge, derived from remote parts of cognition, so that the underdetermination will be alleviated.

Trying to build theories that cover the range of phenomena listed in Figure 1, even if only approximately, is a genuine, stimulating step for cognitive science. The enterprise of producing such unification is difficult, of course, and many scientists tend not to pick up the challenge, preferring to avoid activities that are so strongly synthetic and approximative. Yet it is ultimately much more important to have an approximate theory that encompasses a fair range of detail, than an array of highly specific detailed microtheories for each separate little domain, even though each may be highly accurate. A sociological implication of the attempt to engage in unification is that it cannot possibly be accomplished by one or two persons working in isolation—the typical faculty-*cum*-graduate-student arrangement in university research. Instead, fairly large communities need to grow up to attempt building such unified theories.

Thus, the problem I was posing in the William James lectures was how to make the transition to a psychology that could engage in a quest for unified theories. We don't have any full-blown unified theories of cognition yet and, unfortunately, they can't be talked about effectively in general terms. They must be exemplified, even if only imperfectly, and Soar became the exemplar in the lectures. But Soar is, in fact, only one attempt. There are other attempts at cognitive architectures, though mostly without all the useful properties that Soar has as an exemplar. We can certainly expect that, if the idea of developing unified theories of cognition takes hold, there will be many such attempts. Most will fall by the wayside, because they will fail to recruit a substantial cooperative scientific community to help in their development. But, even with such attrition we can expect several viable efforts to emerge. After all, cognitive science has never had a unified theory, and the natural inclination of all psychological theorists will be to believe that, yes, there should be one, and yes, it should be theirs! Only after some (maybe even many) years of intensive and highly creative development, followed by a radical shake out, will cognitive science pass over into the blessed state of the more mature sciences, in which theorists are quite happy to work within a genuine, operational theory, making their theoretical advances within the constraints set by that theory.

Soar and Its Background

Soar served well as an exemplar for the lectures. But it is now also a serious candidate unified theory of cognition. We are now deeply engaged in this effort—more properly, in the beginnings of this effort, for it is one that will take a long time.

Soar is an outgrowth of thirty years of activity in both AI and cognition —running the full course of the cognitive revolution. My earlier remark about age thirty would seem to apply to Soar too, even if Soar proper only got started in the early 1980s. In an important sense, however, the remark is apt: Soar does build on all this history, integrating and extending the various mechanisms that have been discovered during these thirty years, much more than being a brand-new design. Thus, Soar has a certain maturity about it, gainsaying the immediacy of the current effort.

Figure 2 shows the basic mechanisms in Soar. All of them have have a long history in AI and cognitive science. Soar is, as a whole, a *symbolic computational system*. It manipulates and evaluates symbol structures according to the dictates of programs, that is, of other symbol structures. The stored-program concept, of course, goes back to the beginnings of automatic computation in the 1940s. That these computations are performed, generally speaking, on symbol structures, rather than just on numbers, was one of the two key insights that gave birth to the field of AI in the 1950s.

Soar is organized around *problem spaces*, that is, tasks are formulated as search in a space of states by means of operators that produce new states, where operators may be applied repeatedly, to find a desired state that signifies the accomplishment of the task. Problem spaces derive directly from the second key insight that started AI thirty years ago, namely, to use heuristic search spaces to deal with difficult tasks. Already by the mid 1960s it was understood that heuristic search was ubiquitous in intelligent systems.

Soar is organized entirely as a *production system*, that is, its long-term memory for both program and data consists of parallel-acting condition-action rules. Production systems reflect a twenty-five year old discovery that, rather than follow a fixed program, by moving a pointer through it to do each preordained action in turn—the *fetch-execute cycle*—flexible, intelligent action requires that the data at hand (in a working memory) call forth the knowledge in the memory about what to do—a *recognize-act cycle*. This discovery has not only formed the basis of much of expert systems technology, it has also provided a major organizing principle for modeling human cognition.

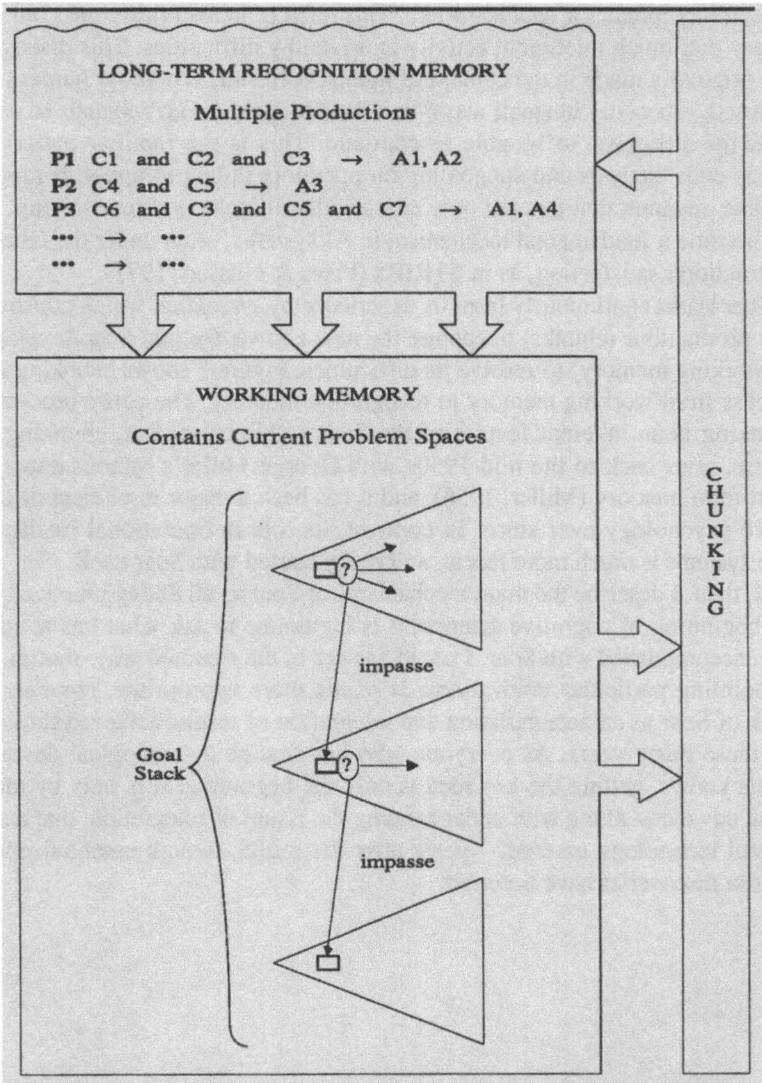

Figure 2. Basic Soar diagram. P1, P2, ... are productions; P1 with conditions, C1, C2, ... and actions, A1, A2, and so on.

Soar incorporates a *goal hierarchy*. This reflects another thirty-year old discovery that much intelligent activity is driven by difficulties. This discovery was originally made in the context of human behavior. Whenever humans are thwarted, especially in small ways, they immediately set up subgoals to overcome the difficulty, to be able to continue. This is the familiar pattern of means-ends analysis and subgoaling on operators failing to apply. It rapidly became apparent that this not only characterizes human problem solving, but has become a fundamental mechanism in AI systems, often under the label of precondition satisfaction, as in STRIPS (Fikes & Nilsson, 1971).

Soar learns continuously from its experience by *chunking*, which constructs new productions (chunks) to capture the new knowledge that Soar developed (in working memory) to resolve its difficulties. Figure 3 shows chunking as a process from working memory to recognition memory. The entire process of chunking is an inherent feature of the Soar architecture. But, chunking, of course, goes back to the mid-1950s with George Miller's famous paper on short-term memory (Miller, 1956), and it has been a major ingredient of cognitive psychology ever since. In contrast, its role in operational intelligent (AI) systems is much more recent, and really started with Soar itself.

If, then, I describe the main mechanisms of Soar as all dating practically to the beginning of cognitive science, it is legitimate to ask what has actually been accomplished with Soar. I could answer in the standard way, that is, by pinpointing particular innovations. It seems more appropriate, however, to think of Soar as an accumulation and integration of results achieved throughout these thirty years. As everyone who has studied technological developments knows, getting the key idea is only the beginning. It is only by many small advances, along with understanding the issues of integration, that a successful technology emerges—years after the initial, though essential inventions or discoveries have occurred.

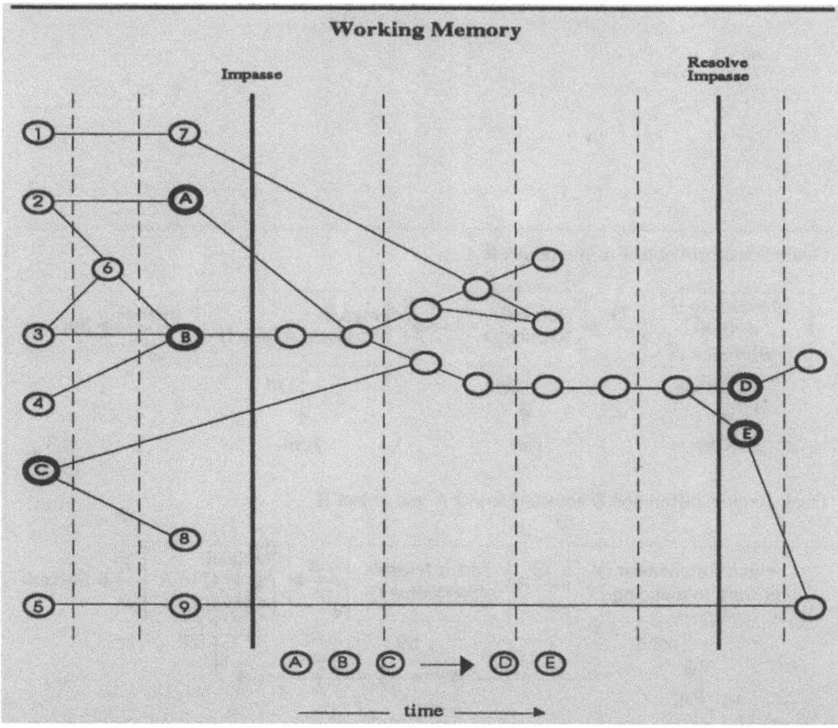

Figure 3. Diagram of the behavior of Soar during chunking. This is a display of working memory, as time flows from left to right. Circles stand for elements in working memory. They come into the working memory one at a time. Each element is produced by some production instantiated to some prior elements. These causal linkages are indicated by the lines connecting the elements. For instance, the element *B* is the result of some production that instantiated on the elements *4* and *6* to its left. The dashed vertical lines show the decision cycles. The left-hand solid vertical line indicates an impasse at that point. After this impasse, Soar creates a new subgoal and proceeds to generate more working-memory elements. Finally, two elements, *D* and *E*, are produced that resolve the impasse. At this point, a new production (the chunk) is created, shown at the bottom of the figure. Its actions are composed from the results, *D* and *E*. Its conditions are composed from the three elements, *A*, *B*, and *C*, that led to the results and that also existed prior to the impasse. This new production is added to the recognition memory and henceforth functions as any other production. Next time, this chunk will fire on available elements, *A*, *B*, and *C*, and put its two actions, *D* and *E*, into working memory. They will enter the decision procedure and the impasse will not occur (Newell, 1990).

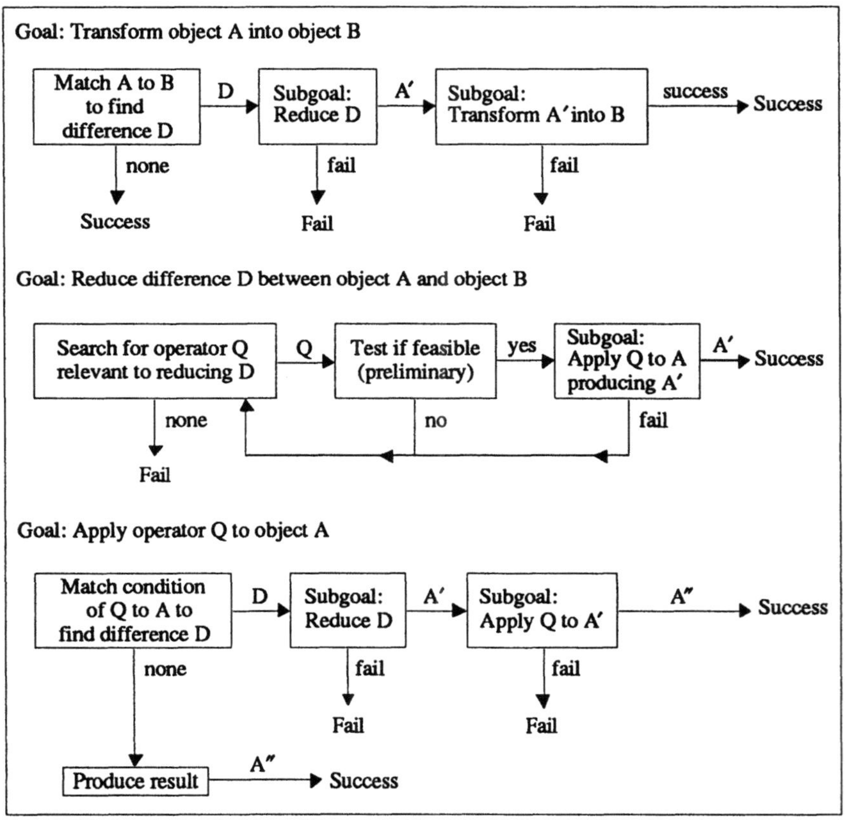

Figure 4. Flow diagram for General Problem Solver (GPS).

The direction in which an AI-systems technology must develop is that of greater flexibility. What has characterized efforts to build intelligent systems is the realization of specific ideas—such as means-ends analysis above—in systems that are, in most other respects, extremely rigid. Yet, what we know of human intelligence—and what must surely be case for ideal intelligence—is complete flexibility of the system to meet the demands of the specific task situations. Flexibility is exactly the sort of characteristic to expect of a maturing technology. It is not something that is attained by a single key idea. Flexibility measures the response of the total system. Thus, an interesting way to see the contributions made by Soar is to consider the increases in flexibility over the intelligent systems of thirty years ago. A useful anchor point for comparison is the *General Problem Solver* (GPS). It actually dates from the late 1950s (Newell, Shaw, & Simon, 1959), though many readers will be familiar with it from the famous edited collection, *Computers and Thought* (Feigenbaum & Feldman, 1963). The key flow diagram for GPS is reproduced in Figure 4.

GPS is an appropriate comparison—it was the 1950s counterpart of Soar. It was an attempt to create a general intelligent system and also to create a theory of human problem solving. It was the first program to have pretensions to generality, because it separated out the program structure for problem solving from the program structure to describe a particular task. It was viewed as novel in many ways. In fact, a number of the important facets mentioned above had their first realization in GPS.

From the viewpoint of flexibility there are many dimensions along which to compare Soar and GPS. Figure 5 gives eight important ones.

Consider problem spaces. GPS did indeed have the concept of problem spaces. But it did everything in a single problem space. Soar, in contrast, has multiple problem spaces and it can generate new ones on the fly.

Consider goals. GPS had goals—indeed it was the first system to have goals that were not just an agenda of task data structures to be processed. GPS had a fixed set of three goal types (see Figure 4): to get from a given state to a desired state, to apply an operator, and to reduce a difference arising from attempting another goal. Soar, in contrast, generates its own subgoals, which may be of unlimited diversity and which do not correspond to any predefined set of types. Soar's subgoals are to make up for a lack of knowledge of any kind—indeed Soar need not be able to specify what knowledge is lacking but only knows that it cannot proceed.[2]

	GPS	SOAR
Problem spaces	Had a single problem space	Has multiple problem spaces Can generate new problem spaces
Goals	Had a fixed set of 3 deliberate subgoal types	Generates its own subgoals of unlimited diversity
Difficulty driven	Had a fixed set of state differences plus operator non-apply	Detects any lack of knowledge (by impasses)
Methods	Had means-ends analysis and operator subgoaling	Has all the weak methods Creates strong methods
What decision to make	Had fixed context-dependent occasions for decisions	Permits any decision to be made on any occasion
Decision making	Had fixed schemes for selecting methods and subgoals	Has open-ended retrieval of knowledge for deliberation Can convert any decision into general problem solving
Communication of results and context	Had prepackaged data communication	Operates in a single open context
Learning	Had no learning ability	Learns continuously from experience on all aspects

Figure 5. Comparison between the basic features of GPS and Soar.

Consider what drives the system. Both GPS and Soar are difficulty-driven. Note that GPS's goal was to reduce a difference. It acted on a fixed set of differences its match routine could detect between two states, and on operators that failed to apply to the current state. Soar, in contrast, detects any lack of knowledge with its impasse structure. It detects that it is stuck, because the process allowing it to proceed fails. This is an *impasse*, not because something labels a condition an impasse, but because, existentially, Soar fails to decide among its preferences and therefore has no way to continue.

Consider methods. Basic GPS had exactly two methods: means-ends analysis and operator subgoaling which, if an operator's conditions were not satisfied, did set up a subgoal to find a state in which an operator could be applied. Both methods are important examples of *weak methods*, which comprise the repertoire of things intelligent problem solvers do when they don't have sufficient knowledge of the domain to permit *strong methods.* But there are many other weak methods, such as hill-climbing, branch-and-bound, and depth-first search. Soar, unlike GPS, has all of the weak methods available. In addition, it creates strong methods of its own by adding search control knowledge as it builds up domain experience. (But Soar does not of itself discover new strong methods, such as a simplex method.)

Consider what decisions have to be taken. GPS, like almost all other AI programs, had fixed occasions when it had to decide, and each such occasion dictated the decision to be made—to work on a subgoal, to choose which of its two methods to use, and so forth. Soar, in contrast, permits any decision to be taken at any time. As Soar builds its hierarchy of subgoals, it can at any point decide to try a particular operator, or reject being at a state, or work in a new problem space, or abandon the subgoal, etc.

Consider how decisions are made. GPS had fixed programs for selecting its methods, that is, fixed codes in the underlying list-processing language that applied built-in heuristics. Soar, in contrast, is entirely open ended. At every decision occasion, it does an open-ended retrieval of knowledge from its long-term memory. If whatever knowledge is retrieved does not suffice to make the decision, then Soar converts the decision into a general problem, to which all the problem-solving resources of Soar can be brought to bear. In effect, Soar can reflect on any decision, to make it by whatever means are appropriate. The reader will have recognized this act of reflection as the occurrence of impassing and subgoaling, that is, as the central act of difficulty-driven problem solving. But that is exactly right—decisions are not made by a separate decision-making process, but by the basic capability of Soar to behave intelligently.

Consider how knowledge is passed between levels. This aspect of system operation is familiar mostly to system programmers. In all standard programming languages there is a fixed scheme by which a called procedure passes its operands into the context in which the procedure will be executed and another fixed scheme by which it packages the results in the evaluation code to be result of the procedure at the point it was called. These conventions seem innocuous enough, but in fact they force strong preplanning constraints. GPS had a typical set of scheme for transfers of operands and results back and forth between contexts. Soar, in contrast, operates in a single working-memory context and has no preset conventions on operand and result passing. Each problem solving context accesses whatever knowledge in working memory is appropriate and places results wherever they are appropriate. So there are no prepackaged communication conventions.

Consider learning. GPS had no learning capability at all. It was just a problem solving system. Soar, in contrast, learns continuously on all aspects of its structure and from all of its experience. Thus, learning for Soar becomes a central process in its operation.

Adding this all up, we seem to have a fair representation of an important strand in the progress of AI over the last thirty years. It indicates how we have progressed from systems that were everywhere rigid, except for some specific problem-solving mechanism of interest, to architectures where such rigidities are largely absent—where almost everything has not been fixed in advance, but instead is allowed to be a function of the knowledge of the task. We are, at last, obtaining systems that have more of the open-ended flexibility that seems to be characteristic of truly intelligent behavior. Soar, no doubt, still has its quota of rigidities, many of them somewhat more subtle than those of GPS, enumerated above, which Soar has basically relieved.

I believe the story of Figure 5 provides a good characterization of the advances that Soar has made. Soar has put together in an integrated fashion all of these mechanisms that have come up in the course of the history of cognitive psychology and AI during the past thirty years, removing rigidities along the way.

Soar As a Candidate Unified Theory of Cognition

We now turn to Soar as a unified theory of human cognition, and not just as a generally intelligent system. The major mechanisms used in Soar as a psychological theory are still those we have just seen. They are central to large parts of cognitive psychology. Problem spaces are the dominant structure for understanding problem solving behavior. Production systems constitute a common language for simulating human behavior in terms of goals and goal hierarchies. Difficulty-driven problem solving and learning through chunking are both pervasive. Even the basic representational medium, which we have not discussed, namely, attribute-value data structures, is closely related to semantic nets, common in cognitive psychology. All of these had already, prior to Soar, been in widespread use within cognitive theory to explain human cognition. Thus, not only does Soar integrate them, which is what we discussed in the previous section, but they, in turn, guarantee that in many respects Soar is a cognitive theory of the right shape.

However, these observations apply at a relatively macroscopic level, that is, to problem solving behavior and to the general use of knowledge. They do not apply to the details of the architecture—that is another matter altogether. We know from both theory and experience in computer science that widely varying architectures can realize the same gross processing, given enough time. Indeed, if architectures have just a few basic properties, they become *universal computers*, which can compute anything that any other computer can compute.[3] This means that the details of an architecture cannot be inferred from its behavior when it has lots of time to process a result.

But there are many important questions about cognition that depend on the detailed nature of the architecture, and that drive a unified theory of cognition, such as Soar, to attend as much to the details of the architecture as to the higher levels of cognitive activity. First of all, as soon as behavior takes times close to the basic times for architectural mechanisms, then the nature of the architecture will show through. Thus, all of what is termed *mental chronometry* in cognitive psychology is influenced strongly by specific architectural details. Second, perception and motor behavior, two vast domains of psychological investigation, are both dominated by architectural concerns. Third, areas such as imagery and emotion are likely to involve special architectural mechanisms. Finally, due mainly to the factors just mentioned, the architecture has much more pervasive effects on the style and character of higher-level cognition than we give it credit for. This is especially true if we move away from a view of creating arbitrary programs in some programming formalism for the production of a result towards viewing all the capabilities of a system, including those that program itself, as being the result of that system's own operations and learning. Then the nature of these architectural mechanisms that mediate everything becomes of the essence. In any event, it is extremely important that Soar not only consist of psychologically valid high-level mechanisms, but that it provide an highly accurate model of the underlying cognitive architecture.

There are ways to get some leverage on how the architecture of human cognition must be structured. A fundamental one comes from the mind being realized in the brain, which is to say, its being realized in a neurotechnology built by evolution. Many constraints on the nature of the cognitive architecture follow from this. One that is especially important is the *real-time constraint on cognition*, namely, that neurons are devices that operate in about one millisecond. Consequently the simplest neural circuits operate in about 10 milliseconds—essentially the time it takes a number of neurons to pass signals back and forth before they reach quiescence. Yet we see cognitive behavior emerging in elementary, but genuine, form in approximately the one second range.[4] This implies that somehow the architecture must fit in between: it succeeds in working with basic components (elementary neural circuits) taking only 10 milliseconds for a processing cycle, yet produces cognitive behavior within a second. This is only 100 basic operation times of 10 milliseconds, which is hardly any time at all. A better way to express this is in terms of system levels: arrangements of elementary neural circuits form some larger subsystems, and then arrangements of these subsystems generate cognitive behavior. There can only be two such system levels, because it takes not much less than ten operation-times of a component to produce a result that can be identified as an elementary action at the next higher system level. Hence subsystems take about 10 times 10 milliseconds or 100 milliseconds to operate, and the organizations of subsystems take about 10 times 100 milliseconds or 1 second to operate—and that is all the time that is available to the architecture. This constraint of the human cognitive architecture to operate in real time, given the slowness of its neural technology, imposes a very strong constraint on the nature of any symbolic architecture that purports to be the architecture of the human mind.

Thus, we are not free in a proposed unified theory of human cognition, such as Soar, to specify how the various theoretical constructs correspond to cognitive structure and operations in the human—as if Soar were a formal theory with arbitrary bridging rules to its domain of application. We must honor the real-time constraint. Figure 6 shows what this entails. It gives the correspondence that *must* hold between Soar and the human if the real-time constraint is to be satisfied.

Soar	Human Cognitive Architecture	Properties
Productions	Symbol System ➪ Access LTM ➪ Retrieve from LTM	➪ ~10 ms level ➪ Recognition system (content addressed) ➪ Parallel operation ➪ Involuntary ➪ Unaware of individual firings ➪ Duration: depends on complexity (simpler match than Ops5)
Decision Cycle	Smallest Deliberate Act ➪ Accumulates knowledge for act, then decides	➪ ~100 ms level ➪ Smallest unit of serial operation ➪ Involuntary (exhaustive) ➪ Aware of products not process ➪ Duration: longest production chain (to quiescence)
Primitive Operators	Simple Selective Operations	➪ ~1 sec level ➪ Serial operations ➪ Primitive observable thinking acts ➪ Goal-oriented ➪ Duration: decision-cycle sequence (minimum of 2 decision cycles)
Goal Attainments	Full Problem Spaces	➪ ~10 sec level ➪ Smallest unit of goal attainment ➪ Smallest nonprimitive operators ➪ Smallest unit of learning (chunk)

Figure 6. Basic mapping of Soar onto the human cognitive architecture; ~ means roughly (Newell, 1990).

Productions, which constitute the elements of recognition memory, must be taking a duration of about 10 milliseconds; they are at the level of elementary neural circuits. They must operate totally in parallel and involuntarily.

Whatever awareness may come to mean in Soar, there can certainly be no awareness of individual productions firing. Productions constitute the bottom-most components of the Soar architecture and everything else is built on top of them.

Consider a mechanism that could realize the Soar decision cycle. Such a mechanism will consist of several elementary retrievals from recognition memory, plus some decision mechanism that sifts through the results of these retrievals to make the decision, plus a phase that executes whatever decision is made. This will be a system that is up one level from the most elementary operation (the production), because it is an arrangement of several such components. With productions in the 10 millisecond range, the decision cycle will be in the 100 millisecond range. The decision cycle is where elementary deliberation occurs—the first level at which a choice can actually be made. Soar will be unaware of what goes on within this elementary deliberation process, because it is happening automatically. It can be aware of the products of the deliberation cycle, but not of the process itself, of exactly what productions fired and in what order to create the result. The decision cycle corresponds to what cognitive psychology calls *automatic*, as opposed to *controlled* behavior (Schneider & Shiffrin, 1977; Shiffrin & Schneider, 1977). It runs to completion until quiescence, thus showing aspects of exhaustiveness, such as not being able to be terminated at will. Thus the decision cycle is the smallest unit of serial operation—the unit where control is exercised.

Putting several decision cycles together gets to the next level of operation. Each decision deals with a choice, such as what problem space to be in, which operator to apply, whether or not the task is accomplished, etc. These are the decisions to move through a problem space. It takes several decision cycles to take a step in a problem space, so that the level of primitive steps in a simple problem space constitutes a level one up from the 100 millisecond decision cycle, about 1 second. This brings the system to where it is making genuine, if elementary, cognitive operations, which can bridge from perception to external action. Examples include reaction tasks where the knowledge to do the simple operations is well known and well prepared, so that the required sequence of two or three decision cycles can be simply run off.

A problem space is elementary when none of its subprocesses—selecting and applying the next operator—does lead to an impasse and thus would require going into subordinate problem spaces. Everything simply runs off. However, in most cases, subspaces are required, not just a single additional level, but many levels. The time it takes to carry out the processing in such a hierarchy of spaces becomes highly variable. Indeed, this is the region of behavior where true problem solving occurs.

We have described the correspondence between Soar and the levels of operation in the human cognitive architecture. Surprisingly, a tightly woven argument can be given which shows that the mapping of Figure 6 is essentially the only way that the behavior of Soar can be mapped into human behavior (Newell, 1990, chap. 3). This argument derives entirely from the real-time constraint on cognition, which is an empirical, if highly general, assertion about the nature of human cognition. From a theoretical perspective, it removes all doubts how Soar should be compared to psychological data.

As we indicated in discussing Figure 1, a unified theory of cognition should be able to handle the full range of cognitive phenomena. Initially, of course, we hardly expect perfection in its coverage or in the depth to which it deals with what it covers. Even if a theory were essentially correct, science takes time to take effect. Meanwhile many questions and domains will remain intractable, until the theory develops the requisite power. What we do expect of a unified theory, especially for cognition, is that there should be a large jump in the number and diversity of phenomena and domains covered. We need to be somewhat relaxed on depth and accuracy, compared with existing microtheories, for there is a certain trade-off of depth for breadth. But such trade-offs stem more from a lag in development than from structural limitations in the theory or clear inabilities to explain details.

In the William James lectures (Newell, 1990) I spent much effort showing the breadth of Soar, mostly because it seemed important to illustrate operationally what was meant by a single theory providing explanations for a really wide range of cognitive phenomena. Here, it is necessary to be much more selective (see Figure 7). It is appropriate to start with two very general points.

First, a theory of human cognition must predict that humans are intelligent and explain how that is possible. No theory of cognition is worth its salt until it succeeds in doing this. Soar makes this prediction. Actually, it makes a slightly weaker prediction, namely that humans are at least as intelligent as Soar. Though it may sound peculiar when phrased this way, Soar cannot do better. This is because the only way for a theory to predict intelligence is for an operational system, constructed according to the theory, to exhibit the requisite intelligence.[5] Soar, as a state-of-the-art AI system, can predict intelligence only up to the level of intelligence it embodies operationally. As we succeed in improving Soar as an intelligent system, the prediction will improve its prediction of the intelligence that humans have.

1. How humans are able to exhibit intelligence
2. Many global properties of human cognitive behavior
3. Human immediate behavior (roughly 1 second)
4. Discrete perceptual-motor behavior (typing)
5. Verbal learning (recognition and recall)
6. Skill acquisition
7. Short-term memory
8. Problem solving
9. Logical reasoning (syllogisms)
10. Elementary sentence verification
11. Instructions and self-organization for tasks

Figure 7. The coverage so far of Soar as a unified theory of cognition.

Second, Soar, in its general structure and behavior, should fit what we know qualitatively and directly about human cognitive behavior. Soar does fairly well on this score, although assessment is subjective. For instance, Soar does not know what it knows. Retrieval from a recognition memory is from the clues assembled in working memory. There is no access to information in memory other than this. So there can be many things that are known, but cannot be retrieved. This feature is often noted of human behavior. Indeed, various authors have made this into a cardinal feature of human cognition. For example, Polanyi's (1958) theory of tacit knowledge in humans (stating, for instance, that it is remarkable that people can drive bicycles and not be able to explain how) formed the basis of an entire philosophical approach to human nature.

SOAR AT THE CHRONOMETRIC LEVEL

Having focused so long on the importance of the details of the architecture, it is now time to show that Soar can model human behavior at the chronometric level—immediate responses that take a second or two. This is behavior that is fast enough to reveal something of the details of the architecture, hence to test architectural details.

The following example comes from work by Bonnie John, who studied aspects of text editing on computers (John, Rosenbloom, & Newell, 1985). The phenomenon of concern is *stimulus-response compatibility* (SRC). Imagine an elevator that has its up-button below its down-button, rather than the other, standard, way around. It takes longer to hit the correct button and there is a greater chance of hitting the wrong button. The directional relationship between the buttons and the elevator's movement is incompatible. The phenomenon is well-known and robust.

Bonnie John's example concerns the intention to DELETE a character while editing with a computer. Editors use abbreviations for their commands. For instance, the command might be DLT, using vowel deletion. The user must go from his intention (DELETE) to typing DLT. Many other abbreviations are possible, for example, ^D where ^ is some special control character and D is the first letter of the command. There is relationship of compatibility between the intention and the abbreviation. Abbreviations that are less compatible will take longer to type and will have an increased chance of being incorrect. This provides a basis for evaluating abbreviations.

We can define a Soar system to perform this task—to start with DELETE, develop from it DLT and then type D,L,T. Such a system will involve the operations of perceiving the initial situation (DELETE), encoding it into working memory, comprehending the important features of the task at hand, generating and intending to make specific responses, decoding these responses into motor commands, and finally moving fingers. Each of these operations is a specific Soar construct: primitive processes (perceive and move), productions (encode and decode), or operators (comprehend and intend), depending on how they are performed by the architecture. More importantly, it requires a sequence of operators to go from the stimulus (DELETE)[6] to the response (D,L,T). Here, Soar goes from from the word (DELETE), to the syllables (DE, LETE), to the spelling of each syllable in terms of letters (D,E and L,E,T,E), from which it can identify which are the vowels (E in three places) and ignore them, so as to evoke the keystroke response only on the non-vowels (D and L,T).

It takes time to run through such a sequence of operations. Indeed each of these operators, which are highly practiced and minimal in their action, take of the order of 50 milliseconds. That allows the total time to respond to be computed. So, by effectively doing a mental time-and-motion study, the total time to do this task can be predicted—it happens to be 2140 milliseconds.[7] John ran an experiment and determined empirically that the task actually takes on average 2400 milliseconds. Thus, Soar gets within about 10 percent, which is quite satisfactory for rough theorizing with parameters determined a priori. The theory also states what is found empirically—that the more complex the mapping, the slower the response—which is the basic SRC effect. Thus, we have a theory that provides quantitative predictions of SRC—indeed, it is the first such one. Notice that this theory is not specific to SRC. It is a theory of how humans make complex immediate responses in general, but it can be applied to the SRC situation to provide predictions of the SRC effect.

There is a second major point to be made about Soar here. Soar is not proposing a new psychological theory of behavior in immediate-response tasks. Rather it is *assimilating* an existing theory, called GOMS (for Goals, Operators, Methods and Selections). GOMS itself is a general theory of routine cognitive skills that permits predictions of the time it takes to perform skilled tasks (Card, Moran, & Newell, 1983). John (John & Newell, 1987) extended this theory to cover SRC effects that result from the internal mappings between stimuli and responses. Thus, John's GOMS theory gets 2573 milliseconds for the task we discussed above, not too different from the values obtained from the subject and from the Soar theory. The GOMS theory maps over into Soar in a direct way, so they are essentially the same theory for their common domain. The assimilation of existing theories is an important aspect of a unified theory of cognition. Many theories of limited domains have captured the essential cognitive mechanism operative in their domains. But a unified theory need not—indeed, should not—explain the same facts from different mechanisms. Instead it has to show how the cognitive mechanisms are expressed as special cases within the framework of the more general theory.

The substantive, rather than methodological, point is that the details of how Soar carries through its algorithm can be converted into a priori predictions of human behavior. With our example we have, of course, just illustrated the process. Figure 8, however, summarizes predicted versus observed behavior for a whole range of stimulus-response experiments, including the classic ones Paul Fitts did in the 1950s to establish the phenomenon of SRC. Fitts' results are the pluses while the dots and squares refer to experiments that John has done later. They show excellent predictions, especially if it is understood that a single set of constants is being used for the perceptual, cognitive, and motor operations (derived from one of these experiments). All of the data are from the John's GOMS theory, but, Soar appropriates these predictions because it reproduces the GOMS theory. More recently we extended the GOMS-like theory to highly detailed theory of transcription typing, which a discrete motor-perceptual skill, dealing with the pipelining from perception to cognition to the keystrokes (John, 1988). As in the SRC work, the predictions for a variety of phenomena related to typing were often quantitative, but—and that is crucial—they were all based on a single set of constants. In addition, Soar predicts the power law of practice, which is an extremely stable quantitative relation between the time to do a task and the number of times a person has already done the task. Soar also provides a partial theory of how recognition and recall occur in classical verbal learning. This is another case of assimilation, in that it shows that the discrimination-net theory of EPAM (Simon, 1989) arises naturally within Soar from the demands of the learning situation.

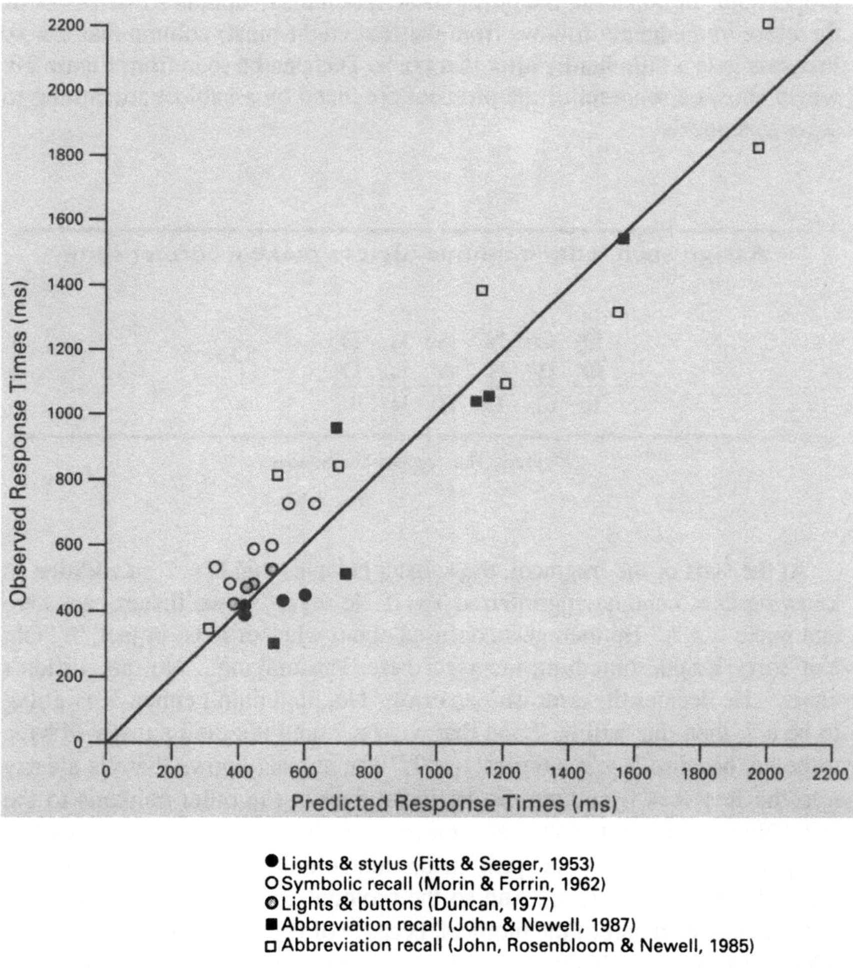

Figure 8. SRC prediction results from GOMS theory (John & Newell, 1987).

SOAR AT THE PROBLEM SOLVING LEVEL

Let us select an example from problem solving. Figure 9 shows a task, *cryptarithmetic*, that Herb Simon and I analyzed in detail back in the late 1960s (Newell & Simon, 1972). This involves a little puzzle in which letters are to be replaced by digits, each letter by a different digit, so as to produce a proper sum. In this case, the puzzle description also stipulates that D = 5. It therefore immediately follows from the first (right-most) column that T = 0. Progress gets a little harder after that point. This can be seen from Figure 10, which shows a segment of the protocol produced by a subject attempting to solve this puzzle.

Assign each letter a unique digit to make a correct sum

```
   D O N A L D        D = 5
 + G E R A L D
 -------------
   R O B E R T
```

Figure 9. The cryptarithmetic task

At the start of the fragment, the subject believes that R = 7, in addition to knowing D = 5 and having inferred T = 0. He says, "So we'll start back here and make it a 7." He then gets confused about whether R is, in fact, 7: "Oh, I'm sorry I said something incorrect here. I'm making... No, no, I didn't either." He decides the error isn't an error: "No, no, I didn't either. R is going to be a 7, then this will be 7 and that will be 7, and it's the Ls that will have to be 3s, because 3 + 3 = 6 plus 1 is 7." The subject knows there is a carry into the R + R = L column. So he looks over at the other columns to the left: "Now, it doesn't matter any more what the Ls are equal to... so I'm independent of L when I get past the second column. But now I know that G has to be either 1 or 2, ..." And so the protocol goes on. This is actually a very complicated part of the protocol, because of the column with O + E = O, which has the same letter above and below the line. Subjects get confused about this. Thus, this segment of behavior is genuinely at the problem solving level.

L1	B61.	So we'll start back here and make it a 7.
	B62.	Now if the . . .
	B63.	Oh, I'm sorry, I said something incorrect here.
	B64.	I'm making . . .
L2	B65.	No, no, I didn't either.
	B66.	R is going to be a 7,
	B67.	then this will be 7,
	B68.	and that will be 7,
	B69.	and it's the Ls that will have to be 3s,
	B70.	because 3 plus 3 is 6
L3	B71.	plus 1 is 7.
	B72.	Now, it doesn't matter anywhere what the Ls are equal to . . .
	B73.	so I'm independent of L when I get past the second column here.
	B74.	But now I know that G has to be either 1
	B75.	or 2,
	B76.	depending on whether or not E plus O is greater than 10
	B77.	or greater than 9.
	B78.	Now I have this O repeating here in the second column from the left.
	B79.	That is, itself plus another number equal to itself.
L4	B80.	This might indicate that E was zero . . .
L5	B81.	In fact, it might have to necessarily indicate that.
L6	B82.	I'm not sure.
L7	B83.	Or, E could be 9
	B84.	and I would be carrying 1,
L8	B85.	which would mean that I was carrying 1 into the left-hand column.
L9	B86.	(E: What are you thinking now?)

Figure 10. Cryptarithmetic protocol fragment during a complex situation.

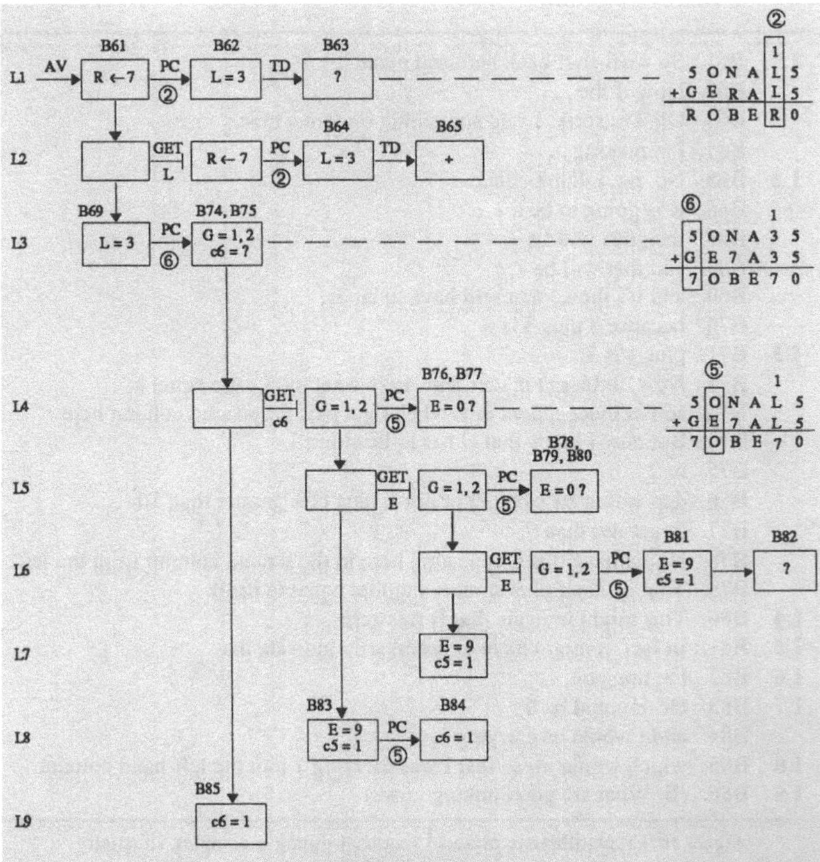

Figure 11. Soar on cryptarithmetic.

Figure 11 shows the fragment of a Soar simulation for this segment. It shows Soar going through impasses, applying operators, etc. The Soar trace follows the subject's behavior very closely, even though the subject is twisting and turning as he tries to figure out what is the case. These twists and turns correspond with the places where Soar is uncertain so that it has to go back over the processing several times.

One reason for doing this simulation is that the subject's behavior is an example of essentially free behavior. A unified theory must be able to describe the twists and the turns of genuinely free problem solving—not just for a little segment, such as the figure shows, but for a much longer segment. A second reason for this particular simulation is to show that we could come back to the old data on cryptarithmetic which played such a strong role in early analyses of problem solving. This is another example of what must be done by a unified theory: it must explain not only the newest results, but it must show it can cover the old results of the old theories. These cryptarithmetic data made their contribution to the 3000 regularities that all need to be covered by a single theory of cognition.

Let me give one more example from the problem-solving level, some recent work by Dirk Ruiz (Ruiz & Newell, 1989) concerning learning. Figure 12 shows the Tower of Hanoi, another puzzle much used to explore issues of problem solving and cognition. There are three pegs with five disks on them. A disk can be moved from the top of one peg to a different peg, but it can never be put on top of a smaller disk. The problem is to start with the stack of all the disks on the left-hand peg (as shown) and to build a stack of all the disks on the right-hand peg, by moving the disks one by one from one peg to another.

When subjects initially attempt this puzzle, most engage in *guided trial and error*—avoiding obvious things, such as moving a disk twice in a row or moving a disk right back to where it came from, but otherwise moving arbitrarily. There is a more effective way of doing this task, called the *goal-recursive strategy*. The reasoning is as follows: the tower of five disks must be moved to the right-hand peg; to do that, the largest disk must be moved to the right-hand peg; to do that, the tower of four smaller disks must be moved to the middle peg; to do that, the largest of these four must be moved to the middle peg; to do that, the tower of three smaller disks must be moved to the left-hand peg; and so on, until it is reasoned that the smallest disk must be moved to the right-hand peg—and since it can be so moved, it is. Thus, the entire goal stack is built up recursively, working backwards from the final goal, and then the behavior is simply read off from the goal stack as the situations occur. Some, but not all, humans shift from guided trial and error to the goal-recursive strategy sooner or later. The interesting phenomenon is that when they do, they do it all of a sudden.

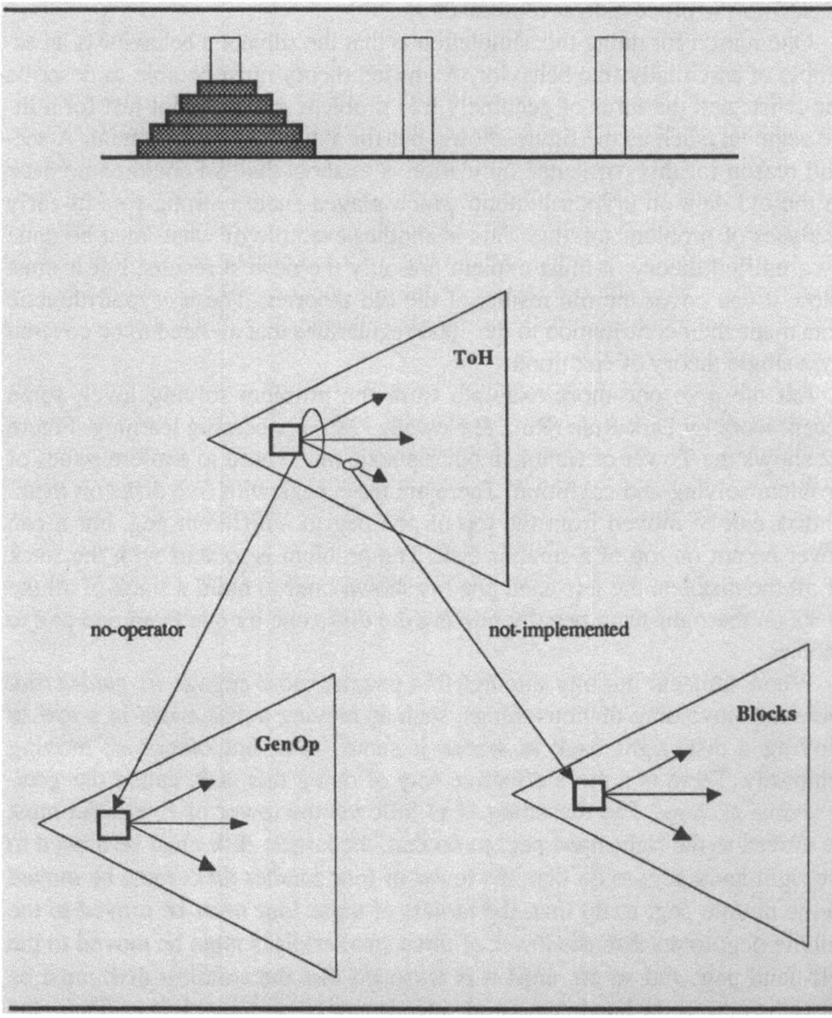

Figure 12. Soar on the Tower of Hanoi. GenOp composes operators for what disk to what peg. Blocks solves how to implement tower operators (Ruiz & Newell, 1989).

There is version of Soar that does the Tower of Hanoi problem and provides an explanation of this sudden strategy change. The two specific strategies of problem solving are easily implemented; the issue is the strategy change. To state the goal-recursive strategy it is necessary to describe the situation in terms of *towers*, not just individual *disks*. For example, the description above said, "... to do that, the tower of four smaller disks...." It doesn't matter whether they are actually called *towers*, of course, what counts is that stacks of disks on a peg be considered together as a unit. *Noticing* that disks form a unit could plausibly be a sudden act of perception, caused by any number of momentary conjunctions of events, such as thinking "tower" in Tower of Hanoi, when attending to disks 4, 2, and 1 on a peg, thus realizing that these form a tower too. This might be sufficient knowledge to initiate a shift of strategy. But it does not answer the question of how to get from the perception of towers to the goal-recursive strategy. This is the step the Soar model explains. It does not explain the act of noticing towers; it does explain how that gets converted into the goal-recursive strategy.

The Soar system for the Tower of Hanoi has a problem space in which it attempts the task, proposing moves and trying them, sometimes with small amounts of look-ahead search before deciding which move to make. However, Soar does not simply select moves from the set of all legal moves, as is typically the case in problem solving programs. Soar *composes* its moves. Moves in Tower of Hanoi involve picking a disk to move and then deciding where to move it. When Soar notices towers, it composes a move to move a given *tower* to some disk. This requires no change in Soar's capabilities; all it does is use a different reference in its move expression. However, it immediately discovers that it does not know how to implement such a move—all it has ever done before is moving single disks. Of course, the Soar theory (like the human subject) does know about moving simple solid things around in space. It has an available blocks-world space—familiar from the AI world of toy tasks. Knowing what a tower is, it solves the problem of moving a tower to a disk in this space. This takes a certain amount of exploration and processing. What happens then—actually over the course of several trials—is that Soar learns (by chunking, naturally) to make tower moves in the same direct way it made single-disk moves. But this leads on to the goal-recursive strategy, since one cannot actually take a tower move until the preconditions are met for moving the smaller tower out of the way. Thus, Soar provides an explanation for an important case of strategy acquisition in problem solving.

These three examples—stimulus-response compatibility, cryptarithmetic and strategy change in Tower of Hanoi—will have to suffice to indicate the way Soar exhibits itself as a unified theory of cognition. These three have been chosen, however, to span a rather large number of basic lessons about how a unified theory should behave itself.

There are still other phenomena we have looked into with Soar—some bits of language comprehension, some tinier bits of language learning, some still tinier bits of conceptual development, and some issues of instructing Soar and how it organizes itself under the instructions. All of these forays are intended to get Soar to cover the wide variety of behaviors, listed in Figure 1. Of course, thus far we only succeeded in getting the first order effects right. It is still too early to have a clear idea whether the Soar theory can be extended to produce a fully detailed unified theory. But there's lots of hope: in some recent work, such as strategy change research in the Tower of Hanoi just discussed, Soar is beginning to provide new explanations of novel phenomena.

Issues for a Unified Theory of Cognition

The story so far has focused on a candidate unified theory of cognition producing detailed explanations and predictions of diverse, but standard, psychological phenomena. But there are other issues surrounding a unified theory that are not dealt very well just by taking a tour along specific phenomena. I take up several of these in the remainder of the paper. They are not the only issues that arise, but they have all actually come up in the course of the short history of Soar, often more than once. Prima facie, they all apply to any candidate unified theory. However, I will look at them strictly from the Soar perspective.

WHY SOAR?

The first question is, Why Soar? Why not John Anderson's ACT* (Anderson, 1983)? Why not the classifier system put forward by Holland, Holyoak, Nisbett, and Thagard (1986)? Why not a connectionist system, even though there are no specific connectionist architectures around yet that make a comparable claim to breadth. What makes Soar *the* choice for a unified theory of cognition? The answer is simple and straightforward: nothing. There should be multiple attempts. Soar is just one attempt, the one that happens to be favored by the Soar research community. But we in cognitive science certainly do not know enough about Soar and its prospects, so perhaps not everyone should go down the Soar path. On the other hand Soar is one of the very few paths that appear to be leading somewhere.

Other architectures are surely both possible and interesting. In fact, I don't think of Soar as the first attempt to get over the threshold of being a unified theory of cognition. John Anderson's ACT* is really the first theory that can make this claim. It is interesting to compare ACT* and Soar at a very general level, to see what makes them both potential, if early, candidates for a unified theory. First, it is essential that the theory be embodied in operational form, that is, as a simulation system. Second, it is essential to deal with both complex behavior, at the level of problem solving, and with learning. It is critical to be able to address why the structures that explain performance are as they are. Third, it is essential to cover both the low-level architecture, as well as the higher-level problem solving. Even when dealing with higher-level cognitive behavior, which is relatively far from the architecture, the architecture is still providing a basis for generalized constraints about higher levels. ACT* and Soar each show all three of these characteristics. There is also a number of substantive commonalities that make them brothers under the skin and make them supporters of each other, rather than competitors. Other candidate unified theories will probably not be so close. But ACT* and Soar definitely both meet the first three criteria that a candidate should really satisfy.

There cannot be indefinitely many different unified theories of cognition. All such theories are attempting to explain and predict the same universe of phenomena, to wit, human perception, cognition and action, and so they have the same 3000 regularities to explain. Ultimately, a shake-out must occur and a single picture emerge. There will always remain differences in how scientists choose to describe things, and such variation is part of the process of continually improving the science. But as matters progress in science, it always becomes clear that all these variations are describing the same underlying structure in the domains that are well understood. The biggest enforcer of scientific convergence, and one that applies strongly to unified theories, is for theories to attempt to explain and predict exactly the same phenomena.

In my view, candidate unified theories should all play the game of "Anything you can do, I can do." We should strive to get our own theories to do what other theories can do well. For a concrete example, consider some work by Gerard Kempen in psycholinguistics (Kempen & Vosse, 1989).[8] Kempen's theory covers the phenomena of real time comprehension of utterances by adults. The architecture is a scheme for parallel searching in the space of fragments of analyses, each fragment being bound together by a certain strength that reflects how well the subfragments satisfy constraints that apply to that fragment. Thus fragments keep forming and dissolving until finally a stable form emerges. The theory has much the flavor of the theory of chemical reactions, according to which all conceivable reactions take place, each at a rate related to its energetic plausibility, until the final energetically stable configurations emerge. Kempen's theory is well formulated and exists in operational form as a simulation system. This theory predicts many regularities, both of time and errors. Therefore, to put words in Kempen's mouth, if Soar is so great, it should be able to predict the same regularities. I think that is a fair challenge. The regularities surrounding sentence comprehension are both important in themselves and indicative of human mental operations—they are an important part of the 3000. That Soar cannot produce these predictions on demand does not count against it. It always takes time and effort to apply scientific theories to particular phenomena. But the challenge stands, not just for phenomena, but for phenomena that can be explained by a well-formed theory. Kempen's theory is not very broad, but it embodies a scheme of information processing that clearly has potential far beyond the linguistic domain. Thus, the counter-challenge is equally appropriate: if this processing scheme is so great, then it should be able to predict the regularities that Soar does in cryptarithmetic and in Tower of Hanoi. Kempen's theory does not immediately yield such explanations, but again, that is no mark against it. These challenges and counter-challenges are meant to keep cognitive theorists from becoming too complacent about their own phenomenological point of view. The challenge is to get everybody to cover the phenomena of everyone else. Not only will we then get appropriate comparisons, but we will also get theories that begin to approach the coverage proper to unified theories.

A high-jump metaphor is useful. As the world record high-jump moves higher, the field establishes an increasing threshold that each new high jumper must get over, just to qualify as a competitor. Similarly, once we can get the process established, each new unified theory must get over a threshold of coverage and adequacy before it can even be considered a candidate. The issue is not who's best—not who momentarily holds the championship—but who can qualify for the event. ACT* established an initial threshold. I think that Soar, even though it has been largely exemplary so far, also qualifies as a candidate. One of my disappointments with the Holland et al. (1986) effort is that, in my estimation, it did not qualify, that is, it did not rise to the level of coherence, coverage, and specificity that I think ACT* established. Qualification is, of course, a question of timing. If Holland et al. had been first, that would have been fine. They would have established the initial qualifying level, but the fact is that ACT* got there first.

CAN AI AND HUMAN COGNITION CO-EXIST?

The second issue is whether AI and human cognition can co-exist in the same system or research program. The Soar effort is committed to making Soar a frontier AI system, that is, a system which is at the research frontier in learning, problem solving, knowledge acquisition, and integrated intelligent systems. But we are also, as this paper makes clear, committed to making Soar a unified theory of cognition. But how is it possible to have an AI system that is also a unified theory of cognition? If you aim for one of these goals, isn't that inconsistent with aiming for the other? There are many people, both in AI and in cognitive science, who believe the two aims are incompatible. Their basic intuition is an optimization argument: it is not possible to optimize two independent payoff functions.

No doubt, the optimization argument is ultimately correct. However, at this moment in history, AI is still missing so many aspects of flexibility that AI systems that attempt at incorporating human flexibility have a great advantage. They can be extremely competitive in the AI domain. In the short run—the next ten years or so—a way to win may be by completely identifying an AI effort with a human cognition effort. That is the bet we are making for Soar—not as an ultimate aim, but one that may serve us well for the next several years.

The argument above is based on the notion of flexibility and non-brittleness, characteristics of AI systems that have been hard to attain. It is also worth noting that many basic mechanisms in AI have been discovered through the study of human behavior—systems with true goals and subgoals, growing discrimination nets, key weak methods such as means-ends analysis and abstraction planning, production systems,[9] and finally chunking. There is a lot of evidence that pushing on psychological aspects of intelligent systems produces big dividends for AI.

The other side of the coin is that there is also an advantage for a theory of cognition to attempt to be an AI system. We have already provided the argument for this. The most important prediction to be made by a theory of cognition is that humans are as intelligent as they are. Historically, the science that has pushed the frontiers in understanding of the functions of intelligence is AI. Psychology, left to its own devices, has essentially ignored the challenge. If you want a symbol of this failure it is the three-quarter century effort in intelligence testing in psychology which, to this day, has contributed almost nothing to the understanding of what it means for humans to be intelligent. In short, perhaps I should add a fourth characteristic that all good candidate unified theories should have, namely, that there must be an associated effort to make the system an AI system.[10]

Altogether, I can be quite content in binding AI and cognition inextricably together in Soar, even while accepting that a time will come when they may finally go their separate ways.

IS SOAR JUST A PROGRAMMING SYSTEM?

The third issue is whether Soar is just a programming system. Why isn't any other programming system just as good a unified theory as Soar is? Why not Lisp? Or C, or Prolog?—pick your favorite. Since one simply programs a Soar system, say for cryptarithmetic, why isn't any programming language equivalent to any other? Several robust fallacies are buried in this question. Chief among them is the notion of universal computation—often referred to as the Turing Tar Pit—whereby all programming languages[11] can compute the same functions, hence are equivalent. So, Why not Lisp? Let me consider the issue at some length.

First, programmability does not imply that everything is possible in terms of human cognition. The times dictated by the cognitive theory for specific operations must be the same as those observed in human performance. This can be stated more abstractly to avoid actual units of measurement. The time-complexity profiles of the human and the program must show the same pattern—what takes a relatively long time in one, must take a relatively long time in the other. This consideration is effective for our *why-not* question, because the equivalence of programming systems (universal computing) specifically abstracts from the duration of the computations. There is no equivalence of programming languages if time complexity is taken into account.

The same consideration applies to other characteristics, such as errors made by the human and by the program (i.e., the theory). It applies to any learning that occurs, such as how long it takes, what errors of overspecialization and overgeneralization occur. These all mean that one cannot write any odd program as long as it does the same task that the human does and expect it to be an adequate theory of cognition. This is particularly evident in the case of learning. If your favorite language is, say, Lisp, and certain learning must occur while doing some tasks (because humans exhibit such learning), there is no direct way to "just program" that in Lisp. A program organization must be invented, including mechanisms of learning as well as performance. Furthermore, if successful, the theory will not be *just Lisp*, but it will also include this organization and these learning mechanisms.

Second, programmability is not a property of unified theories of cognition simply as a convenience to the cognitive scientist. Any such theory must exhibit programmability, because humans are programmable. They program themselves all the time. Just for one instance among millions, they may ask someone else for instructions and then follow those instructions. Any system that is so limited that it doesn't have the flexibility to be programmed nor the capability to program itself, could not possibly be a theory of human behavior. Thus, it is elementary that a theory of human behavior is a theory about a system that exhibits universal computation if given sufficient time and if matters are arranged to keep error rates low enough.

The fear that programmability destroys a theory of cognition is not totally unfounded. A useful way to express this is that human behavior exhibits many degrees of freedom. A theorist attempting to explain the behavior of a subject in an experimental task must postulate a large amount of knowledge that the person has available for doing that task. The person knows about language, about rooms with experimenters in them who give instructions, about how equipment works (more or less), about being civil and compliant, and so on. There is essentially no independent evidence of this knowledge except the theorist's own understanding as a human (which of course cannot be part of his theory). Furthermore if the theorist does not posit this knowledge—even if only implicitly—there is no way to explain the subject's behavior. These postulates may be treated as additional degrees of freedom for the theory. They must be specified, just like the more well-defined parameters in the theory. When the theorist simply posits these assumptions (and there is usually no choice), he is, in effect, making a series of promissory notes about human behavior—about what humans acquired while they were attempting this task, what methods they are deploying, and how they acquired these in the experimental situation. These must ultimately be explained by the theory using other data for verification. When the critic says that she can just as easily program this behavior in some *why-not* language, it is assumed that it is possible to make as many arbitrary assumptions as are needed about what the subject knows. And the cognitive theorist unfortunately must admit that it often sounds that way. Altogether this points to a deep problem for cognitive science: how to reduce the myriad degrees of freedom in cognitive theories. That is the kernel of truth in the fear over programmability.

One purpose of a unified theory is to help cash these promissory notes and contribute to solving the problem of reducing degrees of freedom. Instruction, learning, and performance must all be in the same theory, so that the theorist is no longer forced to make ad hoc assumptions about one, while tinkering with the other. Let us consider what determines behavior—in other words, the cognitive architecture plus all the relevant knowledge that the subject has. One important body of knowledge is the basic task-performance and orienting knowledge that is held in common by all subjects—the basic skills any subject will bring to the experiment. Another important body of knowledge concerns the specific experimental task. No theory can ever predict how a subject will behave in an experiment, if the knowledge of the experimental task is not, in some way, input to the theory. Subjects must know about the task or they could not perform it. And if a human subject must know, so too must the theory. In fact, at the beginning of an experiment, the subject does not know the task. Thus, one basic skill, comprehension, is particularly important. It determines how the subject perceives the instructions, interprets them, and possibly encodes them in ways other than the experimenter intended—the stimulus fallacy. Other bodies of knowledge, including biases, and heuristics are also involved. All these sources of knowledge combine to determine behavior, over and above what explicitly goes into a psychological theory, including the underlying architecture. Which brings us back to the degrees-of-freedom problem: What the theory doesn't provide, the theorist must posit or measure. What a unified theory of cognition should do is to provide as much of these bodies of knowledge as possible—minimizing the degrees of freedom that the theorist must still deal with. The following is a way to tackle this problem by getting the theory to include the reading of instructions that provide the knowledge which organizes the system which then accomplishes this task. This is a far cry from the incorporation of all the bodies of knowledge that a unified theory needs to cover, but the ability to comprehend external instructions is an important component.

Figure 13 shows a fairly abstract picture of a total task being performed, with time running from the top of the figure to the bottom. There are three Soar subsystems called NL-Soar, BI-Soar, and IR-Soar respectively. NL-Soar (Natural Language) is a subsystem for natural-language comprehension. BI-Soar (Behavior Interpreter) is a subsystem for interpreting a representation of a plan of future behavior and guiding behavior. IR-Soar (Immediate Reasoning) is a subsystem for performing an experimental task of reasoning. There are some instructions pertaining to the experimental task at hand: "Read three premises. Then read a statement. If the statement is true, say Yes. If the sentence is false, say No. Then stop" (see Figure 14). Then a start signal for the experiment is presented, followed by a trial of the experimental task, the example in the figure being: "The fork is left of the plate. The cup is above the knife. The knife is right of the plate." Then comes another sentence, "The fork is left of the knife." Soar is supposed to say, "yes," because the fork is, indeed, to the left of the knife.

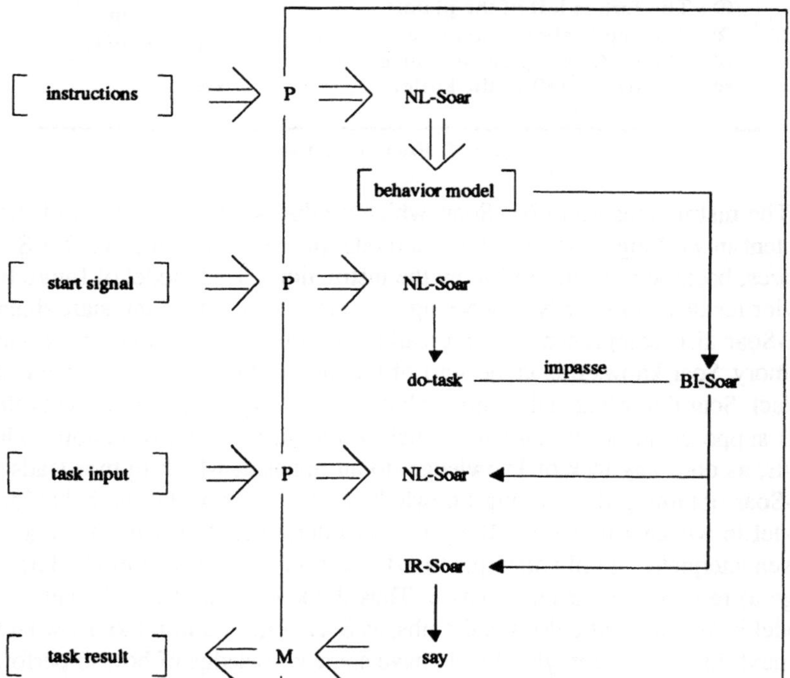

Figure 13. NL+BI+IR-Soar, a collection of problem spaces. NL-Soar comprehends natural language utterances; BI-Soar interprets a representation of behavior as a plan; and IR-Soar does immediate reasoning about a presented situation.

1. **Read three premises.**
2. **Read a statement.**
3. **If the statement is true say "Yes," else say "No."**
4. **Stop.**

< start signal >

① **The fork is left of the plate.**
② **The cup is above the knife.**
③ **The knife is right of the plate.**
→ **The fork is left of the knife.**

		CUP
FORK	PLATE	KNIFE
	Yes	

Figure 14. Example NL task.

The instructions go to NL-Soar, which produces a representation of their content in working memory. This is a model of the future behavior that Soar desires, because it wishes to follow the instructions. This model of future behavior resides temporarily in working memory. Then comes the start signal. NL-Soar also comprehends this, creating additional knowledge in working memory. Soar knows this is the start of the task and proceeds to do the task. In fact, Soar doesn't actually know what task it is supposed to do, except that it is supposed to do the task for which it was just given instructions. This leads, as does any lack of knowledge, to an impasse, which in turn leads to BI-Soar obtaining the missing knowledge. BI-Soar consults the behavioral model in working memory. BI-Soar is an interpreter, but it is an impasse-driven interpreter. It only attempts to extract from the behavior model knowledge to resolve the current impasse. Thus the knowledge from the behavior model is mined in little drips and drabs, as Soar finds it doesn't know what to do next. In fact, Soar might already have some knowledge of how to perform the experimental task. Then, BI-Soar is only consulted on those occasions when not enough knowledge is available. As BI-Soar proceeds, Soar obtains the actual task input and uses NL-Soar to comprehend it, and then evokes the various parts of IR-Soar as they become relevant, until the task is completed.

NL-, BI-, and IR-Soar are not three separate systems. Each is simply a collection of problem spaces, with operators and associated knowledge, all of which constitutes a single Soar system. The passage between them occurs in the same way as it does within each of them, namely, an impasse in one problem space leads to selecting another problem space and formulating within it the problem of resolving that impasse.

While Soar is performing a task by using the behavior model in working memory, it is also learning. It is building chunks every time it impasses from one problem space to another, whether within or between these three "systems." These chunks constitute the acquisition of knowledge for doing the task. On subsequent exposures to the task, Soar won't have to consult the behavior model in working memory, because it will have the chunks available that will provide this same information (and as noted above, Soar is structured to mix whatever it knows with whatever the instructions say). Thus, Soar assimilates a task by interpreting the plan of its own future behavior, and while it is doing so it learns from this experience how to perform this task in the future.

I've glossed over some details, some of which are actually fairly important in their own right. Nevertheless this gives a picture of what a unified theory of cognition should be able to provide. In this situation the theorist does not have to write a flow diagram for how the subject does the task, such as one finds frequently in the psychological literature. Such flow diagrams have a somewhat shadowy status. However, if you inquire, you will find that they represent what *obviously* must be done to accomplish the task, plus the twist that embodies the specific theoretical hypothesis of the study. In fact, the non-twist part of such a flow diagram is exactly the behavior that is implied by the instructions for the task (plus the physical arrangements). Soar, as it assimilates the instructions and performs the task, organizes itself in such a way that it satisfies the general task demands and it therefore implicitly follows the flow diagram. In short, Soar itself provides the non-twist part of the flow diagram. The specific theoretical hypothesis, on the other hand, doesn't come from the instructions, but either from specific knowledge that the subject is supposed to have or possibly from the architecture. These two components would be integrated into Soar's behavior, and, hence into what it projects as the flow diagram that describes its behavior.

The Soar system that carries out this scenario of taking instructions and doing the instructed task (Lehman, Lewis, & Newell, 1991; Lewis, Newell, & Polk, 1989; Polk, Newell, & Lewis, 1989) deals directly, in a quite sophisticated way, with the question of *Why not programming language X?* by converting it into the real question of how to deal with the myriad degrees of freedom that plague all cognitive theories and then showing one way in which a unified theory of cognition can make a dent into this problem.

I have sketched what may seem like a fairly futuristic scenario. But in fact, there is a version of Soar with these three subsystems that does this whole task (Lewis, Newell, & Polk, 1989). We have done several sorts of immediate reasoning tasks: relational reasoning, the example that we used, syllogistic reasoning with quantifiers, conditional reasoning, and the well-known Wason card task. These are all quite similar in some ways, but still show the ability of Soar to go through the entire process described above.

At the moment empirical evidence for the psychological validity of NL- and BI-Soar as the instruction-taking system is limited.[12] Being based on Soar, it is a plausible theory. However, we have not yet tried to obtain data on task acquisition by humans for comparison, and there is not an abundant literature on taking instructions in these situations.

On the other hand, IR-Soar, which explains the immediate verbal reasoning of the subjects, is a very well-developed theory indeed. It explains the qualitative phenomena associated with the four tasks fairly well. But it has been applied most assiduously to the task categorical syllogisms, and there it makes extremely good predictions, not only of all the regularities but also of individual data (Polk & Newell, 1988).[13]

SOAR AND THE BRAIN

Let us turn to yet another issue. Soar is a typical symbol system. Indeed, many people think of it as a prototypical symbolic system. So, what about the brain? Psychological theories are hardly based on knowledge of the anatomy and physiology of the nervous system. With the advent of connectionism, this point has become a little more acute, since it is now claimed that symbol systems are not compatible with the brain, hence are wrong, and that only theories based on a brain-like architecture will lead to genuine models of human cognition. This notion of brain-like architecture is somewhat ill specified, but includes, generally, massive parallelism and, more specifically, excitatory-inhibitory networks of very simple computing elements. The supportive considerations, beyond the surface similarity between artificial and biological neural networks, often focus on the serial nature of many algorithms used to produce intelligent behavior and the impossibility of doing such algorithms as fast as humans do the tasks these algorithms perform. For example, it is simply not possible for humans, who process linguistic utterances in real time, to use the serial parsing algorithms developed in computational linguistics. Thus—so goes the argument—no symbol system can be a reasonable model of human cognition.

Let us see where Soar stands on this. The main point is that Soar, although it is a symbol system, is entirely compatible with the real-time constraint on cognition. Great care and effort were exercised to assure this to be case. Does this mean that the arguments above are without merit? Not entirely. Soar is, in fact, a massively parallel system, although its elements are not artificial neurons. Its recognition memory operates all at once, firing simultaneously all the productions that match working memory. But these very productions also contain the essential feature of a symbol system, namely, they provide an accessing system from currently focused-upon expressions (what is in working memory) to expressions in a long-term memory (the right-hand sides of the productions), which are then retrieved to be added to the expressions being focused upon. So Soar is massively parallel and a symbol system at the same time. Also, of course, if described at the next level up, it is a serial system.

What, more particularly, is the relationship of Soar to connectionist systems? First consider the notion, in connectionism, of a subsymbolic level, that is, of a system level that underlies or supports a symbolic level. Soar implies that there is no room for a subsymbolic level. In Soar, the symbolic access is already occurring at the bottom of the architecture, namely at the level of production firings, which are at the level of retrievals from long-term memory. These immediate retrievals in Soar occur in of the order of 10 milliseconds. There is no way that any subsymbolic processes can proceed at a level lower than this. Ten milliseconds is about as fast as a neural circuits can operate. There can't be any neural circuits of a subsymbolic level, for they would have to operate at 1-2 milliseconds—which is about the time it takes a single neuron to generate a pulse. So if Soar is right, a subsymbolic level cannot exist. Conversely, of course, if a sub-symbolic level exists, then Soar must be wrong. But then a coherent notion must be created of a symbol level that runs at a much slower pace than the 10 milliseconds that Soar requires in the light of the real-time constraint on cognition.

We can look at the issue in a slightly different way, which may be more productive. It also depends critically on the time scales at which various mechanisms operate. Actual connectionist systems that model human cognitive phenomena operate at about the 100 millisecond level (of human time). The settling times for the networks are around 100 milliseconds —perhaps as little as 40, perhaps as much as 150-300 milliseconds. In fact this is also true of other systems. In ACT*, the activation process requires of the order of 100 milliseconds. Thus, anything that occurs faster than that—such as Sternberg's memory scanning with its 40 millisecond per item "rate" (Sternberg, 1975) —will be explained in ACT* by the time it takes activation to settle down and fire the appropriate productions. This also holds in Kempen's annealing system, which we discussed above. For any reasonable system to settle in 100 milliseconds, the elementary steps must not take much longer than 10 milliseconds. Therefore, if connectionist systems turn out to be right, what they displace in Soar is not the production system, that is, the basic retrieval cycle, but the recognition memory plus the entire decision cycle. It is these two together that operate in time scales of about 100 milliseconds.

In sum, all these systems, Soar included, provide substitute explanations for what happens up to the 100 millisecond level. The connectionist models, as well as Kempen's scheme, do not extend to time scales longer than a second or two. But both ACT* and Soar do, ACT* to one level of problem spaces, and Soar to multiple problem spaces. This suggests that the higher levels of systems, such as Soar or ACT*, might be maintained invariantly, while the bottom levels (up to 100 milliseconds) might be constructed various ways. Indeed, John Anderson has recently proposed to abandon the lower levels (activation-based processing) and simply work at the higher levels (Anderson, 1990). A neural implementation of Soar (Cho, Rosenbloom, & Dolan, 1991) would illustrate this, except that it would tend to preserve the Soar architectural structure at the lower levels, whereas the connectionist systems suggest a quite different structure for the lower levels. This might seem to be a subsymbolic level, but the upper level is not a symbolic system, but a problem-space system, which is quite a different thing. The symbols must still be realized at the lower levels, buried in the connectionist or annealing system.

The above considerations are all based on the analysis of the temporal constraints that attend human cognition. Indeed, these are very binding constraints, from which much information about the human cognitive architecture can be extracted. On the other hand, we should not forget that time is not the only constraint on human cognition. The spatial decomposition of processing in the brain is, no doubt, another—one Soar does not yet reflect at all. In the not too distant past there was a feeling that localization of function simply did not occur in the brain, Lashley's *principle of mass action* being the most extreme expression. By now big strides have been made in localizing rather specific functions in rather specific regions of the brain. The most striking of these is the decomposition of the perceptual system in which it has been shown, quite convincingly, that the location of stimulus objects are represented in a different, well defined, subregion from properties of the stimulus objects, such as their color. Gradually we are putting together a spatial map of the brain. Although there is still a long ways to go, at some point the constraint of having to create the cognitive architecture out of a set of anatomically and functionally identified and connected components will be available and have the same kind of binding effect that has been obtained from temporal considerations. Or at least so one can hope.

MAKING NOVEL PREDICTIONS

As a last issue, let me take up novel predictions. A question that my friends ask me very frequently is, "Where are the novel predictions of Soar?" If Soar purports to be a real theory, then it must make novel predictions—for that is what all good theories do. This question is largely motivated by the belief—extending far beyond Soar—that "Simulation theories never give novel predictions, at least I've never seen one, they just put out what you put in." This challenge has forced me to give some thought to the matter. Certainly it is an important matter, and not just for Soar, but for unified theories of cognition generally, with their emphasis on assimilating existing theories.

To talk about novel predictions[14] implies that there is some basis for assessing novelty. Just putting forward a potential prediction simply leaves this judgment in the background. Thus, before we turn to what sorts of novel predictions Soar makes, let us consider some way of judging novelty.

I have invented a scale called the *nov scale*, the *nov* being a unit of scientific novelty. This scale is fashioned after the Richter earthquake scale, and the basic analogy is that something is novel to the extent that it shakes the scientific system on which it is based. As Figure 15 and Figure 16 show, the scale is basically logarithmic. Let me just go through the scale to make clear what the values are.

Nov	Type
0	***Assumption***: Result is exactly what is assumed
1	***Reformulation***: A mild transformation of what is assumed
2	***Routine***: A class of results the theory is known to work on
3	***Confirmation***: Known empirically, but not from the theory
4	***Refinement***: New details, not known empirically
5	***First***: Known empirically, but *no* theory predicts
6	***Discovery***: New result, not empirically known
7	***Home Run***: A widely believed key prediction to make
8	***Revelation***: A new result that restructures the field

Figure 15. The nov scale for the assessment of scientific novelty.

At the lowest level of zero nov, the result is exactly what was assumed in the creating the theory. There isn't any novelty at all. You might think this is an unimportant point, but it is amazing how often conclusions are put forth from a theory which were simply put in somewhere else as an assumption.

Characteristic Effects	Magnitude	Number Per Year	Nov	Type
Damage nearly total	> 8.0	0.1-0.2	8	Revelation
Great damage	> 7.4	4		
Serious damage, rails bent	7.0-7.3	15	7	Home Run
Considerable damage to buildings	6.2-6.9	100		
Slight damage to buildings	5.5-6.1	500	6	Discovery
Felt by all	4.9-5.4	1400	5	First
Felt by many	4.3-4.8	4800	4	Refinement
Felt by some	3.5-4.2	30000	3	Confirmation
Not felt but recorded	2.0-3.4	800000	2	Routine

Figure 16. The analogy between the Richter and nov scales.

At the level of 1 nov, prediction is simply a mild *reformulation* of what is assumed. It involves, for instance, predicting the power law of practice by putting a power law into some component of the system, say the laws of behavior of individual neural elements, and then predicting the overall law by observing the overall behavior of many neurons. In effect, the result is just piped from one part of the model to another. It isn't zero nov because there is some simple aggregation, but it still isn't much of a prediction.

Two nov is where a theory is already known to work for a class of situations and you get more results of the same kind. Certainly this is a prediction, but a fairly *routine* one since you know already that the theory works.

Three nov reflects *confirmation*, by a theory, of facts that are already known empirically, but of which it was not yet known that your theory can produce them. This is beginning to be little bit better.

Four nov stands for *refinement*, new details that no theory has ever shown.

Five nov can be called a *first*—something is known empirically but no theory predicts it. If a theory gets that far, it is really beginning to be noticeable. This is why the nov scale is like the Richter scale. The question is how much it shakes the scientific world.

Discovery is a new result, not empirically known, which no other theory has demonstrated. Its nov value is 6. An example is Dirac's prediction of the positive electron from theory.

The *home run* (I didn't have a better name) occurs when there is a widely known key result that everyone believes it is critical to predict, and the theory finally comes up and predicts it. This is 7 nov, a result like the perihelium shift of Mercury that was predicted by relativity theory.

Then there are scientific *revelations*—new results that restructure their field. Einstein's marvel, $E = mc^2$ is an example. With that result whole new subfields open up.

The descriptive labels for the Richter earthquake magnitude scale correspond to these notions pretty well. An interesting correlated measure is how many earthquakes of a given magnitude can be expected per year. Translating this into the scientific realm, there are some 800,000 routine predictions, not felt by anyone, but recorded. Discoveries at 6 nov give slight damage to the structure of the existing scientific world. Great damage, damage nearly total occurs at eight on the Richter scale, which is one of the revelations. So this scale works. Thus, using earthquakes in place of any empirical validation whatsoever, we have generated the nov scale to help us assess the novelty of purported predictions of a cognitive theory.

With this scale in hand let us look at some candidate Soar predictions.

Whether a prediction is known to be true or not is not a relevant consideration. Some of these predictions may well turn out to be false. That is the way it is with predictions. The question is simply, if they were true, how novel would they be?

Soar shows the power law of practice. I put that at about 1.3 nov, just above a simple transformation. From the beginning, we built our model of Soar with a concern for chunking as an explanation of the power law (Newell & Rosenbloom, 1981). So we don't get novelty for that. It is not the case that the explanation is simply piped from one place to the other—the power law is not simply put in. Rather, it can be demonstrated in Soar systems that are organized in a particular way, which is why the nov value is a little greater than 1.

However, it turns out that Soar appears to exhibit the power law quite generally, without being specifically organized to do so. For example, a Soar system for exploring production scheduling in a factory exhibited the power law when it happened to be arranged to do the same scheduling task repeatedly —the task arrangement in which the power law is likely to arise. The prediction from Soar of the ubiquity of the power law is worth, say, 2.2 nov.

Soar's prediction of the existence of the automatic processing level is a 3 nov prediction. This feature of human cognition is well known empirically, but not from the Soar theory. However, theories of automatic behavior do exist.[15] Furthermore, the feature was not built into the theory deliberately by the scientists. The entire structure of the decision cycle—the production memory being a recognition memory that operates completely in parallel, the repeated cycles of retrieval until quiescence, the accumulation of preferences that form the input to the decision procedure—all these were created and shaped by the functional requirements for Soar to operate as an intelligent system (Laird & Newell, 1983). The relation with automatic processing became apparent after the fact during the preparation of the William James lectures in 1986-87. For instance, that the exhaustiveness of much automatic behavior arises from the quiescence mechanism of the decision cycle, came as a complete surprise. That elevates this prediction to 3 nov.

Consider chunking, which is posited as the only learning mechanism in Soar and one that operates pervasively. Chunking is tied to impasses, which occur and are resolved within a few seconds. Thus it follows that any memory that is used in a task and lasts more than a few seconds, is really long-term memory that arises from chunking. Indeed, increasingly, as we come to understand how Soar systems should be built, we see that chunking, that is, learning, enters into the very fabric of the performance system. Since the a priori expectation, from the study of learning systems, is that learning is separate from performance, this comes as something of a surprise. (For one thing, it means that the system cannot operate in a no-learning mode.) This seems to me to provide new details, not previously known. This is actually pretty interesting, and I give this prediction 4 nov.

There are several 5 nov predictions—known empirically, but predicted by no prior theory. The formulation of these predictions from Soar is not yet completely solid, so the predictions are actually not entirely derived from the theory but rather from the theorists. But we are getting close. One such close hit is that declarative memory is reconstructive. This is a feature of memory, known since Bartlett (1932), and confirmed in all kinds of experiments. However, there is no theory that explains why memory has to be reconstructive —no explanation that didn't in effect start from the assumption of memory being reconstructive. But there is a version of the Soar theory that actually predicts this feature.

A second prediction is the cause of the well-known, fast-read/slow-write feature of human memory. Writing into long-term memory takes much more time than reading information out of long-term memory. Retrieving information occurs in well under 100 milliseconds, but chunks do not seem to be learned faster than about one chunk every two seconds. There are no theories that adequately explain this arrangement, although it has received some attention, most notably in consolidation theories, which postulate that it takes some time-consuming process to fixate memories in long-term memory. However, Soar predicts this feature of human cognition. Retrieval from long-term memory is the retrieval from recognition memory in Soar and requires approximately 10 milliseconds. This aspect is part of the basic assumptions about Soar. Writing to long-term memory in Soar is just chunking. Now the time to construct a chunk is essentially of this same order, that is, it happens almost instantaneously. There is no time gap at all between when knowledge is acquired (chunking) and when it is available for performance. Consequently consolidation theories can't be right because it does not take a sufficiently long time to manufacture a chunk. What counts, rather, is the rate at which chunks get created. That is what governs the rate at which new knowledge can be added to long-term memory. This, in turn, is governed by the rate of impassing, since chunks only arise in response to resolved impasses. And impasses, in their turn, are governed by performance—they occur only so often and their resolution requires time—a new problem space must be created and the resolution sought in this new space. Each such period of preparatory activity requires many retrievals from long-term memory, so there is a characteristic ratio between read and write. There are some empirical indications from many Soar systems that a ratio of 1 to 20 may not be too far off, but there are many things which influence this that we do not yet understand.[16]

There is another 5 nov Soar prediction that is worth mentioning. Cognitive psychology has revealed a veritable zoo of short-term memories, from the sensory stores and the verbal STM, to the articulatory loop, to the visual scratch pad, to a number of others. There are serious experimental and methodological issues in determining a definitive catalog of such memories, but there is little doubt about the empirical reality of the zoo. There is no theory about why there should be such a zoo in the first place, except that a few of its inhabitants have been grounded in the requirements of the senses. Soar offers a prediction of the basic mechanism that gives rise to multiple short-term memories (Newell, 1990, chap. 6). Briefly, it arises from the connection between the perception and motor systems and cognition, in which the coupling is via an internal attention operator. An internal act of moving and returning attention to a given internal region provides a short-term memory whose residence times are determined by the nature of the internal region and whose accessing characteristics are determined by the ability of central cognition to identify the items available on return with the items it left there when attention shifted. The system (Soar) must learn to exploit these short-term memories—their operation and role are not wired in.

We can actually find a couple of Soar predictions at 6 nov. Recently, we discovered that Soar predicts that the short-term and long-term goal structures are independent. Research in AI provides us with most of our knowledge about the nature of goals, how they form goal-subgoal hierarchies and how they are used. All this work leads to the view that there is a single goal structure, possibly with a tangled hierarchy of relations that describe which goals are subgoals of others, which are related disjunctively or conjunctively, etc. In this arrangement the long-term goals of the system—e.g., its career goals, so to speak—are at the top of the goal hierarchy and the immediate, momentary goals are down at the bottom. There is a single big hierarchical structure. Soar, which builds its goal hierarchy from impasses, cannot be that way. And it thus predicts that human goal organizations cannot be that way either. If it really were that way—if all goals were in this impasse hierarchy—then the first impasse that ever happened to a person after or before he or she was born would be the one sitting at the top. Life's goal, so to speak, would be to resolve this primeval impasse! It seems hardly plausible. The problem is not difficult to discern. The goal hierarchy in Soar is ephemeral. It is impasse-created and has an existence only as long as the impasses are maintained. But these are a function of the momentary situation. One would not expect to wake up in the morning with the impasses that one went to sleep with, except perhaps in some pathological conditions. The content of all the goals in the hierarchy are of the form, "such and such knowledge is needed to resolve an impasse," and not of the form, "I want to be a doctor when I grow up." The implication from this is that there exists a long-term structure that holds these content goals, makes them available, and makes contact with the other sorts of knowledge that is necessary to understand them and to face the problems of adjudication between them. We do not yet know what the structure is. Conceivably it could be a special architectural structure. But the more likely prediction from the nature of Soar is that it is built up, like all long-term memory structures, by chunking, reflecting experiences in the world (including experiences of the state of the body). This Soar prediction is not yet specific about the detailed nature of this second goal structure. It only maintains that the existing goal structure, which has all the processing properties of a general goal structure, is a short-term affair and that a second long-term goal situation exists.

The second 6 nov prediction is that the learning rate is tied to the impasse rate. This is an obvious structural feature of the Soar architecture and it is used in the discussion of a number of other aspects, such as the fast-read/slow-write characteristic of human memory. But its obviousness in Soar does not keep it from predicting a very deep identity between performance and learning processes. Like so many other things in the Soar architecture it was not placed there deliberately. Rather, it arose from the functional demands of getting Soar to be an intelligent system. A learning system that is not tied to the goal-oriented aspects of the performance system simply does not learn anything useful. For instance, an earlier chunking system that simply learned whatever was in working memory—that, in other words was focused only on the gross level of attention of the human—learned lots of stuff, but none of it relatable to future behavior. So this link between chunking and impasses is a consequence of the Soar architecture, not an assumption of it. Unlike most of the other predictions, it is not actually clear yet what this one means for human cognition. It is not cast in terms of a specific external phenomenon. But if this deep connection between performance and learning exists, and if it exists in this specific form, then we can expect many consequences, which will make us aware of an important constraint in human cognition. That is good enough for 6 nov.

1. Soar shows power law (Seibel task: 1.3 nov; any: 2.2 nov)
2. Existence of automatic processing (3 nov)
3. Exhaustiveness of automatic processing (3.2 nov)
4. Learning is used for all (> 3 sec) performance (4 nov)
5. Declarative memory is reconstructive (5 nov)
6. Fast-read/slow-write characteristic (5 nov)
7. Source of multiple short-term stores (5 nov)
8. Short- and long-term goal structures independent (6 nov)
9. Learning rate = impasse rate (6 nov)

Figure 17. Summary of Soar novs.

Figure 17 summarizes the list we have just been through. Its main purpose is to lay to rest the canard that operational (i.e., simulation) systems such as Soar are not able to make novel predictions. The nov scale, I hope, can have some uses beyond this one exposition of Soar. It may provide some discriminations which are useful in discussing and comparing unified theories of cognition.

Summary

Let me come back to the top-level issue, which is not Soar but the need for the cognitive science community to attempt unified theories of cognition. I am much in favor of non-Soar candidate unified theories. I also don't think that unified theories all start with an overall view of how to deal with all of cognition—and perception and motor action as well. Mostly, they grow from being successful in some domain. The history of ACT* provides an excellent lesson in this respect. It started out as HAM (Anderson & Bower, 1973), a pure memory model, acquired an action component in ACT-E (Anderson, 1976), and then became cast as a full architecture in ACT* (Anderson, 1983). Kempen's system, discussed above, could potentially follow an analogous path. The annealing mechanism seems to provide a basis for handling a wide range of cognitive tasks, and I would hope Kempen and his colleagues will grow his system, as Anderson has done ACT*.

There are many arguments for unified theories of cognition. Maybe I believe too much in the lash over the carrot, but I would like to raise once more the specter of the 3000 regularities. If cognitive psychology has learned anything, it is how to generate new, robust regularities and to explore them thoroughly, so they have a permanent existence. Cognitive psychology will continue to ply its trade—the 3000 regularities will become 4000, then 10,000. What will we do then? Unified theories of cognition are the only way to bring this wonderful, increasing fund of knowledge under intellectual control. Then, as in other sciences, the number of regularities will no longer matter. They will find their place in an established theoretical order. A precious few will not, of course, and these will provide the necessary continuous challenge to existing theory. But there will not be hundreds of such major challenges per year.

This paper has not been just about unified theories of cognition, of course. It has also been about Soar, our own attempt. Whilst being democratically enthusiastic about all the world's candidates, I do not conceal my special zeal and conviction for what is now the theory of the Soar community. Soar seems to me to have made it over the qualifying threshold established by ACT* and to have helped raise that threshold somewhat. New candidate unified theories must do modestly well *vis-à-vis* Soar (as well as ACT*) in order to be considered serious candidates. The notion of the qualifying hurdle, however unquantifiable because of so many dimensions of comparison, seems to me quite useful. It prevents theorists from simply exhibiting a single neat result from a specific microdomain, and claiming this is all that counts. And whereas the Soar of the William James Lectures in 1987 was essentially an exemplar, the current Soar is truly a serious candidate for being a unified theory of cognition.

Acknowledgements

The work on Soar is now carried out by an entire community of scientists. I would like to thank them for their help in developing Soar. I would especially like to acknowledge John Laird and Paul Rosenbloom, who have been my colleagues for a decade in the creation of Soar, and all those whose particular efforts I have used here: Bonnie John, Jill Lehman, Rick Lewis, Thad Polk, Dirk Ruiz and Olin Shivers. Over the years my research on Soar has been supported primarily by the Defense Advanced Projects Agency, and in part by the Office of Naval Research, both of the US Department of Defense.

NOTES

[1]And perception and motor action as well, but it is burdensome to repeat this too often.

[2]Descriptions of Soar often refer to impasses of various types, e.g., *tie impasses*. But this does not define a typology of goals, since the goal is to *find additional knowledge that will resolve the impasse*, not to *select an element of the tied set.*

[3]A more familiar term may be *Universal Turing Machines*, Turing Machines being one class of computational devices that are capable of universal computation.

[4]Fast reaction times take only about 200 milliseconds, but these situations involve so much preparation and practice that it is unclear how much cognition remains. So it is better to stay with a one-second duration, where it is clear the cognition plays a strong role.

[5]This is worth pondering quietly for a bit. If a theory is to predict that a human is intelligent, it must predict what the human does when faced with the need for an intelligent action. If it predicts the intelligent action, then it provides a prescription for that action, so that a machine built to embody the principles of the theory would be able to take the intelligent action. A fortiori, the machine would be an intelligent system.

[6]In the experiments subjects see the command, DELETE, rather than having it arise internally during the course of editing.

[7]There are a priori primitive times for perception and motor movement in addition to the 50 milliseconds for fast cognitive operators, but they are all determined a priori (Newell, 1990, chap. 5).

[8]Kempen gave a talk under the title "A cognitive architecture for human sentence processing," based on this work at the Symposium on Soar and Unified Theories of Cognition, June 1989, held in Groningen, The Netherlands, and illustrated it with a very neat dynamic display of his simulation.

[9]Even though called "Post production systems," after the logician Emil Post, they were introduced into AI through the study of human behavior, and in fact attained thereby the form required to become reasonable processing systems, namely, working memory as a set of independent elements, variables for the instantiation of productions, and task-related conflict resolution. None of these features characterizes Post productions or the related Markov algorithms. Post and Markov systems, of course, focused on entirely different issues, namely logic and foundations.

[10]Interestingly, some support for this can be found in the development of connectionist systems, where the emergence of a vigorous "pure AI" effort in connectionism is having the same salutary effort there as symbolic AI has had for classical cognitive science.

[11]Each language must contain a basic set of mechanisms and have access to an indefinite (expanding) amount of memory, but these conditions are easily met.

[12]The work on NL-Soar has progressed well beyond the requirements of the example being discussed here (Lehman, Lewis, & Newell, 1991).

[13]The theoretical account here, including the work on individual differences, is based on more recent research by Thad Polk, and has not yet been published.

[14]Although for some purposes predictions, postdictions, explanations and descriptions are all different, here it simplifies matters to just fold them all into the notion of a theory's *prediction*.

[15]For instance, the original effort of Shiffrin and Schneider (Schneider & Shiffrin, 1977; Shiffrin & Schneider, 1977), but others as well. It is a little unclear whether any of these theories actually predicts automatic behavior, rather than taking it as a given and then proposing explanations of it.

[16]On the empirical side we have a few Soar systems that learn chunks at a much higher rate; on the definitional side, the chunks that get measured in an experiment on rate of long-term acquisition are not all the chunks that get created.

REFERENCES

Anderson, J. R. (1976). *Language, memory, and thought*. Hillsdale, NJ: Erlbaum.

Anderson, J. R. (1983). *The architecture of cognition*. Cambridge, MA: Harvard University Press.

Anderson, J. R. (1990). *The adaptive character of thought*. Hillsdale, NJ: Erlbaum.

Anderson, J. R., & Bower, G. (1973). *Human associative memory*. Washington, DC: Winston.

Bartlett, F. C. (1932). *Remembering: A study in experimental and social psychology*. Cambridge, UK: Cambridge University Press.

Card, S. K., Moran, T. P., & Newell, A. (1983). *The psychology of human-computer interaction*. Hillsdale, NJ: Erlbaum.

Cho, B., Rosenbloom, P. S., & Dolan, C. P. (1991). Neuro-Soar: A neural-network architecture for goal-oriented behavior. In *Proceedings of the Thirteenth Annual Conference of the Cognitive Science Society* (pp. 673-677). Hillsdale, NJ: Erlbaum.

Crowder, R. G. (1976). *Principles of learning and memory*. Hillsdale, NJ: Erlbaum.

Crowder, R. G. (1982). The demise of short-term memory. *Acta Psychologica, 50,* 291-323.

Feigenbaum, E. A., & Feldman, J. (Eds.). (1963). *Computers and thought*. New York: McGraw-Hill.

Fikes, R. E., & Nilsson, N. J. (1971). STRIPS: A new approach to the application of theorem proving to problem solving. *Artificial Intelligence, 2*, 189-208.

Holland, J. H., Holyoak, K. J., Nisbett, R. E., & Thagard, P. R. (1986). *Induction: Processes of inference, learning, and discovery*. Cambridge, MA: MIT Press.

Hull, C. L. (1943). *Principles of behavior: An introduction to behavior theory*. New York: Appleton-Century-Crofts.

John, B. E. (1988). *Contributions to engineering models of human-computer interaction*. Unpublished doctoral dissertation, Carnegie Mellon University, Pittsburgh, Pennsylvania.

John, B. E., & Newell, A. (1987). Predicting the time to recall computer command abbreviations. In J. M. Carroll & P. P. Tanner (Eds.), *Proceedings of the 1987 Conference on Human Factors in Computing Systems and Graphics Interface* (pp. 33-40). New York: Association for Computing Machinery.

Kempen, G., & Vosse, T. (1989). Incremental syntactic tree formation in human sentence processing: A cognitive architecture based on activation decay and simulated annealing. *Connection Science, 1*, 273-290.

Laird, J., & Newell, A. (1983). *A universal weak method* (Tech. Rep. CMU-CS-83-141). Pittsburgh, PA: Carnegie Mellon University, Department of Computer Science.

Lewis, R. L., Newell, A., & Polk, T. A. (1989). Toward a Soar theory of taking instructions for immediate reasoning tasks. In *Proceedings of the Eleventh Annual Conference of the Cognitive Science Society* (pp. 514-521). Hillsdale, NJ: Erlbaum.

Lehman, J. F., Lewis, R. L., & Newell, A. (1991). Integrating knowledge sources in language comprehension. In *Proceedings of the Thirteenth Annual Conference of the Cognitive Science Society* (pp. 461-466). Hillsdale, NJ: Erlbaum.

Miller, G. A. (1956). The magical number seven, plus or minus two: Some limits on our capacity for processing information. *Psychological Review, 63*, 81-97.

Newell, A. (1973). You can't play twenty questions with nature and win: Projective comments on the papers of this symposium. In W. G. Chase (Ed.), *Visual information processing* (pp. 283-308). New York: Academic Press.

Newell, A. (1990). *Unified theories of cognition*. Cambridge, MA: Harvard University Press.

Newell, A., & Rosenbloom, P. S. (1981). Mechanisms of skill acquisition and the law of practice. In J. R. Anderson (Ed.), *Cognitive skills and their acquisition*. Hillsdale, NJ: Erlbaum.

Newell, A., Shaw, J. C., & Simon, H. A. (1959). Report on a general problem-solving program. In *Proceedings of the International Conference on Information Processing* (pp. 256-264). Paris: UNESCO House.

Newell, A., & Simon, H. A. (1972). *Human problem solving*. Englewood Cliffs, NJ: Prentice-Hall.

Polanyi, M. (1958). *Personal knowledge: Towards a post-critical philosophy*. London: Routledge & Kegan Paul.

Polk, T. A., & Newell, A. (1988). Modeling human syllogistic reasoning in Soar. In *Proceedings of the Tenth Annual Conference of the Cognitive Science Society* (pp. 181-187). Hillsdale, NJ: Erlbaum.

Polk, T. A., Newell, A., & Lewis, R. L. (1989). Toward a unified theory of immediate reasoning in Soar. In *Proceedings of the Eleventh Annual Conference of the Cognitive Science Society* (pp. 506-513). Hillsdale, NJ: Erlbaum.

Ruiz, D., & Newell, A. (1989). Tower-noticing triggers strategy-change in the Tower of Hanoi: A Soar model. In *Proceedings of the Eleventh Annual Conference of the Cognitive Science Society* (pp. 522-529). Hillsdale, NJ: Erlbaum.

Schneider, W., & Shiffrin, R. M. (1977). Controlled and automatic human information processing: I. Detection, search, and attention. *Psychological Review, 84*, 1-66.

Shiffrin, R. M., & Schneider, W. (1977). Controlled and automatic human information processing: II. Perceptual learning, automatic attending, and a general theory. *Psychological Review, 84*, 127-190.

Simon, H. A. (1989). *Models of thought* (Vol. 2). New Haven, CT: Yale University Press.

Sternberg, S. (1975). Memory scanning: New findings and current controversies. *Quarterly Journal of Experimental Psychology, 27*, 1-32.

Watson, J. B. (1913). Psychology as the behaviorist views it. *Psychological Review, 20*, 158-177.

ON A COMPUTATIONAL MODEL OF HUMAN PLANNING

ALADIN AKYÜREK
Department of Psychology, University of Groningen
Groningen, The Netherlands

ABSTRACT. In this paper, I discuss various computational models of planning, specifically one that is derived from "case-based reasoning" that appears to provide a plausible process model to account for planning behavior of some interest in humans, and consider extending it with a temporal component. The key idea underlying the model is that plans are more or less frozen structures marked by the characteristics of the situations (e.g., goals) in which they are constructed or implemented. They are retrieved from episodic memory for reuse. If needed, retrieved plans are elaborated to fit current situations by problem solving. The results of such problem solving episodes constitute new plans which are again stored in the planner's episodic memory. Whilst there exists a number of computer programs that implement this model to various extents, the interest of this paper lies in showing a possible mapping of the model onto Soar, an architecture intended as a unified theory for covering all of cognition. Some issues such an undertaking has to solve are identified. It is concluded that modeling the behavior of case-based planners in Soar may provide a valuable test of the computational assumptions subtending the architecture.

Introduction

Plans represent courses of action. More specifically, a plan is a set of more or less consecutive actions that achieve one or more goals. Planning is often construed as deciding on a course of action (e.g., Wilensky, 1983). As Hoc (1987) notes, planning does not constitute a well-defined area of research in psychology as do the fields of learning, memory, and perception, for example. Yet, like learning, planning intervenes in most of the cognitive activities. Actually, planning can be taken as part of central cognition and, as such, it is subsumed by problem solving (Miller, Galanter, & Pribram, 1960). But, what is an action? What is a goal? By and large, these being rather difficult

J. A. Michon and A. Akyürek (eds.), Soar: A Cognitive Architecture in Perspective, 81–108.

concepts (Brand, 1984), I will not seek to circumscribe them, but, give instead an approximate definition by examples. An action is something that an agent does: walking into the dentist's office, giving a lecture, buying something, or pointing to an object in order to direct someone's attention, and so on. A goal is something that an agent wants to possess or achieve: a Renault 4, a Mexican meal, attending a party, or passing an examination. Actions are commonly modeled by operators in problem solvers as well as in planners. A temporal ordering of operators is constitutive of planning. This point is crucial for systems that purport to function as planners because they have to deal with multiple goals and interactions that may occur among the goals and subplans. The issue of interactions is of course related to issues of causation and temporalization of action. At any rate, I will utilize the notions of actions and goals in this paper in a problem solving perspective as is stipulated in Newell (1990).

This paper reviews, briefly, different types of planners, those deriving from the framework that construes problem solving as search, and those deriving from a recent framework, called case-based reasoning. The latter appear to involve a process model capable of describing significant aspects of human planning behavior. The prospect of mapping this model onto Soar, a cognitive architecture which constrains and extends the theory of problem solving as heuristic search in problem spaces, is considered, and some issues such an undertaking has to solve are indicated.

Types of Planners

Although a sound classification of existing planners would require a conceptual in-depth study, I consider the typology given in Figure 1 as adequate for the present purposes. In any case, the classification reflects a growing concern for cognitive plausibility among designers of planning systems (cf. Hoc, 1987). Research in the field of planning appears to gradually move towards knowledge level mechanisms related to (a) causation, (b) temporalization, (c) analogical reasoning, (d) memory, and (e) learning in specifying and constraining planning processes, as can be seen in attempts to design adaptive planners (e.g., see Agre & Chapman, 1989; Alterman, 1988; Hammond, 1989; Kaelbling, 1987).

The earliest systems (e.g., STRIPS, HACKER, ABSTRIPS, and NOAH) were all derived from the state-space approach to problem solving. State-space systems represent the world at each moment of time as being in some state, describable in terms of a set of objects having certain properties. It is only through the application of legal operators that states change. The collection of states that are reachable from an initial state defines the state space. Since each action (i.e., operator) is considered to bring about a new state, concurrent actions and actions with attenuated effects are not allowed, or their effects, however minute, are forced to map into distinct states. Under the state-space paradigm, a task is envisioned as consisting of an initial state, a set of possible task states, a collection of admissible operators, and a goal state. A plan is a sequence of operators that will transform the initial state into the goal state. Various weak methods such as heuristic search and means-ends analysis are utilized to focus the search to find a suitable operator sequence that leads to the goal state.

---

linear planners
[STRIPS, HACKER]

abstraction planners
[ABSTRIPS, NOAH, MOLGEN]

opportunistic planners
[OPM]

case-based planners
[CHEF, JULIA, PLEXUS]

Figure 1. A typology of planner systems with some examples. STRIPS, HACKER, ABSTRIPS, and NOAH are all domain-independent, weak method planners. The STRIPS system was applied in the domain of robot planning tasks. HACKER's task was to plan the actions of a virtual robot in a blocks world. NOAH was designed for dealing with assembly tasks in the domain of electromechanical equipment. MOLGEN was developed to assist geneticists in planning gene-cloning experiments. OPM is a simulation of think-aloud protocols collected from subjects performing a hypothetical errand-planning task. CHEF's domain is Szechwan cooking. JULIA is an interactive catering advisor that assists users in meal planning. PLEXUS is intended as a system that is capable of re-using abstract (or generic plans) as well as specific plans in new situations.

The means-ends analysis, a problem solving method introduced with GPS (Newell & Simon, 1963, 1972), plays a prominent role in planners such as STRIPS, ABSTRIPS, MOLGEN, and in the 'analogy' framework due to Carbonell (1983, 1986). Briefly, this method consists of (1) choosing a difference from a set of differences, found by a difference function that compares the current state to the goal state, (2) identifying an operator that can reduce that difference, and either (3a) applying the operator if possible to the current state, or (3b) executing means-ends analysis, in case the identified operator fails to apply, on this operator's preconditions and the current state. The method requires, moreover, a means of associating operators with differences that they can reduce. GPS stores this knowledge, for instance, in a table of connections.

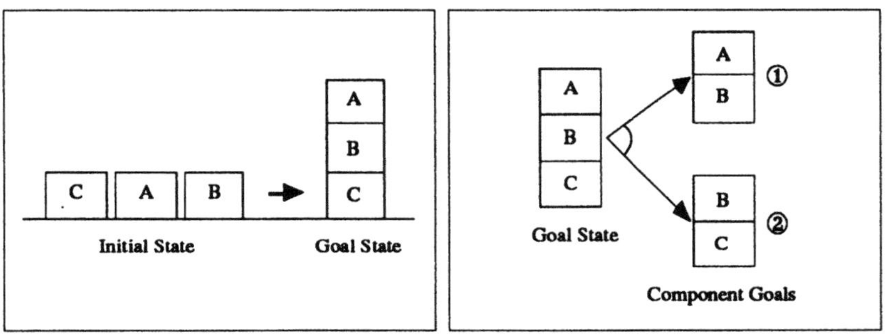

Figure 2. A goal state may consist of either a compound goal or multiple goals. A compound goal is commonly decomposed into its components (problem reduction). A planner that operates under the linearity assumption has to reconsider the plans that it produces when the component goals interact. For example, if the planner first achieves the goal component [on(A, B)] above, it will have to undo this result to achieve [on(B, C)], a state of affairs which ensues from the interdependence of these goals.

LINEAR PLANNERS

A planner is called linear if it operates under the assumption that the components of a goal or multiple goals do not interact and can be achieved one after another in an arbitrary order (see Figure 2). This is known as the *linearity assumption* (Sussman, 1975). STRIPS (Fikes & Nilsson, 1971), uses the heuristics of problem reduction (i.e., dividing a problem into a set of subproblems) and means-ends analysis to solve planning tasks. It constructs plans for multiple goals by planning for each individual goal at a time and attempts to cope with interactions between steps as they arise. When all of the individual goals are solved, STRIPS reconsiders any compound goal that fails to match the current state, because this is indicative of harmful interactions among the individual goals. This problem solver plans bottom-up, in that it always produces a plan directly in terms of essential (i.e., concrete) operators. For example, it will immediately try to establish an essential operator (e.g., one of *Walk*, *Take a cab*, or *Ride the subway*) as a step to achieve the goal of getting to an airport.

inRoom(ROBOT, r1) connects(d, r1, r2) status(d, OPEN) inRoom(b, r2) object(b) door(d)	GoTo(d) GoThru(d, r2) GoTo(b)	nextTo(ROBOT, b) inRoom(ROBOT, r2)

Figure 3. A generalized plan or MACROP in STRIPS. The left panel shows the preconditions, the middle panel the constituent operators (i.e., suboperators), and the right panel the effects of the plan. This MACROP can be used in multiple ways during planning for a new task or problem. For example, it may be used as the initial part of a plan for collecting an object from an adjacent room. Also, if the first two suboperators are used alone, the planner would attain the goal of getting the robot from a room to an adjacent room.

The initial STRIPS system had to solve each new task from scratch, without the benefit of stored experience. In a later version (Fikes, Hart, & Nilsson, 1972) the system was augmented with the capability to accumulate its experiences in planning as *macro-operators*. A macro-operator (MACROP) is an operator sequence that is generalized and stored for reuse in subsequent planning and plan execution. A macro-operator is retrieved either as a whole or in fragments depending on the goal STRIPS attempts to achieve (see Figure 3).

HACKER (Sussman, 1975) was put forth by its author as a model of skill acquisition that exploits "the programming metaphor." A skill is viewed as a connected set of procedures, each indexed by what it can achieve. A procedure corresponds to a plan in that, when interpreted, an ordered set of actions is taken that can bring about the situation as described by its access pattern. The HACKER system attempts a task (in the blocks world) by first searching its Answer Library for a plan whose access pattern matches *all* of the goals given in the task. If none is found, the system "writes one," using general knowledge stored in its Programming Techniques Library in conjunction with the available domain knowledge. In the process of writing a plan, the system may retrieve plans that can achieve some of the original goals and insert these in the evolving plan. A plan so built is inspected by "plan critics" that look for "bugs" (i.e., interaction problems) in the plan, and if needed, propose appropriate "patches" (i.e., repairs) to correct the plan. If a retrieved plan (or a new one which is possibly patched as suggested by plan critics) fails to run, the system "debugs" that plan. To this end, HACKER applies its general planning knowledge of possible types of bugs and associated patches to the faulty plan. From this experience, the system learns in two ways: it builds plan critics which it stores in the Critics Gallery, and saves the successful plan, indexed by the goals the plan achieves, in the Answer Library.

ABSTRACTION PLANNERS

Whilst weak methods are good at directing search, the combinatorics involved in traversing a complex problem space becomes rapidly unwieldy. Significant gains can be obtained in reducing the amount of search required to solve a task if a problem solver is to explore, before going through a problem space *p*, an *abstraction space* that simplifies the representation of *p* (Sacerdoti, 1974; Tenenberg, 1988). Human subjects make use of abstractions when asked to plan meals for a dinner party (Byrne, 1977)[1] or a day's errands (Hayes-Roth & Hayes-Roth, 1979).

ABSTRIPS (Sacerdoti, 1974) and NOAH (Sacerdoti, 1977) both solve planning tasks in a hierarchy of abstraction spaces before they progressively fill in the details of a solution in the ground space. That is, abstractions are used to focus the planner's attention on the difficult parts of a task, so that less critical parts or details of the task can be dealt with by subsequent problem solving. An abstract plan for a dinner party, for example, may comprise the steps *Invite guests, Cook meal, Serve meal,* and so on. In the next abstraction space, the details of the meal can be worked out—for example, the style of cooking for each part of the meal. This mode of operation has a top-down character. ABSTRIPS, for instance, abstracts over preconditions of operators, NOAH over operators themselves.

```
MicroWave(x,y,z)
   P:  in(x,y)
       inMicroWave(y,z)
       raw(x)
   D:  raw(x)
   A:  microWaved(x)

Bake(x,y,z)
   P:  in(x,y)
       inOven(y,z)
       raw(x)
   D:  raw(x)
   A:  baked(x)

Cook(x,y,z)
   P:  in(x,y)
       inCooker(y,z)
       raw(x)
   D:  raw(x)
   A:  cooked(x)

Sautee(x,y,z)
   P:  in(x,y)
       onBurner(y,z)
       raw(x)
   D:  raw(x)
   A:  sauteed(x)
```

Figure 4. Example of abstracting over operators. Concrete operators such as *MicroWave, Bake,* and *Sautee* can all be mapped onto the abstract operator *Cook*. Concrete properties—predicates and objects—can also be mapped onto abstract properties as in *baked* → *cooked* and *burner* → *cooker.* Abstractions are known to impart efficiency gains in reasoning. P stands for preconditions of an operator; D and A (abbreviations of Delete and Add) represent together the operator's effects (Tenenberg, 1988).

NOAH plans in terms of generalized operators which it later refines to essential operators that are available in its problem space. Thus, to get to an airport, an abstraction planner[2] will first consider an abstract operator, say, *Travel* and later refine this to an essential operator such as *Walk, Take a cab,* or *Ride the subway.* Figure 4 shows *Cook* as an example abstract operator that can be made concrete in terms of operators such as *MicroWave, Bake,* or *Sautee.* NOAH constructs plans under the guidance of plan critics which contain knowledge to actually propose modifications to a faulty plan. If an action, proposed to attain one goal, thwarts some other action related to another goal, the *resolve-conflicts* critic, for example, detects this interaction problem and attempts to reorder the conflicting actions. Thus, instead of committing itself to an arbitrary ordering of essential operators and fixing the sequence afterwards for interaction problems, NOAH commits itself to an ordering of problem-solving operators as late as possible. This is often referred to as *least-commitment strategy.*

MOLGEN (Stefik, 1981a) devises plans for gene-cloning experiments in molecular genetics by elaborating skeleton plans, pre-stored in memory. MOLGEN abstracts both the operators and properties of objects in its problem space. It uses a method called *constraint posting* to defer decisions involving objects and operators to handle problems caused by interacting goals. A plan is produced when all of the formulated constraints are satisfied. A key feature of MOLGEN is that plans—sequences of essential operators in its domain of application—are generated by means of *design operators* such as *Propose-Operator,* the behavior of which is controlled in turn by so-called *strategy operators* such as *Guess* and *Undo* (Stefik, 1981b). To give an example, *Propose-Operator* may put forth *React* (an abstract operator) to reduce a relevant difference. *Refine-Operator* (another design operator) replaces *React* with *Cleave* "which cuts a DNA molecule with a restriction enzyme" (a specific operator).

Planners like ABSTRIPS, NOAH, and MOLGEN tend to limit *backtracking* as a side effect of operating in abstraction spaces. Backtracking means that, after a failure, the problem solver simply returns to the decision point closest to the point where the failure has occurred to consider an alternative. This is a costly operation in terms of memory load, one that humans avoid as much as possible. These systems, on the other hand, have no structural capability for learning and reusing plans. SIPE (Wilkins, 1988) is a recent system that consolidates and extends the various elements to be found in "classical planners" as the ones discussed thus far.

AN OPPORTUNISTIC PLANNER

Hayes-Roth and Hayes-Roth (1979) studied the behavior of human subjects in an experiment in which the subjects were requested to verbalize while planning a day's errands in a hypothetical town. Errands consisted of various items such as *Pick up medicine for your dog at the vet* and *Buy a fan belt for your refrigerator at the appliance store.* Also, explicit constraints were imposed on some errands, for example, *Pick up your car by 5:30.* The analysis of protocol data (see Ericsson & Simon, 1984, for a description of this method) shows that subjects tend to plan bottom-up as well as top-down. For example, one of their subjects first classifies the errands as either primary or secondary, according to their importance. This subject then starts reasoning in terms of a series of immediately achievable goals (i.e., individual errands), hence bottom-up. As soon as he notices that these errands can all be done in a specific part of the town, he creates an abstract goal, *Do southeast errands*, and attempts to incorporate other errands into a plan which includes "heading southeast" as a subplan. This leads the subject to reason top-down, that is, to break up the town into sections and cluster the errands by section. While moving through a section, the subject notices a newsstand and, driven by this opportunity, he instantly inserts a secondary errand, *Buy a gardening magazine*, into the plan he is developing. Hayes-Roth and Hayes-Roth realized this opportunistic, "multi-directional" planning in a blackboard architecture, a particular system organization that has the potential for being an architecture for general intelligence. In this blackboard planner, plan steps are decided by various specialists (realized as condition-action rules) that operate in an asynchronous mode, a mechanism that generates the ordering of operators in a piecemeal fashion like human subjects carrying out the errand-planning task. An errand plan is developed from abstract as well as concrete, essential operators. It is driven by opportunities to introduce goals or actions into the plan it is building or executing, hence it has a bottom-up component to it.

CASE-BASED PLANNERS

Whenever there exists a prior case, an example or analogy, or metaphor that may be drawn upon to meet the demands of a situation, humans will do so (e.g., Bobrow & Norman, 1975; Carbonell & Minton, 1985; Hoc, 1987; Miller, Galanter, & Pribram, 1960; Schank, 1982).[3] For case-based planners like CHEF (Hammond, 1989), JULIA (Hinrichs, 1988; Kolodner, 1987), and PLEXUS (Alterman, 1988) as well as in the "analogy" framework (Carbonell, 1983, 1986), this entails searching the long-term memory for episodes of past planning experiences in situations (i.e., cases) that resemble the current task situation. Episodic memory (Tulving, 1972) is assumed to hold cases that are indexed by features which reference the relevant properties of the situation (e.g., goals) that called for them. This *reasoning from cases* proceeds basically as follows:

- Retrieve a previous case
- Adapt the retrieved case to the current task
- Store the result obtained from adapting the retrieved case

The notion of reasoning from cases is increasingly exploited in various areas of application (e.g., Riesbeck & Schank, 1989). The following example illustrates what is involved. When in New York for the first time, a Parisian who wants to ride the subway is likely to try a series of actions appropriate to riding the Paris métro. When the sequence of actions fails, as it certainly will, what one does is to "tweak" the sequence. The Métro sequence has an action slot that says *Buy a ticket* to gain access to the métro station, which in fact does not apply to the New York subway. Such failures start a problem solving episode to adapt the plan at hand to the current circumstances. The resulting Subway sequence or plan will instead have a corresponding action slot saying *Buy a token*. On the other hand, someone who has never taken an underground transport system before will probably resort to actions resembling those of taking a bus. The Bus plan would of course require more elaborate problem solving to generate a Subway plan. This plan-editing allows the planning agent to construct new memory structures so that it may be reminded of them at appropriate time. Editing a past plan that is retrieved from memory because it meets the agent's current set of goals in some way or another may involve distinct but interconnected operations as will become clear later.

CHEF operates in the cooking domain. A task for CHEF is formulated as a set of goals for different tastes, textures, ingredients, and types of dishes. To give an example, a task may consist of the following goals: Include beef in the dish, Include broccoli in the dish, Make stir-fry dish. The planner seeks to produce a recipe (i.e., plan) that meets all of the goals it is given. The basic approach of CHEF consists of examining the goals in its input for possible interaction problems (i.e., failures) and finding a past recipe in memory that will avoid predicted problems as well as satisfy as many of the most important goals (according to a goal value hierarchy) as possible. For the example task, the planner retrieves the recipe Beef-With-Green-Beans because it is a stir-fry dish that includes beef as ingredient and there is a partial match between broccoli and green beans, an ingredient in the recipe Beef-With-Green-Beans, in that they are both vegetables. Afterwards, CHEF adapts the retrieved recipe by *modifying* it in order to satisfy all of the goals, simulating the resultant recipe, and *repairing* it for failures that may occur. The simulator in CHEF simply interprets (*reads and runs*) the steps of a recipe in sequence and collects the results of steps run in a table. This table enables the system to assess whether or not the adapted recipe meets its goals. If the simulation succeeds, the new recipe is saved in memory, indexed by the goals that it satisfies and the failures that it avoids. Organizing plans not only under the goals they can achieve, but also under the conditions of failures encountered while constructing them, makes it possible for CHEF to foresee possible interactions among its goals, and to predict these interactions in future situations.

JULIA plans meals for users in interaction with them. JULIA first splits the meal task into an ordered set of subtasks (problem reduction), establishes the constraints that the meal must satisfy (constraint posting), and retrieves previous cases from which it attempts to put together a meal that satisfies all of the prevailing constraints. The initial subtasks, which are ordered in accordance with domain knowledge, are achieved one at a time. Consider the following example. While planning for a dinner, JULIA attempts the subtask of selecting a main course with the constraint that the meal be Mexican. When the user accepts the system's suggestion to serve chili, it is reminded of a past meal with chili as the main course, which was unsuccessful in that some guests did not eat spicy food. JULIA now tries to avoid repeating the same mistake again by requesting information about the participants and finds out that some of them, indeed, do not favor spicy food. This observation leads JULIA to formulate the constraint "non-spicy-food" which causes ruling out Mexican as a cuisine. If this meal had succeeded, the case would instead provide suggestions about outstanding parts of the current meal (e.g., appetizer or dessert) that the system is trying to assemble. As shown by Byrne (1977) and replicated in our laboratory, the preferred order in which human subjects plans a meal is: starter, main-course, dessert, whereas JULIA appears to always use the order: main-course, starter, dessert where starter consists of appetizer and salad.

In PLEXUS, retrieving an old plan and refitting it to the current situation is called *situation matching*. The planning agent is modeled as one that acts on differences (categorized into failing preconditions, failing outcome, differing goals, and step out of order) that occur between the actual situation and the plan that is recalled. In PLEXUS, these differences direct the retrieval of background knowledge related planning and thereby the retrieval of other specific plans. An example (Alterman, 1988, p. 410) of the type 'step out of order' would show up in the situation in which an American student intends to eat at a cafeteria in Paris. The student recalls Cafeteria-Eating with step1 = *Select food* and step2 = *Pay cashier*, and tries *Select food* that instantly fails, due to the unsatisfied precondition 'access food.' PLEXUS will reorder the steps involved in Cafeteria-Eating to meet the French situation.

Carbonell's (1983) *analogy* framework (not listed in Figure 1 above) can be viewed as a proposal to incorporate reasoning from cases or by analogy into the perspective of goal-directed problem solving. The framework under consideration posits a *base* problem space (B-space) and a *transform* problem space (T-space). Problem solving in the B-space as well as in the T-space is driven by means-ends analysis, outlined earlier. The purpose of the T-space is to adapt a retrieved solution, using a set of *transform operators*, into one that solves the task at hand. Recall that a solution is an operator sequence that, if applied to the initial state of a task, achieves that task's goal state. Assume a pair *(t, G)*, where *t* is a task and *G* is *t*'s goal state. If the problem solver retrieves a past solution, say, *Sol1*, for a task *t1* similar to *t*, the current state in T-space is set to *Sol1* while the goal state is to find a solution *Sol* that, when applied—in the B-space of course—to the initial state of *t*, achieves *G*. The problem solving in T-space proceeds, as required in means-ends analysis, by finding the *differences* that transform operators can reduce. When no past solution is recalled, the problem solver attempts the task by means of essential operators available in the B-space. Carbonell (1986) suggests using also the "trace" of reasoning that is associated with a past solution. Such a trace contains information which can be transferred to the new task situation (e.g., derivations that were needed to obtain the past solution).

The planners reviewed above involve contrasting approaches to planning (Carbonell, 1986; Riesbeck & Schank, 1989; Rosenbloom, Laird, Newell, & McCarl, 1991), if not, to cognition in general: planning as search, derived from the problem solving framework (Newell & Simon, 1972) and case-based reasoning, derived from the work of Schank (1982), with formulations by McDermott (1978) and Wilensky (1983) in between but close to the latter. Both approaches assume that the planning agent possesses a repertoire of primitive actions and that planning involves "the creation (or retrieval) and use of a data structure that represents a sequence of actions" (Rosenbloom et al., 1991, p. 318) to attain a set of goals. The case-based approach emphasizes the organization of memory, the retrieval of already existing data structures, and adapting the retrieved structures to new situations. As will become clear in the following sections, the process model underlying the case-based approach appears to be supported by psychological research and theorizing. The remainder of this paper will present an attempt to bring the elements of this process model into the problem solving perspective embodied by the Soar architecture which is intended to cover all of cognition (Newell, 1990). The attempt is similar to that of Carbonell (1983, 1986).

The Soar Architecture As Planner

Since my aim is here to consider how to map the process model underlying case-based planning onto Soar, the following provides a brief summary of some basic features of the architecture and existing Soar work on planning. For more extended treatments, see Laird, Congdon, Altmann, and Swedlow (1990), Rosenbloom et al. (1991), or Newell (1990); and for "psychological reviews" devoted to Soar, see Norman (1991) and Lindsay (1991). Soar is often described as a system that *accepts and formulates* tasks in terms of problem spaces, operators, and states. In effect, it is a system that operates by means of heuristic search and/or extensive domain knowledge through multiple problem spaces, each with operators and a state space of its own. This is one important characteristic distinguishing the Soar system from its state-space counterparts. A parallel production system structures the memory in Soar: all knowledge, including search methods, is encoded in productions (condition-action pairs) which also act as memory retrievers. In Soar, a task is solved in a cascade of *decision cycles.* Each decision cycle is said to gather knowledge from the long-term memory by allowing to fire, in parallel, all of the productions whose access patterns—that is, condition sides—match the working memory. This knowledge contains *preferences* indicating the relative or absolute worth of problem spaces, states, or operators. When there are no more productions that fire, a decision procedure is invoked to examine these preferences in order to determine what problem space, state, or operator to consider. If the preferences, taken collectively, permit the decision procedure to produce an unequivocal choice, the architecture is said to have made a decision for an action implied by that choice, upon which it enters the next decision cycle. An *impasse* arises when the knowledge is insufficient or just ambiguous to allow an unequivocal choice. This is the occasion for Soar to create a subgoal and an associated problem space (often referred to as a subspace) in which to acquire the missing knowledge.

Every time an impasse manifests and is later resolved in a subspace, chunking brings together the conditions that gave rise to the impasse with the results that eliminated it in a chunk—that is, a new production. Obviously, chunking can be said to "program" Soar, but the architecture is not necessarily at the mercy of this learning element. It can also use chunking to "program" itself in ways it sees fit; this is already the case in some Soar systems, for instance, in NL-Soar (Lehman, Lewis, & Newell, 1991).

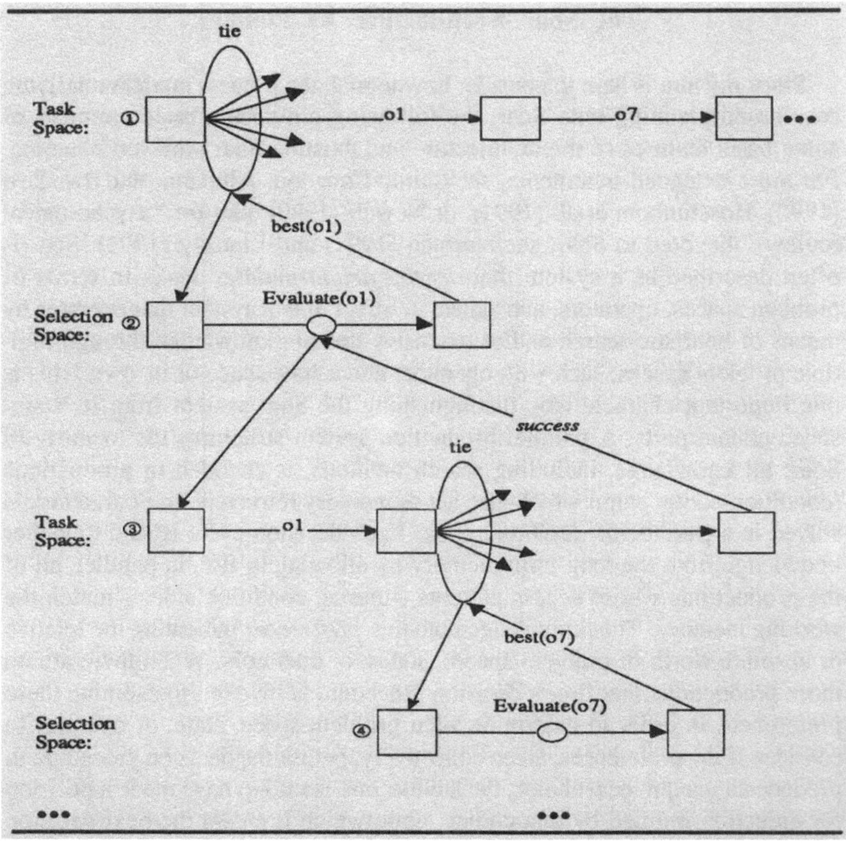
tie
Task Space:
①
o1
o7
best(o1)
Selection Space:
②
Evaluate(o1)
success
tie
Task Space:
③
o1
best(o7)
Selection Space:
④
Evaluate(o7)

As stated before, problem solving subsumes planning. It is therefore natural to expect a general architecture like Soar to incorporate planning behavior. There is already some research effort to model planning. Much of this is essentially based on weak methods: look-ahead search (e.g., Hucka, 1989; Laird, 1988; Laird & Rosenbloom, 1990; Rosenbloom, Lee, & Unruh, 1990; Unruh & Rosenbloom, 1989) and means-ends analysis (Akyürek, 1992; Young & Whittington, 1990). A substantial part of default knowledge, available in Soar, concerns the impasse that arises when the preferences for selecting operators fail to suggest a unique best choice. In the associated subgoal, this knowledge brings in the *selection* problem space to find out which operator to select. The processing that occurs in the selection space is said to implement look-ahead search (see Laird et al., 1990 for a detailed outline), which is depicted in Figure 5. In conjunction with chunking, look-ahead search causes Soar to acquire *search-control knowledge*, which consists of productions that create preferences for operators (e.g., Laird, Rosenbloom, & Newell, 1986; Minton, 1988). Figure 6 shows an example. Although default knowledge does not implement the whole of means-ends analysis, it provides for the component which involves working through the unsatisfied preconditions of an operator, selected for reducing a difference. In the Soar literature, this is known as operator subgoaling (see Figure 7). In Akyürek (1992), I have shown how learning in operator subgoals creates *macrochunks*—procedures that can directly modify the state.

If	the goal is to have a block on top of another block
	and each one of the blocks is clear
	and an operator is proposed to stack one block on top of another
Then	this operator is best

Figure 6. Example of a search-control production.

Although the work cited above establishes Soar as a weak method planner, at least to some extent, this does not cover yet all of planning as a cognitive activity. Cognition is bounded by knowledge inclusive of experience that can be brought to bear. The question of how knowledge is represented in memory and put to use, appears to be a core issue in diverse approaches to problem solving and planning (e.g., see Carbonell, 1986; Carbonell & Minton, 1985; McDermott, 1978; Schank, 1982; Wilensky, 1983).

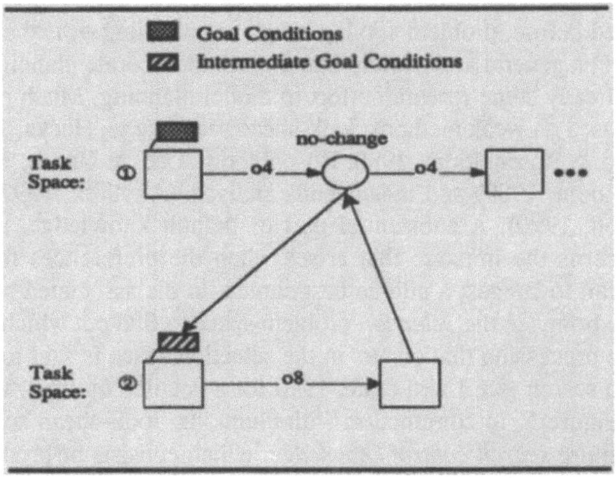

Figure 7. Operator subgoaling (or precondition satisfaction) in Soar. Squares represent states, horizontal arrows the operators that are selected and/or applied; downward arrow points to the subgoal that is created, upward arrow to the results. The example shows that the operator o4 is selected, but it fails to apply to the current state. The preconditions of o4 are cast as intermediate goal conditions in the subsequent subgoal. The current state changes as a result of applying o8 in the subgoal, which enables o4 to execute in turn. Both ① and ② share same problem space and state. The difference lies in the respective goal conditions. The operator sequence that obtains is: o8, o4, ... (Akyürek, 1992).

A basic distinction regarding representation is that between "declaratives" and "procedures." Kirsh's (1991) definition is exceptionally clear:

> "Declaratives release their information upon being *read*, whereas procedures release their information upon being *run*" (p. 166).

Soar's productions are procedures, but they can also encode declaratives. The condition side of the production is an access pattern to what is encoded in its action side. Thus, productions may be viewed as retrieving either procedures or declaratives (cf. Rosenbloom et al., 1991; Rosenbloom, Newell, & Laird, in press). In Soar, procedures are the predominant form. Hence, experiences, which accumulate into search-control chunks and macrochunks, are procedures. A plan, in the Soar systems cited above, is a structure jointly determined by a set of procedures that just run off to solve a task. Thus, declarative structures like MACROPs in STRIPS, recipes in CHEF, or meals in JULIA are not created in these Soar systems or, for that matter, in Soar in general (cf.

Ellman, 1989). Declarative structures, however, are required if Soar is going to account for the behavior modeled in case-based systems. Recall that such behavior consists of retrieving a past plan, fitting it to the current situation, and storing the result. A case-based agent is a "tweaker." One can believe and even defend the thesis that (human) agents as such are *tweak-free*, but speaking of a *tweak-free case-based agent* (Rosenbloom et al., 1990) is a contradiction in terms.

But this leads to a significant question: how can reasoning from cases be fit into the Soar theory which formulates cognition as goal-directed problem solving? Figure 8 shows a Soar draft model, set up to answer this question. The components involved are taken up in the next section.

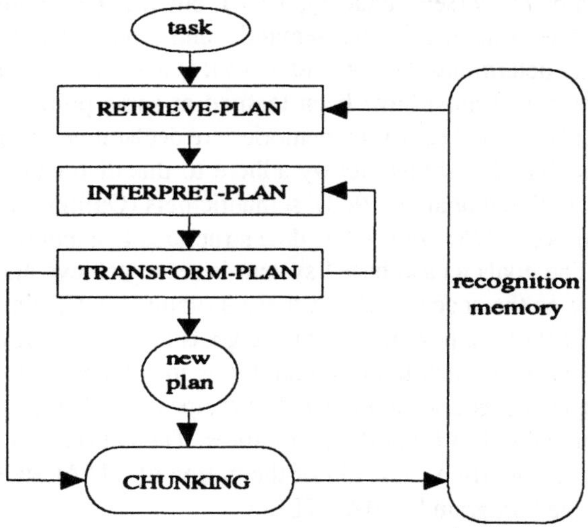

Figure 8. A draft model for Soar as case-based planner.

Reasoning from Cases: A Mapping Onto Soar

The processing of inputs from a situation at time *t* leads humans to be reminded of memories laid down in situations, prior to *t*, and to recall those memories (Schank, 1982). The "match" between what is processed and what is retrieved appears to be a continuum, from identical, to similar, to analogical (Burstein, 1989; Gentner, 1983, 1989; Keane, 1988; Michon, 1990; Ross, 1989). The Parisian who recalls the Métro plan in New York apparently does so because métro and subway are perceptually similar objects that also do have a similar function, that of being used for moving about in big cities. A case-based system is likewise reminded of past plans that match its current goals. The phenomenon appears to be real. When asked for a menu that must meet certain constraints (e.g., a vegetarian meal), the subjects appear to respond almost immediately: they recall dishes they prepared in the past (Byrne, 1977; Morton & Byrne, 1975). Also, when we asked subjects in an experiment[4] to plan a hypothetical symposium, one subject did not hesitate to add a step into his plan to make reservations for "lecture rooms" in agreement with the single experience, we knew, he had had.

There exists a multitude of conceptualizations in psychology regarding human long-term memory (see Baddeley, 1990), but it is commonly characterized as a tripartite system: episodic, semantic, and procedural (Tulving, 1983, 1985). Learning determines the contents—what is learned must be retrievable, and what is retrieved must have been learned at some point prior to its retrieval. Both episodic and semantic memories are declarative (or propositional) in nature. Case-based systems closely adhere to this distinction, in that discrimination nets (Feigenbaum, 1963), semantic nets (Quillian, 1968), as well as frames (Minsky, 1975) are used as data structures to encode knowledge as declaratives. The goals a case-based system is set to achieve and other situation cues serve as the access paths to these structures. CHEF's memory is a discrimination net of recipes indexed by the goals they can achieve. In JULIA, meals are stored in an abstraction hierarchy as in semantic nets. PLEXUS's memory is organized as a semantic net. The recipes of CHEF and the meals of JULIA are both stored in frame-like structures. The notion of a plan in case-based planners is clearly a close kin of the notion of a MACROP in STRIPS or an examinable "program" in HACKER.

The Soar theory takes, however, a different stance on memory (Newell, 1990, chap. 2). It asserts the functional unity of long-term memory, meaning that the distinctions above do not occur as separate memories but as types of encoding of knowledge in the same memory. Chunking (i.e., learning) is the process that does the encoding. Not everyone is prepared to accept this uniform memory hypothesis (e.g., Norman, 1991). As already discussed earlier, in Soar, productions are organizing units for all long-term memory. In a recent model (Morton, Hammersley, & Bekerian, 1985), human memory is conceptualized as consisting of individual *headed records*, not connected to each other in any direct way. A record is retrievable only by addressing the heading attached to it. The contents of the heading itself, on the other hand, cannot be retrieved. As such, headed records are not far from the Soar productions.

```
(sp p40
    (goal <g> ^operator <q>)
    (goal <g> ^problem-space <p> ^state <s>)
    (operator <q> ^name memory ^retrieve? T ^cue coffee)
    -->
    (state <s> ^plan <e> + & )
    (object <e> ^id i608 ^name have-coffee))

(sp p41
    (goal <g> ^operator <q>)
    (goal <g> ^problem-space <p> ^state <s>)
    (operator <q> ^name memory ^expand <e>)
    (state <s> ^plan <e>)
    (object <e> ^name have-coffee ^id i608)
    -->
    (object <e> ^name have-coffee ^next <a1>)
    (action <a1> ^name goto
            ^location kitchen
            ^duration 60
            ^before <a2>)
    (action <a2> ^name boil
            ^object water
            ^duration 140
            ^meets <a3>)
    (action <a3> ^name make
            ^object coffee
            ^duration 240
            ^before <a4>)
    (action <a4> ^name pour
            ^object brewed-coffee
            ^duration 40
            ^next end))
```

Figure 9. Example Soar chunks that can retrieve past plans for goal conditions that are similar to the ones prevailing in the current situation (for *P40*, see the text). The action side of the production *P41* contains a declarative plan for the goal condition *Have coffee*. This plan specifies four steps, temporally linked to each other: *GoTo(kitchen)*, *Boil(water)*, *Make(coffee)*, *Pour(brewed-coffee)*, which, when retrieved, must be interpreted to take effect.

PLAN RETRIEVAL AND LEARNING

It is, by now, clear that declarative structures are required for reasoning from cases to occur and that Soar's productions do, in principle, allow such structures. Moreover, a Soar system implemented by Reich (1988) shows the use of declaratives in combination with look-ahead in a design task. Another example comes from Driver-Soar.[5] When this system needs to execute the operator *ChangeGear* to slow down the vehicle it is operating, the subactions required to do this are determined in multiple subspaces and returned as a subgoal result, consisting of temporally interlinked "objects" that are interpreted as operators in the top problem space.

In what follows, I will assume a weak method throughout—means-ends analysis, for example. The reason for this is that, in the absence of a past plan, Soar can still attempt to achieve a set of goal conditions given by a task. The first process involved in the draft model for Soar as a case-based planner is Retrieve-Plan (see Figure 8). For Soar to recall the appropriate plans, the goal conditions that it is set to achieve in a task domain have to be associated with past plans in memory. For example, if Soar ever to build a plan for how to make coffee, it must have stored that plan in memory indexed by the goal condition *Have coffee* (see the action side of *P41* in Figure 9 for such a plan). This can be done in Soar by *data chunking* (see Newell, 1990, chap. 6; Rosenbloom & Aasman, 1990), a procedure that was first used for modeling the recognition and recall tasks of the verbal learning literature in psychology. Note that learning involved in associating a plan with each goal condition that it satisfies resembles the cued-recall situation: given a goal condition, recall the associated plan. This is done after the means-ends process has created a plan or transformed a past plan. At this point, a memorization operator is selected, with goal conditions as the cue set, to create two type of chunks (*P40* and *P41* in Figure 9): the first associates the cues with an internal name, the second associates cues with the plan. If the plan for *Have coffee* is associated just with "coffee," it can only be used again when the same goal condition arises. By generalizing a cue, however, a wider range of application for a plan can be obtained (e.g., coffee to aromatic-drink, broccoli to vegetable). This means that the goal condition "aromatic-drink" can be added to the cue set during memorization. This will enable the Soar planner intending to *Have tea* to generate the goal condition *Have aromatic-drink*—from the domain knowledge that "tea" ISA "aromatic-drink." The presence of this abstract goal condition will evoke the retrieval and use of the plan for *Have coffee* to create a plan for *Have tea.*

If the retrieval process delivers multiple plans, problem solving in a *plan valuation problem space* can be used to select an initial plan that can best help in achieving a particular set of goal conditions.

PLAN MODIFICATION AND REPAIR

Modification and repair of retrieved plans involve knowledge that is invoked to fit a plan to the current situation. In CHEF, modifying plans means altering them to satisfy additional goal conditions, while repairing means invoking planning knowledge and a causal domain model to explain and remedy plan failures (e.g., see Sacerdoti, 1977; Sussman, 1975; Wilensky, 1983). To adjust a plan, the modification process relies primarily on the knowledge encoded in a collection, domain-dependent modifier rules, each of which correlates a set of steps to be added to an existing plan and a goal condition. These rules also include information indicating where in a plan the new steps are to be inserted. This is a limited form of temporalization based on the *before* relation. Another source of knowledge for this process consists of the role specifications that define a plan type (i.e., skeleton recipe). For example, a role associated with MEAL, a plan type for all meals, would be "dessert" which can be filled with, say, ice cream or yogurt. Using such information, this process can substitute a new object for the old. To repair plans, CHEF exploits a set of *Thematic Organization Packets* or TOPs (Schank, 1982) that describe potential planning problems and relevant sets of repair strategies to deal with them. These TOPs are stored in a discrimination net, indexed by the features of the problems they describe.

For instance, a TOP may refer to situations in which the side effect of one plan step (e.g., an operator application) violates the preconditions of another step later on. Whenever the planner encounters a problem of this type, it will locate the related TOP and use one of the strategies suggested there to solve that problem (recall the "plan critics" in HACKER and NOAH). Possible repair strategies in this case could be: (a) find a different operator that does not undo the preconditions of the operator that is required later in the plan, (b) reorder the operators, or (c) introduce an additional step to recover from the side effect that occurred. These repair strategies, while situation specific, are not domain specific. Rather, expressed as rules in a causal vocabulary, they are instantiated as domain specific repairs, a process that depends on detailed causal descriptions of the problems the planner encounters in its domain of interest. A planning step *Paint ladder* to apply paint to a ladder that is needed for painting the ceiling, for example, disables a precondition of the action *Paint ceil*-

ing by making the ladder unavailable. A causal description of this problem might be *blocked precondition* which could invoke a related TOP that proposes in turn a repair—for example, *reorder steps,* that is, execute *Paint ceiling* before *Paint ladder*. The assumption here is that the planner is able to describe the problems it encounters in a causal language which can be correlated with the language in which the TOPs are expressed. In the context of Soar systems that create procedural plans, an analog process takes place, known as *recovery from error* (Laird, 1988). Recovery from errors involves replanning, that is, problem solving that leads to the creation of new chunks that can dominate the chunks learned earlier.

Insert adds a new step to *X*.
Delete removes a step from *X*.
Splice inserts a sequence of steps into *X*.
Substitute replaces a step in *X* by a new step or sequence of steps.
Concatenate adds a sequence to the beginning or the end of *X*.
Mesh merges two complementary solutions (*X1* and *X2*) that are retrieved.
Reorder rearranges the temporal order of the steps in *X*.
Replace-Objects replaces the objects affected by *X* with the new task objects.
Truncate eliminates unnecessary steps from *X*.
Inverse-Sequence reverses *X*.

Figure 10. A list of transform operators that can be used to adapt a recalled operator sequence *X* to the demands of a new task situation (After Carbonell, 1983).

An attractive idea is to allow the means-ends process to modify and repair retrieved plans, as suggested in Carbonell (1983), using general problem solving operators (see Figure 10). This strategy corresponds to the Transform-Plan component in the draft model. The purpose of Interpret-Plan is to interpret a plan for inspection as well as performance.

A difficulty that must be overcome is reasoning with temporal knowledge. Reordering steps of a plan, chopping a difficult step in a plan into two or more steps and running them independently, or adding a step to an existing plan to recover from a side effect—all involve some kind of temporal reasoning. Also, altering the duration of a step in a plan requires explicit treatment of time as a resource. The template given in Figure 9 to represent plans includes some of the elements required to explicitly *temporalize* action (Allen,

1984; Allen & Kautz, 1985; McDermott, 1982; Michon, 1985, 1990). My present intuition is that plans so stored will not be too hard to "interpret" in the current architecture.

Summary

Classical planners that viewed planning as search led to the development of important computational mechanisms such as abstraction, plan critics, plan repair, and constraint satisfaction which recur in more recent systems that view planning as memory-driven activity. Soar and systems that are based on reasoning from cases are all memory-driven, that is, they emphasize experience. For Soar, this means creating sets of effective "procedures" that easily transfer to tasks in the same domain. Case-based systems, on the other hand, attempt to model the retrieval of experiences by analogy, similarity judgment, or metaphors and the deliberate manipulation thereof to cope with new situations. Psychological research, though sparse, appears to provide some support for the notion of reusing experience by adapting it to new situations. A closer examination shows that the process model involved in the case- or analogy-based systems requires a particular memory organization to work at all, that is, declarative data structures to represent the episodic experience. A preliminary draft Soar model is proposed to cover the behavior of such systems, in which plans are stored and retrieved by memorization operators and retrieved plans are adapted by general problem solving operators, used by a means-ends process. The proposal may eventually lead to a valuable test of the computational assumptions that subtend the Soar architecture.

Acknowledgements

I thank John A. Michon for helping me clarify the ideas and for his support. I would like to thank Jans Aasman for his helpful suggestions that I freely used in writing the section on plan retrieval and learning.

NOTES

[1]The think-aloud data collected in our laboratory (by Agnes van den Berg), in replication of Byrne (1977), confirm the use of abstractions in planning the menu for a dinner party.

[2]Systems that plan at successive levels of detail by means of abstractions are also referred to as hierarchical planners. Wilkins (1988) includes an interesting discussion concerning the confusion that surrounds the notion of hierarchical planning.

[3]It should be noted that case, plan, or solution are interchangeable notions, especially in the field of planning.

[4]From the think-aloud data collected (by H. Numan, F. Pakes, J. G. Schuurman, and N. Taatgen) in our laboratory.

[5]This system is built by J. Aasman to simulate driver behavior at intersections (see also Aasman and Michon, 1992).

REFERENCES

Aasman, J., & Michon, J. A. (1992). Multitasking in driving. In J. A. Michon & A. Akyürek (Eds.), *Soar: A cognitive architecture in perspective* (pp. 169-198). Dordrecht, The Netherlands: Kluwer.

Agre, P. E., & Chapman, D. (1989). *What are plans for?* (AI Memo 1050a). Cambridge, MA: Massachusetts Institute of Technology, Artificial Intelligence Laboratory.

Akyürek, A. (1992). Means-ends planning: An example Soar system. In J. A. Michon & A. Akyürek (Eds.), *Soar: A cognitive architecture in perspective* (pp. 109-167). Dordrecht, The Netherlands: Kluwer.

Allen, J. F. (1984). Towards a general theory of action and time. *Artificial Intelligence, 23*, 123-154.

Allen, J. F., & Kautz, H. A. (1985). A model of naive temporal reasoning. In J. R. Hobbs & R. C. Moore (Eds.), *Formal theories of the commonsense world* (pp. 251-268). Norwood, NJ: Ablex.

Alterman, R. (1988). Adaptive planning. *Cognitive Science, 12*, 393-421.

Baddeley, A. (1990). *Human memory: Theory and practice*. Hove, UK: Erlbaum.

Bobrow, D. G., & Norman, D. A. (1975). Some principles of memory schemata. In D. G. Bobrow & A. Collins (Eds.), *Representation and understanding: Studies in cognitive science* (pp. 131-149). Orlando, FL: Academic Press.

Brand, M. (1984). *Intending and acting: Toward a naturalized action theory*. Cambridge, MA: MIT Press.

Burstein, M. H. (1989). Analogy vs. CBR: The purpose of mapping. In *Proceedings of a Workshop on Case-Based Reasoning* (pp. 133-136). San Mateo, CA: Morgan Kaufmann.

Byrne, R. (1977). Planning meals: Problem-solving on a real data-base. *Cognition, 5*, 287-332.

Carbonell, J. G. (1983). Learning by analogy: Formulating and generalizing plans from past experience. In R. S. Michalski, J. G. Carbonell, & T. M. Mitchell (Eds.), *Machine learning: An artificial intelligence approach* (pp. 137-161). Los Altos, CA: Morgan Kaufmann.

Carbonell, J. G. (1986). Derivational analogy: A theory of reconstructive problem solving and expertise acquisition. In R. S. Michalski, J. G. Carbonell, & T. M. Mitchell (Eds.), *Machine learning: An artificial intelligence approach* (Vol. II, pp. 371-392). Los Altos, CA: Morgan Kaufmann.

Carbonell, J. G., & Minton, S. (1985). Metaphor and commonsense reasoning. In J. R. Hobbs & R. C. Moore (Eds.), *Formal theories of the commonsense world* (pp. 405-426). Norwood, NJ: Ablex.

Ellman, T. (1989). Explanation-based learning: A survey of programs and perspectives. *ACM Computing Surveys, 21*, 163-221.

Ericsson, K. A., & Simon, H. A. (1984). *Protocol analysis: Verbal reports as data*. Cambridge, MA: MIT Press.

Feigenbaum, E. A. (1963). The simulation of verbal learning behavior. In E. A. Feigenbaum & J. Feldman (Eds.), *Computers and thought* (pp. 297-309). New York: McGraw-Hill. (Original work published 1961)

Fikes, R. E., Hart, P. E., & Nilsson, N. J. (1972). Learning and executing generalized robot plans. *Artificial Intelligence, 3*, 251-288.

Fikes, R. E., & Nilsson, N. J. (1971). STRIPS: A new approach to the application of theorem proving to problem solving. *Artificial Intelligence, 2*, 189-208.

Gentner, D. (1983). Structure-mapping: A theoretical framework for analogy. *Cognitive Science, 7*, 155-170.

Gentner, D. (1989). Finding the needle: Accessing and reasoning from prior cases. In *Proceedings of a Workshop on Case-Based Reasoning* (pp. 137-143). San Mateo, CA: Morgan Kaufmann.

Hammond, K. J. (1989). *Case-based planning: Viewing planning as a memory task*. San Diego, CA: Academic Press.

Hayes-Roth, B., & Hayes-Roth, F. (1979). A cognitive model of planning. *Cognitive Science, 3*, 275-310.

Hinrichs, T. R. (1988). Towards an architecture for open world problem solving. In *Proceedings of a Workshop on Case-Based Reasoning* (pp. 182-189). San Mateo, CA: Morgan Kaufmann

Hoc, J. M. (1987). *Psychologie cognitive de la planification* [Cognitive psychology of planning]. Grenoble, France: Presses Universitaires de Grenoble.

Hucka, M. (1989). *Planning, interruptability, and learning in Soar.* Unpublished manuscript, University of Michigan, Electrical Engineering and Computer Science Department, Ann Arbor.

Kaelbling, L. P. (1987). An architecture for intelligent reactive systems. In M. P. Georgeff & A. L. Lansky (Eds.), *Reasoning about actions and plans* (pp. 395-410). San Mateo, CA: Morgan Kaufmann.

Keane, M. T. (1988). *Analogical problem solving*. Chichester, UK: Ellis Horwood.

Kirsh, D. (1991). Today the earwig, tomorrow man? *Artificial Intelligence, 47*, 161-184.

Kolodner, J. L. (1987). Extending problem solver capabilities through case-based inference. In *Proceedings of the Fourth International Workshop on Machine Learning* (pp. 167-178). San Mateo, CA: Morgan Kaufmann.

Laird, J. E. (1988). Recovery from incorrect knowledge in Soar. In *Proceedings of the Seventh National Conference on Artificial Intelligence* (pp. 618-623). San Mateo, CA: Morgan Kaufmann.

Laird, J. E., Congdon, C. B., Altmann, E., & Swedlow, K. (1990). *Soar user's manual: Version 5.2* (Tech. Rep. CMU-CS-90-179). Pittsburgh, PA: Carnegie Mellon University, School of Computer Science.

Laird, J. E., & Rosenbloom, P. S. (1990). Integrating execution, planning, and learning in Soar for external environments. In *Proceedings of the Eighth National Conference on Artificial Intelligence* (pp. 1022-1029). San Mateo, CA: Morgan Kaufmann.

Laird, J., Rosenbloom, P., & Newell, A. (1986). *Universal subgoaling and chunking: The automatic generation and learning of goal hierarchies*. Boston, MA: Kluwer.

Lehman, J. F., Lewis, R. L., & Newell, A. (1991). Integrating knowledge sources in language comprehension. In *Proceedings of the Thirteenth Annual Conference of the Cognitive Science Society* (pp. 461-466). Hillsdale, NJ: Erlbaum.

Lindsay, R. K. (1991). Symbol-processing theories and the SOAR architecture. *Psychological Science, 2*, 294-302.

McDermott, D. (1978). Planning and acting. *Cognitive Science, 2*, 71-109.

McDermott, D. (1982). A temporal logic for reasoning about processes and plans. *Cognitive Science, 6*, 101-155.

Michon, J. A. (1985). The compleat time experiencer. In J. A. Michon & J. L. Jackson (Eds.), *Time, mind, and behavior* (pp. 20-52). Berlin: Springer-Verlag.

Michon, J. A. (1990). Implicit and explicit representations of time. In R. A. Block (Ed.), *Cognitive models of psychological time* (pp. 37-58). Hillsdale, NJ: Erlbaum.

Miller, G. A., Galanter, E., & Pribram, K. H. (1960). *Plans and the structure of behavior*. New York: Holt, Rinehart and Winston.

Minton, S. (1988). *Learning search control knowledge: An explanation-based approach*. Boston, MA: Kluwer.

Minsky, M. (1975). A framework for representing knowledge. In P. H. Winston (Ed.), *The psychology of computer vision* (pp.211-277). New York: McGraw-Hill.

Morton, J., & Byrne, R. (1975). Organization in the kitchen. In P. M. A. Rabbitt & S. Dornic (Eds.), *Attention and performance* (Vol. 5, pp. 517-529). London: Academic Press.

Morton, J., Hammersley, R. H., & Bekerian, D. A. (1985). Headed records: A model for memory and its failures. *Cognition, 20,* 1-23.

Newell, A. (1990). *Unified theories of cognition.* Cambridge, MA: Harvard University Press.

Newell, A., & Simon, H. A. (1963). GPS, a program that simulates human thought. In E. A. Feigenbaum & J. Feldman (Eds.), *Computers and thought* (pp. 279-293). New York: McGraw-Hill. (Original work published 1961)

Newell, A., & Simon, H. A. (1972). *Human problem solving.* Englewood Cliffs, NJ: Prentice-Hall.

Norman, D. A. (1991). Approaches to the study of intelligence. *Artificial Intelligence, 47,* 327-345.

Quillian, M. R. (1968). Semantic memory. In M. Minsky (Ed.), *Semantic information processing* (pp. 227-270). Cambridge, MA: MIT Press.

Reich, Y. (1988). *Learning plans as a weak method for design.* Unpublished manuscript, Carnegie Mellon University, Department of Civil Engineering, Pittsburgh.

Riesbeck, C., & Schank, R. C. (1989). *Inside case-based reasoning.* Hillsdale, NJ: Erlbaum.

Rosenbloom, P. S., & Aasman, J. (1990). Knowledge level and inductive uses of chunking (EBL). In *Proceedings of the Eight National Conference on Artificial Intelligence* (pp. 821-827). San Mateo, CA: Morgan Kaufmann.

Rosenbloom, P. S., Laird, J. E., Newell, A., & McCarl, R. (1991). A preliminary analysis of the Soar architecture as a basis for general intelligence. *Artificial Intelligence, 47,* 289-325.

Rosenbloom, P. S., Lee, S., & Unruh, A. (1990). Responding to impasses in memory-driven behavior: A framework for planning. In *Proceedings of the Workshop on Innovative Approaches to Planning, Scheduling, and Control* (pp. 181-191). San Mateo, CA: Morgan Kaufmann.

Rosenbloom, P. S., Newell, A., & Laird, J. E. (in press). Towards the knowledge level in Soar: The role of the architecture in the use of knowledge. In K. VanLehn (Ed.), *Architectures for intelligence.* Hillsdale, NJ: Erlbaum.

Ross, B. H. (1989). Some psychological results on case-based reasoning. In *Proceedings of a Workshop on Case-Based Reasoning* (pp. 144-147). San Mateo, CA: Morgan Kaufmann.

Sacerdoti, E. D. (1974). Planning in a hierarchy of abstraction spaces. *Artificial Intelligence, 5,* 115-135.

Sacerdoti, E. D. (1977). *A structure for plans and behavior.* New York: Elsevier North-Holland.

Schank, R. C. (1982). *Dynamic memory: A theory of learning in computers and people.* New York: Cambridge University Press.

Stefik, M. J. (1981a). Planning with constraints (MOLGEN: Part 1). *Artificial Intelligence, 16*, 111-140.

Stefik, M. J. (1981b). Planning and meta-planning (MOLGEN: Part 2). *Artificial Intelligence, 16*, 141-170.

Sussman, G. J. (1975). *A computer model of skill acquisition*. New York: American Elsevier.

Tenenberg, J. D. (1988). *Abstraction in planning* (Tech. Rep. No. 250). Rochester, NY: University of Rochester, Computer Science Department.

Tulving, E. (1972). Episodic and semantic memory. In E. Tulving & W. Donaldson (Eds.), *Organization of memory* (pp. 381-403). New York: Academic Press.

Tulving, E. (1983). *Elements of episodic memory*. Oxford: Clarendon Press.

Tulving, E. (1985). How many memory systems are there? *American Psychologist, 40*, 385-398.

Unruh, A., & Rosenbloom, P. S. (1989). Abstraction in problem solving and learning. In *Proceedings of the Eleventh International Joint Conference on Artificial Intelligence* (pp. 681-687). San Mateo, CA: Morgan Kaufmann.

Wilensky, R. (1983). *Planning and understanding: A computational approach to human reasoning*. Reading, MA: Addison-Wesley.

Wilkins, D. E. (1988). *Practical planning: Extending the classical AI planning paradigm*. San Mateo, CA: Morgan Kaufmann.

Young, R. M., & Whittington, J. E. (1990). *Using a knowledge analysis to predict conceptual errors in text-editor usage*. In J. C. Chew & J. Whiteside (Eds.), *Proceedings of the 1990 Conference on Human Factors in Computing Systems* (pp. 91-97). New York: Association for Computing Machinery.

MEANS-ENDS PLANNING: AN EXAMPLE SOAR SYSTEM

ALADIN AKYÜREK
Department of Psychology, University of Groningen
Groningen, The Netherlands

ABSTRACT. Although Soar is intended to cover the full range of weak problem-solving methods—often hypothesized in cognitive science as basic for all intelligent agents, earlier attempts to add means-ends analysis to Soar's repertoire of methods have not been particularly successful or convincing. Considering its psychological significance, stipulated by Newell and Simon (1972), it seems essential that Soar, when taken as a general cognitive architecture, should allow the means-ends analysis to arise naturally from its own structure. This paper presents a planner program that interleaves a difference reduction process with Soar's default mechanism for operator subgoaling that it modifies in order to map means-ends analysis onto Soar. The scheme advanced is shown to produce "macro-operators" of a novel kind, called *macrochunks*, which may have important implications for explaining routine behavior. The approach taken and the problems that had to be dealt with in implementing this planner are treated in detail. Also, *SoarL*—a language used for state representations—is reviewed with respect to the frame problem.

Introduction

Soar is a computer program that embodies a theory of the architecture of human cognition. As such, it provides a basic set of mechanisms by means of which the full range of human cognition can be studied. Having such an architecture available makes it possible to discover, it is hoped, elements that are common to models grounded in psychological research (Newell, Rosenbloom, & Laird, 1989). Soar embraces the *problem space hypothesis* according to which heuristic search of problem spaces is constitutive of problem solving (Newell, 1980; Newell & Simon, 1972). In addition, another hypothesis, called *universal subgoaling*, has been decisive in defining the Soar architecture

J. A. Michon and A. Akyürek (eds.), Soar: A Cognitive Architecture in Perspective, 109–167.

in its present form (Laird, 1984).

The architecture's organization is such that its repertoire of basic acts supports a problem-space system (Laird & Newell, 1983; Newell, Yost, Laird, Rosenbloom, & Altmann, 1990). There are four core processes that determine the behavior of a problem-space system: Formulate-Task, Select-Operator, Apply-Operator, and Terminate-Task. *Formulating* a task involves adopting a particular problem space p, a goal state, and an initial state. A problem space is defined by a set of states and a finite set of operators, where each operator is a state to state function. A task is accomplished by attempting, that is, by taking a sequence of steps in p, and *terminating* the attempt. Each step consists of *selecting* an operator from the available set and *applying* that operator to the current state. If this operator is applicable, the modified state becomes the current state. The task attempt is terminated when the current state is the desired goal-satisfying state, or when there is sufficient evidence showing that the goal state cannot be achieved from the current state.

Universal subgoaling (Laird, 1984) refers to the fact that, in Soar, subgoals come into existence following *impasses* encountered in performing any of the above processes. For example, Select-Operator is said to fail when it cannot propose any operator for transforming the current state. This impasse will induce Soar to set up a subgoal, capable of activating Formulate-Task to define a task for resolving it. Apply-Operator will fail to execute when the current operator does not succeed in producing the next state. This situation too leads Soar to create a subgoal, allowing Formulate-Task to define a task appropriate to the impasse. Various types of search behavior arise as a function of the amount of knowledge that can be used by these processes. A weak method of search is a scheme that specifies behavior in terms of problem space processes to accomplish a task, and to formulate subtasks for resolving impasses that may occur in executing these processes. The weak methods such as generate-and-test, branch-and-bound, hill-climbing, and means-ends analysis are generally believed to be among the fundamental methods for all intelligent agents. Soar contains a package of productions that provides default responses to the types of impasses it can recognize. An important conjecture is that the weak methods should be realizable in the Soar architecture as natural extensions of this default knowledge (Laird, 1984; Laird & Newell, 1983).

In what follows, I will attempt to show how means-ends analysis may be added to the architecture's repertoire of problem solving methods. There are two good reasons for such an attempt. The first is that means-ends analysis can probably be used as a component of a comprehensive model of human planning based on reasoning from cases (Akyürek, 1992). The second and perhaps more important reason is that, given the psychological significance of this heuristic as established in Newell and Simon (1972), a cognitive architecture simply cannot afford to exclude it from its scope of problem solving strategies. Note that a recent architecture, called Prodigy, has as its kernel an advanced means-ends problem solver (Minton, 1988; Minton et al., 1989).

The paper is organized as follows. First, means-ends analysis is reviewed in detail in state-space problem solvers. Then, a Soar system (Robox-Soar) is introduced that interleaves a difference reduction process with the architecture's default mechanism for operator subgoaling that it modifies in order to map means-ends analysis onto Soar. And, a component of the difference reduction process, called operator valuation, is treated in a separate section as a potential weak method for resolving tie impasses. Then, operator subgoaling is discussed in relation to learning macrochunks along with what it reveals about the current Soar architecture. Next, SoarL, a particular language for representing states in Soar, is considered in relation to the frame problem. The last two sections summarize the results.

Means-Ends Analysis in State-Space Problem Solvers

The means-ends heuristic revolves around the detection of differences between what is given and what is desired, and taking steps that can reduce those differences. This heuristic was essential to GPS, and later also to STRIPS. Both were state-space problem solvers, that is, they worked on state-space problems. A state-space problem is said to consist of an initial state, a set of possible states, a set of admissible operators, and the specification of a desired state or a set of goal conditions. This is, in fact, quite similar to the task formulation in Soar, discussed in the previous section. A solution to a problem in this view (and in Soar as well) is a sequence of operators that changes the initial state into a state in which the problem is solved. This definition implies that each intermediate state created by one of these operators either must satisfy or not block the conditions of application (e.g., the preconditions) of the next operator in the sequence. It is obvious that a plan is like a solution: a sequence of operators that can transform an initial state into a state that satisfies a given goal specification. Thus, a planner can be said to solve problems in its domain of application.

MEANS-ENDS ANALYSIS IN GPS

Means-ends analysis in GPS requires knowledge, not contained in the specification of a task. The method uses a finite set U of *differences*, assumed to exist in the task domain, a *difference ordering*, and a *table of connections* that relates the differences in U to the domain operators. Difference ordering, which is in fact a partial ordering on the set U, ranks differences according to how difficult they are to reduce or eliminate. GPS represents such an ordering in a table of connections, which lists the highest ranking (i.e., the most difficult) differences first. The table also lists domain operators, indexed by the differences that they can reduce.

GPS organizes means-ends analysis in terms of three processes (Newell & Simon, 1963). Find-Differences computes differences between the current state and the goal state. Identify-Operator retrieves operators which can reduce the highest ranking difference among the computed differences, and identifies the operator to apply.[1] Apply-Operator applies the identified operator to the current state. If this operator is applicable, a new state will be generated that becomes the current state, hence the target difference it is associated with will be reduced. This *difference reduction process* is repeated until Find-Differences detects no further differences between the last state generated and the initial goal state. If the identified operator is not applicable, Apply-Operator sets this operator's preconditions as an intermediate goal state, which must be achieved first. As a result, the difference reduction process is restarted, with as input the intermediate goal state and the current state. The intent is to reach a state in which the identified operator under question can succeed. It should be noted that Find-Differences recognizes a difference only if it is in U, and Identify-Operator consults the table of connections to locate operators relevant to the highest ranking difference.

```
Procedure GPS(G)
  until S matches G do:
     begin
♣       u ← a difference between S and G;
♣       o ← an operator relevant to reducing u;
        p ← preconditions of appropriate instance of o;
        GPS(p);
        S ← result state that obtains after applying o to S;
     end
```

Figure 1. A procedural description of GPS where S refers to the current state and G to the goal state.

The procedure given in Figure 1 defines recursive GPS, driven by means-ends heuristic (Nilsson, 1980). Let *S* be the initial state and *G* be the goal state. The procedure is called initially with *G* as its argument. The steps marked with the symbol ♣ are points where backtracking may occur, that is, the procedure may have to consider a set of differences and/or operators at these points. It is easy to see that the main loop of the procedure is iterative. Recursion occurs at step 6 when GPS works on the preconditions of the operator that is selected. Note that Robox-Soar is intended to model precisely this computational process in Soar.

MEANS-ENDS ANALYSIS IN STRIPS

STRIPS (Fikes & Nilsson, 1971) attempts to find a sequence of operators in a space of "world models" (i.e., states) that can transform a given initial world model into another in which a set of goal conditions can be proven to be true. STRIPS represents states as collections of facts, and the goal conditions as a conjunction of literals, all expressed in first order logic.

This problem solver defines each operator by a description consisting of three components, expressed also in logic as literals: a *precondition formula*, a *delete list*, and an *add list*. The first component corresponds to the preconditions, and the last two to the effects of the operator. Whenever an operator is applied to a state, the facts mentioned in its delete list are first removed from that state and then the facts mentioned in its add list added to it.

A theorem prover is used to retrieve operators that are applicable within a model and to determine whether or not goal conditions have been satisfied in it. But, for searching a space of world models, STRIPS reverts to means-ends analysis to acquire knowledge, indicating operators that can achieve a given goal condition, or relevant to reducing a difference. While GPS obtains such knowledge from a table of connections, STRIPS derives it from the operator descriptions and uncompleted proofs. The behavior of this problem solver on a task is best explained by going through an example.

Assume that STRIPS is trying to accomplish the trivial task in which a robot must go from *LOC-A* to *LOC-B*. Unless the robot is at *LOC-B* in the state *M*, the attempt to prove that the goal condition *G = At(ROBOT, LOC-B)* follows from *M* will certainly fail. The uncompleted proof will contain the unsatisfied goal formula *At(ROBOT, LOC-B)*, which is taken to be the difference between *M* and *G*. Next, the theorem prover looks for operators whose effects on *M* would enable it to complete or to continue the proof. In this case, the operator *Go(x, y)*, instantiated as *Go(x, LOC-B)*, is relevant to reducing this difference. Accordingly, *Go*'s preconditions, say, *At(ROBOT, x)*, is taken as G', an intermediate goal condition. If the state M contains the fact *At(ROBOT, LOC-A)*, an instance of G' can be proven from M. This leads to the application of the operator instance *Go(LOC-A, LOC-B)* to M, producing M'. After this stage, it is trivial for STRIPS to prove G from M'.

The procedure displayed in Figure 2 defines a recursive STRIPS with backtracking as control regime (Nilsson, 1980). As above, let S be the initial state and G the goal state. The procedure is called initially with G as its argument. The symbol ♣ again indicates points where backtracking may occur, that is, the procedure may have to consider a set of goal conditions (or differences) and/or operators at those points. Notice that, again, the main loop of the procedure is iterative. Recursion occurs at step 6 when STRIPS works on the preconditions of the operator that is selected. The recursive STRIPS above can be seen as a special case of GPS where differences between S and G are the literals in G that are not in S, which can be reduced by operators whose add lists contain those literals as their effects.

```
Procedure STRIPS(G)
1     until S matches G do:
2        begin
3 ♣         g ← a component of G that is not in S ;
4 ♣         o ← an operator whose add list contains
                      a literal that matches g;
5           p ← preconditions of appropriate instance of o;
6           STRIPS(p);
7           S ← result state that obtains after applying o to S;
8        end
```

Figure 2. A procedural description of a recursive STRIPS where S refers to the current state and G to the goal state.

Means-Ends Planning: A Soar System

The program Robox-Soar is a Soar system that uses means-ends analysis to plan in a microworld of rooms and boxes (shown in Figure 3) in which a robot can transform an initial state into a goal state. The domain the program operates on is fairly common in the literature on planning (e.g., see Fikes, Hart, & Nilsson, 1972; Fikes & Nilsson, 1971; Tenenberg, 1988). Here, it consists of four rooms interconnected by doors, and two boxes. Operators have been specified that model actions of a robot to go to any object or location within a room, to open or close a door, to push boxes within a room or through a door, and to go through a doorway. The tasks the planner Robox-Soar can solve are similar to the example task given in Figure 3 and Figure 4 which specify an initial state and a goal state to be achieved.

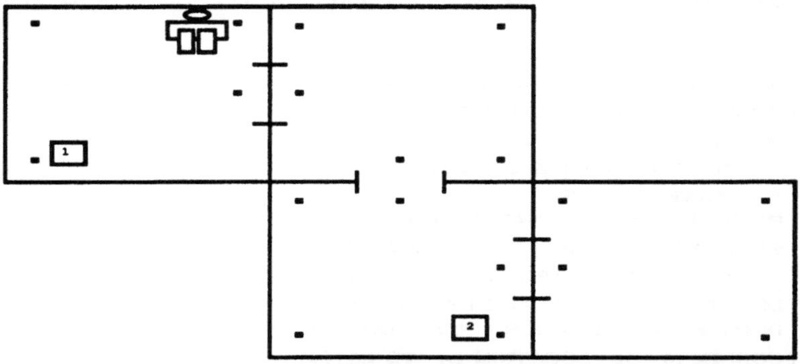

Figure 3. An initial state in the microworld on which the planner Robox-Soar operates. Dots stand for named locations. The robot, named FRED, is at LOC-8 and BOX-1 at LOC-9, both in the same room ROOM-1. BOX-2 is at LOC-15 in ROOM-3. DOOR-1 and DOOR-3 are closed while DOOR-2 is open. Available operators are: ***PushThru, GoThru, Push, Go, Open,*** and ***Close***. In this world, the action of going through a door means that the robot is at one location in front of the door prior to the action and at the other location behind the door after the action. The same also applies to the action of pushing a box through a door. Note that Figure 4 shows a possible goal state in the same microworld.

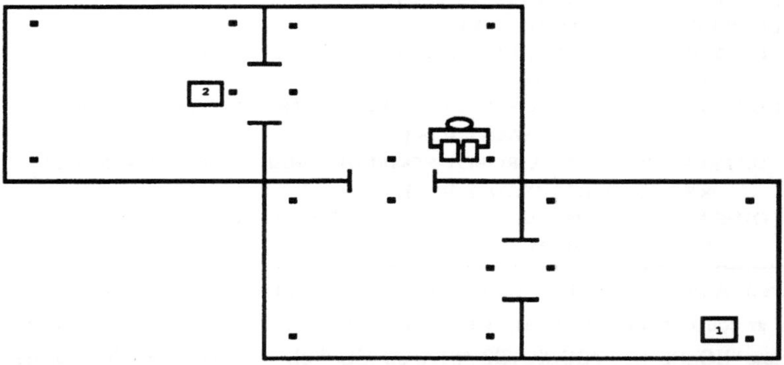

Figure 4. A goal state in the microworld on which the planner Robox-Soar operates. It consists of having FRED at LOC-12 in ROOM-2, BOX-1 at LOC-18 in ROOM-4, and BOX-2 at LOC-1 in ROOM-1.

Before proceeding any further, first consider Figure 5 which reproduces a fragment of Soar's working memory while the planner is attempting to solve the example task. The fragment shows how Soar represents a task to itself. This representation is essentially a collection of related assertions, encoded in data structures consisting of attribute-value pairs. Of special interest is that goal conditions are represented as values of the `^desired` slot of the goal.

```
[GOAL G1 ^PROBLEM-SPACE P2 ^STATE S3
     ^DESIRED D41 D42 D43
     ^DIFFERENCE U49 U51 U53
     ^OPERATOR O56 ]
[PROBLEM-SPACE P2 ^NAME ROBOX ]
[STATE S3 ^LOCATION L4 ... ^DOOR K22 ... ^ROOM R25 ...
     ^BOX B29 B30 ^ROBOT F31 ^HOLDS H32 ... ]
[LOCATION L4 ^NAME LOC-1 ^NEXTTO D22 ^IN R25 ] [...]
[DOOR K22 ^NAME DOOR-1 ^TYPE DOOR ^CONNECTS C38 ] [...]
[CONNECTS C38 ^LOCATION L4 ^TO L5 ] [...]
[ROOM R25 ^NAME ROOM-1 ^AFTER R26 R27 R28 ] [...]
[BOX B29 ^NAME BOX-1 ^TYPE OBJECT ] [...]
[ROBOT F31 ^NAME FRED ]
[HOLDS H32 ^ROBOT F31 ^AT L11 ]
[HOLDS H33 ^BOX B29 ^AT L12 ]
[HOLDS H34 ^BOX B30 ^AT L18 ]
[HOLDS H35 ^DOOR K22 ^STATUS CLOSED ]
[HOLDS H36 ^DOOR K23 ^STATUS OPEN ]
[HOLDS H37 ^DOOR K24 ^STATUS CLOSED ]
[DESIRED D41 ^ROBOT R31 ^AT L15 ]
[DESIRED D42 ^BOX B29 ^AT L21 ]
[DESIRED D43 ^BOX B30 ^AT L4 ]
[DIFFERENCE U49 ^ISA BOX-ROOM-DIFFERENCE ^INVOLVES B30
     ^CURRENT R27 ^WANT R25 ]
[DIFFERENCE U51 ^ISA BOX-ROOM-DIFFERENCE ^INVOLVES B29
     ^CURRENT R25 ^WANT R28 ]
[DIFFERENCE U53 ^ISA ROBOT-ROOM-DIFFERENCE ^INVOLVES SELF
     ^CURRENT R25 ^WANT R26 ]
[OPERATOR O56 ^NAME PUSHTHRU ^DIRECTED-AT B29
     ^FOR U51 ^FROM L8 ^TO L9 ]
```

Figure 5. A snapshot of a fragment of Soar's working memory. Soar represents the world to itself as collections of assertions, coded in attribute-value data structures. For example, the structure "HOLDS H35 ^DOOR K22 ^STATUS CLOSED" is an assertion which can be taken to mean that *Door-1 is closed.*

Since planning tasks involve reasoning about actions, it is important to state at the outset how the *frame problem* is dealt with. In the present planner, all changes to dynamic facts that hold in the state follow from operator actions—for example, there are no non-operator rules that delete objects or relations from the state or change static facts in it. Thus, what does *not* change is the collection of static facts. This is essentially STRIPS's solution to the frame problem (see Fikes & Nilsson, 1971; Hayes, 1973; McDermott, 1987; Schubert, 1990; Wilkins, 1988). How states are represented in the present planner will be discussed in more detail in the section on *SoarL*.

Table 1. *Difference Types and Associated Operators*

Differences	Operators
Box-room	PushThru
Robot-room	GoThru
Box-location	Push
Robot-location	Go
Closed->open	Open
Open->closed	Close

DIFFERENCES

As we saw in the previous section, a requirement for means-ends analysis in GPS style is that knowledge must be available about the possible differences that characterize the task environment. The domain differences that the present planner must deal with are divided into three main categories. First, a *room difference* exists when an entity is at a location in some room while it should be at a location in some other room. If the entity is a box, it is called a *box-room difference*. If the entity involved is the robot itself, there is a *robot-room difference*. Second, a *location difference* exists when an entity is at some location in a room while it should be at some other location in the same room. Consequently, a *box-location difference* is derived if the entity involved is a box. A *robot-location difference* is derived when the object of the difference is the robot itself. Third, a *status difference* is said to exist in relation to the doors. Thus, either a *closed->open difference* or an *open->closed difference* is inferred depending on whether a door should be open or not. Operators that are relevant to reducing these differences are shown in Table 1.

THE PLANNER

Robox-Soar is structured in terms of three problem spaces. The top problem space, where planning occurs, is called "robox." The state of this space is set to the initial task state. There are six operators available in the robox space, suited to the domain of the system. These task operators are defined in Figure 6. The code given in Appendix A shows their representations in Soar. In addition, there is a domain-independent operator, *Goal-Test*, that supports task termination.

On its own, the robox problem space is however unable to propose operators without the knowledge of differences between the task state and the goal conditions. As a result of not having an operator to change the current task state, the architecture faces a *state no-change* impasse that activates another problem space, called "compute-diffs." This subspace contains a *Differentiate operator* that extracts the differences between the current state and the current goal conditions (*step 3* in the procedure GPS, shown earlier in Figure 3), and returns each difference that it finds to the robox problem space. All computed differences are stored in a `^difference` slot of the goal (see Figure 5).

Once the differences to focus on are known, task operators are proposed in the top space that are relevant to reducing them. If there is just one operator proposed, that operator is instantly selected. If there are several operators proposed and there is no information available for comparing them to make a selection, the architecture experiences another difficulty, this time an *operator tie* impasse. When this happens, another problem space is entered that enables the top space to make that selection (*step 4* in GPS). This subspace is called the "valuation" space. It encodes task dependent knowledge, that is, it contains information regarding the relative ranking of differences. Here the task operators are valuated by creating preferences for them that reflect the ranking of the differences they are proposed for, so that the architecture's decision procedure can select an operator which pertains to the current highest ranking difference. Generally, if u_1 is easier to reduce than u_2, operators associated with the second difference will be favored, through appropriate preferences, over those associated with the first. The valuation problem space has a *Valuate operator* to realize this process of preference assignment. The ranking of the differences (i.e., their linear ordering) is addressed separately along with the rules of preference assignment in the following section.

To summarize, the activities of differentiating, proposing, and valuating enable Robox-Soar to employ a difference-guided process of operator selection (cf. Newell et al., 1990).

PushThru(b,x,y,d)
"Push box b from location x to location y thru door d"
P:Location(x), Location(y), Box(b), Door(d), Robot(FRED),
At(b,x), Status(d,OPEN), At(FRED,x), In(x,r1), In(y,r2),
Room(r1), Room(r2), Connects(d,x,y)
D:At(FRED,x), At(b,x)
A:At(FRED,y), At(b,y)

Push(b,x,y)
"Push box b from location x to location y in room r"
P:Location(x), Location(y), Box(b), Robot(FRED),
At(b,x), At(FRED,x), In(x,r), In(y,r), Room(r)
D:At(FRED,x), At(b,x)
A:At(FRED,y), At(b,y)

GoThru(x,y,d)
"Go from location x to location y thru door d"
P:Location(x), Location(y), Door(d), Robot(FRED),
Status(d,OPEN), At(FRED,x), In(x,r1), In(y,r2),
Room(r1), Room(r2), Connects(d,x,y)
D:At(FRED,x)
A:At(FRED,y)

Go(x,y)
"Go from location x to location y in room r"
P:Location(x), Location(y), Robot(FRED),
At(FRED,x), In(x,r), In(y,r), Room(r)
D:At(FRED,x)
A:At(FRED,y)

Open(d,x)
"Open door d from location x in room r"
P:Location(x), Door(d), Robot(FRED), Status(d,CLOSED),
At(FRED,x), NextTo(x,d), In(x,r), Room(r)
D:Status(d,CLOSED)
A:Status(d,OPEN)

Close(d,x)
"Close door d from location x in room r"
P:Location(x), Door(d), Robot(FRED), Status(d,OPEN),
At(FRED,x), NextTo(x,d), In(x,r), Room(r)
D:Status(d,OPEN)
A:Status(d,CLOSED)

Figure 6. Definitions of task operators used by Robox-Soar. In Soar, operators are represented by three or more productions. Soar productions that *implement* operators in particular correspond roughly to these definitions.

If the preconditions of the selected operator are met in the current state, the operator is applied immediately to that state in the top space. As a result, the difference for which this operator was selected is reduced. Notice that the problem solving activity that starts with difference computation and ends with the application of a task operator does realize the difference reduction process.

If the preconditions of the selected operator are *not* met in the current state, an *operator no-change* impasse arises. At this point Robox-Soar follows a modified default strategy of operator subgoaling that makes the *preconditions* of the selected operator—*and not the operator itself as the original default rules for operator subgoaling would have it*—the intermediate goal conditions which, in turn, it attempts to achieve (*steps 5 and 6* in GPS). The idea behind this strategy is that the selected operator not being applicable to the current state, another state must be found to which it is, that is, some state of which the selected operator's preconditions are true (*step 7* in GPS). Whenever this process of subgoaling on operators creates any intermediate goal conditions, the difference reduction process is restarted to eliminate the differences between these goal conditions and the current state. Thus, Robox-Soar interleaves the processes of difference reduction and operator subgoaling to embody the heuristic of means-ends analysis. Operator subgoaling will be taken up in more detail in a later section.

Operator Valuation

This section provides a more detailed description of the process that occurs in the valuation problem space. As noted before, knowledge of differences is brought to bear on which operators to propose in the task space. Any number of them may be proposed. Recall that problem solving is a sequential activity, where a single operator is selected and applied to move through a problem space. Selection and application are *decisions* that the architecture makes at a time (see Newell, 1990, chap. 4). Thus the Soar architecture will detect an operator tie impasse when it cannot select from a collection of operators that are all acceptable and automatically create a subgoal for resolving that impasse. A tie impasse can be resolved by creating additional preferences that favor one alternative, bar all alternatives but one, or make them all indifferent. As was pointed out above, whenever an operator tie impasse occurs in the task space, Robox-Soar selects the valuation space to resolve that impasse. The valuation space relies on domain knowledge, particularly on the available difference ordering, to create additional preferences for operators to indicate the relative worth of each. Hence, I refer to this process as *operator valuation*.

The following defines a partial ordering over the set of room, location, and status differences in the present domain, described in the foregoing section:

```
[1]   robot-related-differences
        ≤ door-related-differences
          ≤ box-related-differences
```

This is an "is-easier-to-reduce-than" relation from the domain theory, that is, it ranks the differences in terms of how difficult they are to deal with. As stated before, means-ends analysis depends on this kind of relationships. The domain theory, likewise, tells which operator(s) can remove which difference (recall Table 1). Hence, the operators are themselves partially ordered, that is,

```
[2]   {Go,GoThru}
        ≤ {Open,Close}
          ≤ {Push,PushThru}
```

The valuate operator indeed effectuates following rules in the valuation problem space that translate [2] in terms of the preference language that Soar uses in making decisions.

```
[3]   [tokenOf(x,Open) ∨ tokenOf(x,Close)]
        ∧ directedAt(x,y) ∧ door(y)
          ⊃ indifferent(x) ∧ worst(x)

[4]   directedAt(x,y) ∧ box(y) ⊃ indifferent(x)

[5]   [tokenOf(x,PushThru) ∨ tokenOf(x,Push)]
        ∧ for(x,u) ∧ box-related-difference(u)
          ∧ [tokenOf(y,Gothru) ∨ tokenOf(y,Go)]
            ∧ for(y,v) ∧ robot-related-difference(v)
              ⊃ better(x,y)

[6]   directedAt(x,y) ∧ ¬robot(y)
        ∧ ∃z. [in(SELF,z) ∧ in(y,z) ∧ room(z)]
            ⊃ best(x)
```

The first three rules above assign preferences to operators in accordance with the ranking of the differences they are associated with. The rule in [6] is a of least-effort heuristic: if an environment-directed action can be carried out in a room where the robot is, that action is given a best preference. Given two differences, say, a robot-room difference and a box-room difference, two operators will be proposed to reduce them: *GoThru* and *PushThru*. It follows from [5] above that *PushThru* is better than *GoThru*. Consequently, the architecture will decide on selecting *PushThru* in the task space.

One might think that this model will fail in a domain where there is no one-to-one correspondence between differences and operators. This is simply not the case. Suppose we have four differences and an ordering over them that says: $u_1 \leq u_2 \leq u_3 \leq u_4$. Let's also assume that the following operators are relevant to reducing them:

u_1: *A*, *B*, *C*
u_2: *B*, *D*
u_3: *C*, *E*, *F*
u_4: *G*

Imagine that we have two computed differences at some moment: u_1 and u_2. Assume also that following operators are proposed, say, {a1, b1, c1} for u_1 and {b2, d1} for u_2. Notice that b1 and b2 are different instantiations of the same operator, that is, of *B*. A valuation rule will prefer both b2 and d1 over a1, b1, and c1 because of $u_1 \leq u_2$. Another valuation rule will make each element in {a1, b1, c1} indifferent just because each is capable of reducing a difference of the same type (i.e., u_1). This same rule will also fire to make each element in {b2, d1} indifferent, again because each can reduce a difference of the same type (i.e., u_2). Soar will then select either b2 or d1 at random. If there is more knowledge about *B* and *D*, for example, one being cheaper than the other, an operator valuation rule can make the cheaper operator better than the other.

In fact, the valuation problem space might be taken to embody a table of connections, though it is more powerful than such a table.

Operator Subgoaling

As was established in the foregoing sections, acting on operators failing to apply is crucial to the means-ends heuristic. The following example illustrates this. Suppose that Fred intends to *call Mike*. While attempting to call, he discovers that he does not have *Mike's telephone number*. Upon deciding to get Mike's telephone number, he *looks up* Mike's number in the telephone directory. Obviously, looking up the number in the directory brings Fred in a situation where he can proceed with his original intention. A subset of Soar's default productions is intended to implement this form of commonsense reasoning, often called precondition satisfaction in artificial intelligence and cognitive science, as a weak method of problem solving. In the Soar theory, this becomes: If a selected operator cannot be applied to the current state, a reasonable strategy is, as the universal subgoaling hypothesis also implies, to create a subgoal to find a state where the operator can be applied (Laird, Swedlow, Altmann, Congdon, & Wiesmeyer, 1989). It is called operator subgoaling for obvious reasons.

Operator subgoaling is considered appropriate in Soar when a selection has been made for an operator and a no-change impasse arises. It is implemented by setting up the same context in the subgoal as that prevailing before the impasse, but with a different objective: that of achieving a state in the domain of the selected operator. To this end, both acceptable and worst preferences are created to enable selecting the operator's problem space in the subgoal. If there are no competing problem spaces, this one will be selected in the subgoal so that a search can be undertaken in the same problem space as the supergoal. Obviously, reaching a state in the domain of an operator failing to apply amounts to finding another operator or an operator sequence that can produce that state. When the parent problem space has been chosen, the new goal is labeled `operator-subgoal` and the target operator is attached to it as its `^desired`. According to Laird et al. (1989), this establishes a convention that, when the filler of a goal's `^desired` slot is an operator, the objective of the subgoal is to attain a state to which that operator can be applied. This convention raises two problems. First, if we do this, the "semantics" of the slot becomes unclear. Since this slot is ordinarily used to encode the goal state Soar is set to accomplish, it is hard to see how an operator can be a state. Second, if used as advertised, it will become unnecessarily difficult for Soar to infer or know the characteristics of the state it is supposed to find.[2] In fact, the `^desired` slot should indicate—that is, it should contain information on—what must hold in a goal state. In operator subgoaling, these are evidently objects and/or relations specified in the preconditions of the superoperator, not the superoperator itself. Therefore, I have replaced all references to `^desired` in the rules for operator subgoaling to `^achieve`,[3] so that the structure `^desired` is now reserved to house an operator's preconditions instead of the operator itself. This relatively small modification allows reasoning from superoperator's preconditions to search for other operators having those preconditions as their effects, hence a state where the superoperator can be executed.

Given this modification, the telephone case above, for example, translates into Soar as follows. Upon Fred's failure to *call Mike*, an operator no-change impasse will occur. The `^achieve` slot will come to point to the operator *call Mike* in the subgoal. A task specific production will interpret this as the occasion for creating a `^desired` slot, pointing to a description that casts *Mike's telephone number* as the intermediate goal state, which must be attained first.

There is likewise a default rule that creates an acceptable preference for the superstate, which is in fact the task state. Consequently, the task state is transformed directly in the subgoals. This *state sharing* across subgoals is, of course, efficient compared to the state copying that would otherwise be necessary, or to techniques that would defer operator applications. Also, it makes all changes to the task state that would occur through perception *downward visible* to all subgoals for immediate consideration. Likewise, any change to the task state in a subgoal will be *upward visible* throughout the goal hierarchy, a property that may enable Soar to interleave planning and plan execution and act on interrupts in real time (cf. Laird & Rosenbloom, 1990; McDermott, 1978). But I will not elaborate further on these aspects here. Suffice it to say that state sharing appears to be a significant advantage for a system that must interact with the external world.

Figure 7 shows a typical goal-subgoal hierarchy that obtains during operator subgoaling. Once operator o84 is executed in state s3, the changed state becomes immediately available to the goals g70, g42, and g1, and o51 gets applied to the state as modified by o84. The resulting state is again immediately available to the goals g42 and g1. Finally, o40 is applied to the state as modified by o51. In other words, the result states obtained in subgoals are upward visible to all pending goals.

The operator subgoaling structure, mentioned above, forms for Soar an excellent source of experience in that the architecture learns "procedures" which appear better suited to explain routine behavior in skills such as driving, typing, or making coffee. As will become apparent later on, operator subgoaling also reveals an interesting, if not serious, problem in the current Soar architecture, related to its mechanism of operator termination. Although there is a perfectly reasonable solution to it at the level of programs that Soar runs (of which Robox-Soar is an example), its "proper solution" entails changes to the architecture itself.

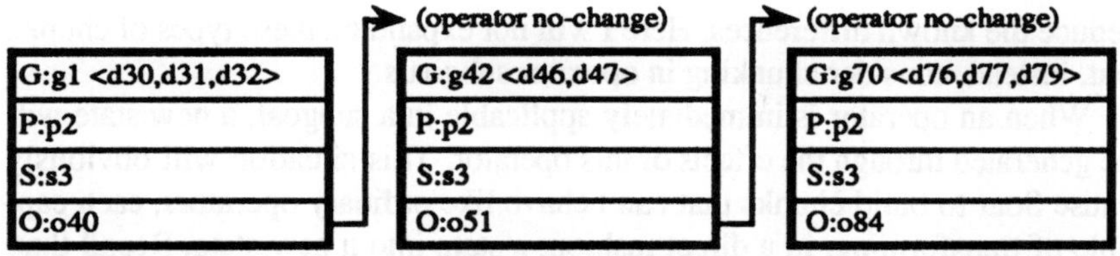

Figure 7. A hypothetical example of operator subgoaling as modified in the present paper. *Left:* the top goal context with <d30,d31,d32> as the planner's initial set of goal conditions, where operator o40 is selected but not applicable. *Middle:* the subgoal context with preconditions of o40 as the intermediate set of goal conditions <d46,d47>, where the operator o51 is selected that can achieve (a part of) <d46,d47> but cannot be applied yet. *Right:* the subgoal context with preconditions of o51 as the intermediate set of goal conditions <d76,d77,d79>, where the operator o84 is selected that can achieve (a part of) <d76, d77,d79>. If o84 is applied, then o51 will be applied, and after that o40. Note that when o84 is applied, the changes made to s3 are also immediately available under all goals (i.e., g70, g42, and g1).

MACROCHUNKS

A key feature of Soar is that it is a goal-based learner. In this subsection, I deal in particular with what Soar can learn in operator subgoals. The architecture learns through *chunking,* which is stipulated to be a general learning mechanism (Laird, Rosenbloom, & Newell, 1984, 1986). Chunking bears some similarity to knowledge compilation (Anderson, 1986) and is essentially a form of explanation-based learning (e.g., DeJong & Mooney, 1986; Minton, 1988; Mitchell, Keller, & Kedar-Cabelli, 1986).

Briefly, chunking turns problem solving in subgoals into productions (i.e., chunks). A chunk's actions are based on the results obtained in the subgoal, while its conditions are composed from aspects that were necessary to produce the results. Chunks contain knowledge that enables Soar to bypass subgoaling in situations similar to the ones in which they were created. Chunking in Robox-Soar occurs in subgoals *cum* problem spaces for computing the differences, valuating operators related to the computed differences, and in subgoals that are set up for operators with unsatisfied preconditions. Example chunks that can ensue from these subgoals are given in Appendix C. Chunking in the compute-diffs problem space yields chunks that can directly detect differences between a state and a set of goal conditions. Chunking in the valuation problem space, on the other hand, yields chunks that contain search-control knowledge—information pertinent to the selection of operators, proposed to reduce the known differences. Here I will not expand on these types of chunks but, instead, consider chunking in operator subgoals.

When an operator is immediately applicable in a subgoal, a new state will be generated through the effects of this operator. This situation will obviously cause Soar to build chunks that can behave like ordinary operators, each capable of transforming, in a direct fashion, a state into a new state. Recall that, in contrast, an ordinary operator has to be first proposed and selected before it can be applied to a state that it will modify. Also, an operator must be explicitly terminated. None of these is required for a chunk. Now, consider the following: suppose that operator o84 in the subgoal g70 in Figure 7 applies and thereby modifies the state s3. Chunking will include the effects of o84 in the action side and the working memory elements referring to o51 along with other elements in the condition side of the chunk that it builds. Thus, such a chunk is a procedure that effectively packages an operator, some conditions of *non* applicability of that operator, and the effects of another operator, either of the same type or of a different type. This *sequencing* of two or more operators in a single procedure is often called a *macro-operator* or MACROP (Fikes, Hart, & Nilsson, 1972). Put more generally, the Soar architecture learns two-step MACROPs of the following general form:

Op1 & some conditions needed for Op1 to apply → effects-of (Op2)

If *Op1* and *Op2* are of the same type, these operators are, of course, instantiated differently. Two examples from Robox-Soar are given below.

```
[7]    If    the operator PushThru(box,x1,y1,d1) is
                 selected,
             and done? = NO,
             and the location y1 in room r1,
             and the location x1 in room r2,
             and the door d1 is open,
             and the box and the robot both are at
                 location x2,
             and the location x2 in room r3,
             and the door d2 that connects x2 to y2
                 is open,
             and the location y2 in room r2,
             and r3 and r2 are adjacent,
       Then modify the state such that the robot and
                 the box both are at y2 in room r2.
```

```
[8]    If    the operator Push(box,x,y) is selected,
             and done? = NO,
             and the box is at location x,
             and the robot is at location z,
             and x, y, z are all in the same room,
             and x ≠ z,
       Then  modify the state such that the robot
                  is now at x.
```

These examples can be found in Appendix C in Soar's native language as *P421* and *P107*, respectively. The first *macrochunk* above will fire to implement the actions of a *PushThru* to get a box in a room adjacent to another room which is in turn adjacent to the room that is the destination of the box for which a *PushThru* is selected. Macrochunks of this type resemble most the "macroproductions" in ACT, which Anderson (1986) illustrates with dialing a phone number as an example. Similarly, the second macrochunk will do the actions of a *Go* whenever a *Push* is selected but is not applicable. These macrochunks are in fact *specializations* of the operators that they implement. For example, *P107* specializes the rule `implement*go` (which is given in Appendix A) for the *Go* operator. To my knowledge, these types of macro-operators have never been described before in the Soar literature.

STRIPS, for instance, constructs multi-step macro-operators from strings and substrings of primitive task operators that appear in a solution to a problem or a plan (see Fikes, Hart, & Nilsson, 1972). In the REFLECT system (Dawson & Siklóssy, 1977) and the Macro Problem Solver (Korf, 1985), however, macro-operators are constructed in a preprocessing stage, that is, they are not learned during problem solving. For example, REFLECT generates a two-step macro-operator, called BIGOP, if the effects of a primitive operator match the preconditions of some other operator. These types of macro-operators are costly and not flexible enough (e.g., Carbonell, 1983; Russell, 1979). Macrochunks differ, however, from these macro-operators in that they mesh well with primitive operators and with each other. It is perfectly possible that *Op1* or a primitive task operator or another macrochunk will apply after a macrochunk including *Op1* gets applied. This is due to the fact that a macrochunk does not have to satisfy *all* of the preconditions of *Op1*, but *only some* of them. After applying a macrochunk Soar can also fall back on ordinary problem solving, if needed. Furthermore, these macrochunks are not expensive (Minton, 1988; Tambe, Newell, & Rosenbloom, 1990). Another characteristic of the Soar macrochunks is that they ignore the goal conditions they can achieve. This makes them flexible. If, for example, an agent wants to have some coffee (a goal condition) *and* decides to *make coffee*, this decision will be sufficient to activate macrochunks having *make coffee* as the first operator to execute one after another, thereby leading to the goal state of having coffee to drink. Thus, macrochunks serve to execute a decision to do something, not to produce that decision. Of course, there will be other productions or chunks that generate that decision in the agent.

OPERATOR IMPLEMENTATION PROBLEM

This subsection deals with the problem that derives from a subtle interaction between operator subgoals and the way Soar implements and terminates operators. A selected operator modifies the current state only when production rules sensitive to that operator fire and implement its effects. Applying an operator is a complex process in itself. For instance, it may occur incrementally and require feedback from the environment as well. One component of this process is ascertaining that the operator is completed. In Soar, an additional rule tests that the operator is successfully implemented and signals that the operator has terminated.

As a close examination of the code for Robox-Soar would reveal, the productions that propose, implement, and terminate operators all have a *done?* attribute, with as possible values *YES* and *NO*. The reason for adding this attribute to the operator-related productions has to do with the fact that, if it is removed, Soar will run into the *operator implementation problem*, and would not be able to learn macrochunks discussed above.[4] This problem occurs when there are a number of operators selected, in a hierarchy of goals as is the case in Figure 7, and productions sensitive to these operators start firing to implement their effects *and* terminate them in succession. The following is an attempt to show what the problem is and under which circumstances it arises. To this end, I use a trace of the architecture's behavior, extracted from a run of Robox-Soar while it attempts a task whose initial state contains the following dynamic facts:

```
[ 9]   Status(DOOR-1,CLOSED)
       Status(DOOR-2,OPEN)
       Status(DOOR-3,CLOSED)
       At(FRED,LOC-8)
       At(BOX-1,LOC-9)
       At(BOX-2,LOC-15)
```

Furthermore, the set of goal conditions to be achieved is:

```
[10]   At(FRED,LOC-8) ∧ At(BOX-1,LOC-7)
          ∧ At(BOX-2,LOC-12)
```

The trace below omits many irrelevant details and intendedly disregards the distinction between problem space and symbol level events to make it easier to understand. *SELECT* means that a decision is made on an operator to apply. *IMPLEMENT* indicates the fact that the selected operator is applied to the current state. The consequences of applying a selected operator take effect after executing *DEL*ete and *ADD* operations. *TERMINATE* displaces the selected operator so that another operator can be selected; a selected operator, however, goes out of existence only after an explicit *DEL* operation that will remove it from working memory. For this particular run, the done? attribute mentioned above has been omitted from all operator-related productions, and chunking has not been activated. Notice that with this predicate, it is secured that an operator instance is not re-applied if it has already been applied.

```
17      SELECT(PushThru(BOX-2,LOC-4,LOC-3,DOOR-2))        [g1]
```

The Pushthru operator is not applicable because BOX-2 is not at LOC-4. FRED is, in fact, at LOC-7 in ROOM-1. Since BOX-2 is not at LOC-4 but at LOC-15, Robox-Soar plans to get this box in front of DOOR-2 (i.e., at LOC-4).

```
   PROPOSE(Push(BOX-2,LOC-15,LOC-4))
      ADD(operator(Push(BOX-2,LOC-15,LOC-4)))
27 SELECT(Push(BOX-2,LOC-15,LOC-4))                      [g89]
```

This Push is not applicable because FRED is not at the same location as BOX-2 to push it. Robox-Soar generates a number of steps (not shown here) after which FRED is at LOC-4, next to DOOR-2. Since FRED is at LOC-4 and BOX-2 is at LOC-15 both in ROOM-3, the Push that is selected at 27 now can be made applicable if FRED goes to LOC-15.

```
   PROPOSE(Go(LOC-4,LOC-15))
      ADD(operator(Go(LOC-4,LOC-15)))
60 SELECT(Go(LOC-4,LOC-15))                              [g84]
   IMPLEMENT(Go(LOC-4,LOC-15))
      DEL(At(FRED,LOC-4))
      ADD(At(FRED,LOC-15))
   TERMINATE(Go(LOC-4,LOC-15))
   IMPLEMENT(Push(BOX-2,LOC-15,LOC-4))
      ADD(applied(Go(LOC-4,LOC-15)))
      DEL(At(BOX-2,LOC-15))
```

```
        ADD(At(BOX-2,LOC-4))
        DEL(At(FRED,LOC-15))
        ADD(At(FRED,LOC-4))
    TERMINATE(Push(BOX-2,LOC-15,LOC-4))
    IMPLEMENT(PushThru(BOX-2,LOC-4,LOC-3,DOOR-2))
```

At this point, the Pushthru planned at 17 becomes applicable, so Soar IMPLEMENTs it. But it attempts to IMPLEMENT the operator Go(LOC-4, LOC-15) too.

```
    IMPLEMENT(Go(LOC-4,LOC-15))
```

This happens after the last Push, as a side effect, got FRED back at LOC-4. That FRED is at LOC-4 makes the rule that implements Go refire. The reason for this is that the operator Go, although TERMINATEd, is not yet DELeted from working memory, so it gets a second chance with FRED coming back at LOC-4. Since this happens in parallel with the production that implements PushThru, there arises uncertainty about the location of FRED.

```
        ADD(applied(Push(BOX-2,LOC-15,LOC-4)))
        DEL(At(BOX-2,LOC-4))
        ADD(At(BOX-2,LOC-3))
        DEL(At(FRED,LOC-4))
```

Soar now runs into an impasse concerning FRED's location: is it LOC-15 or LOC-3?

Briefly, the issue arises when the planner tries to attain the goal condition $At(BOX, L_1)$, while the state contains the following facts that $At(FRED, L_1)$ and $At(BOX, L_2)$. To achieve $At(BOX, L_1)$, it creates the operator subgoaling structure: (a) $Push(BOX, L_2, L_1)$ and (b) $Go(L_1, L_2)$. At this point, the rule that implements *Go* operator fires with the result that $At(FRED, L_2)$. After that, within the same Soar elaboration phase, the rule that implements *Push* fires with obvious results that $At(BOX, L_1)$ and $At(FRED, L_1)$. The problem is that, while in the same elaboration phase, the rule to implement *Go* re-fires on $At(FRED, L_1)$, an event that moves *FRED* back to his previous location: $At(FRED, L_2)$, which is in fact an unintended outcome.[5] The reason for this to happen is that the operator *Go* is still around—*terminated but not yet deleted from the working memory* after the rule to implement *Push* has fired. When *Go*'s first argument re-appears in the working memory, the rule that implements this operator gets a second chance to fire. What has been shown is that Soar's symbol level mechanism for operator termination can fail when multiple operators must be implemented in succession in a single elaboration.

The attribute done? with NO as its initial value is added in Robox-Soar as argument to the task operators by productions that propose them. When they fire, the productions that implement these operators modify the value of the attribute to YES, whereas other productions, including macrochunks, can test its value before they act. This solution effectively catches the "architectural error," described above.[6] A proper solution to the problem within the architecture itself appears also possible. There are at least two alternatives to consider. First, if a production has already implemented an operator in the subgoal, that production can be excluded by the architecture itself from firing again on data modified by productions that implement operators in the supergoal during the same elaboration phase.[7] Second, the architecture can execute a *DEL* to delete a selected operator from working memory *immediately after* a *TERMINATE* (i.e., a *reconsider*) related to that operator occurred. As Laird has also noted, however, the issue requires more thought and theoretical justification.

SoarL

This section deals with representing states in Soar, particularly with respect to the frame problem whose solution requires an efficient way to compute what persists from one situation to another. SoarL is a principled, albeit tentative, language that I use to represent states in Soar.

State descriptions contain objects and relations that must be represented in a sufficiently expressive and efficient language to model situations of concern to an agent. In Soar, everything is encoded as an *augmentation*. Augmentations are minimal *symbolic structures* which are used to represent objects and relations, and to compose productions and preferences. An augmentation is an ordered set of four elements:

```
(class identifier ^attribute value)
```

An identifier can be said to reference a description unit. Below is a collection of augmentations which represent some objects and relations between the objects. Such Soar expressions might be considered as *ground* expressions, and are produced either by the actions of productions, or by the architecture itself. As such, they appear only in the working memory. Under some conditions, however, such expressions may also appear in the productions, hence in the recognition memory.

```
[11]   (object o43 ^color red)
       (object o43 ^on o53)
       (object o43 ^isa box)
       (object o43 ^size small)
```

Attribute-value pairs in Soar actually allow building arbitrary data structures in the working memory, having all sorts of attributes which may be difficult to interpret (cf. Woods, 1975). Describing states as in [11] above is more or less standard practice, but such a description does not make a distinction between dynamic and static relations or objects. Dynamic relations and objects are the only things that can change from state to state through operator actions (e.g., the location of a box or the position of the agent itself). Static relations and objects, presumably, do not change (e.g., the name of a city). In order to make this distinction visible, I have opted for a representational scheme in which the attribute `^holds` is used to indicate dynamic relations. Supposing that the relation `^on` is the only changeable relation above, in SoarL we would obtain:

```
[12]  (object  o43  ^color  red)
      (object  o43  ^isa  box)
      (object  o43  ^size  small)
      (holds  h1  ^object  o43)
      (holds  h1  ^on  o53)
```

This SoarL expression can be rendered in first order logic as

```
[13]  color(o43,RED)
        ∧ isa(o43,BOX)
          ∧ size(o43,SMALL)
            ∧ holds(on(o43,o53)),
```

where o43 and o53 are regarded as "unique names." Goal conditions, headed by `^desired`, are represented in SoarL in a structure similar to that of dynamic relations, headed by `^holds`. As said before, the operators of the present planner act only on relations headed by the `^holds` predicate. Any other relation or object persists (i.e., does not change) from one situation to another, which is essentially the STRIPS solution to the frame problem. The scheme likewise imparts the Soar architecture to acquire non-expensive macrochunks. Note that the manual for Soar5 has adopted a state representation scheme identical to SoarL, which was developed independently (Laird, Congdon, Altmann, & Swedlow, 1990).

Performance On the Example Task

Having described the organization of the planner and its important components, let us examine briefly how it solves the example task introduced earlier. With Soar's chunking mechanism switched off, Robox-Soar generates the operator sequence given in Figure 8. While correct, this plan is rather lengthy. This "suboptimal" behavior is caused by the fact that there exist operators with indifferent preferences still awaiting in the top space, and that there are no competing chunks available to shadow them.

```
Go(LOC-8, LOC-9)
Push(BOX-1, LOC-9, LOC-1)
Open(DOOR-1, LOC-1)
PushThru(BOX-1, LOC-1, LOC-2, DOOR-1)
Push(BOX-1, LOC-2, LOC-3)
PushThru(BOX-1, LOC-3, LOC-4, DOOR-2)
Push(BOX-1, LOC-4, LOC-5)
Open(DOOR-3, LOC-5)
PushThru(BOX-1, LOC-5, LOC-6, DOOR-3)
GoThru(LOC-6, LOC-5, DOOR-3)
Go(LOC-5, LOC-15)
Push(BOX-2, LOC-15, LOC-4)
PushThru(BOX-2, LOC-4, LOC-3, DOOR-2)
Push(BOX-2, LOC-3, LOC-2)
PushThru(BOX-2, LOC-2, LOC-1, DOOR-1)
Gothru(LOC-1, LOC-2, DOOR-1)
Go(LOC-2, LOC-3)
GoThru(LOC-3, LOC-4, DOOR-2)
Go(LOC-4, LOC-5)
GoThru(LOC-5, LOC-6, DOOR-3)
Push(BOX-1, LOC-6, LOC-18)
Go(LOC-18, LOC-6)
GoThru(LOC-6, LOC-5, DOOR-3)
Go(LOC-5, LOC-4)
GoThru(LOC-4, LOC-3, DOOR-2)
Go(LOC-3, LOC-12)
```

Figure 8. The plan Robox-Soar generates, without chunking being activated, to solve the example task in which the initial state consists of the following dynamic facts: FRED is at LOC-8 and BOX-1 at LOC-9, BOX-2 is at LOC-15, and both DOOR-1 and DOOR-3 are CLOSED while DOOR-2 is OPEN, and the goal conditions are: FRED at LOC-12, BOX-1 at LOC-18, and BOX-2 at LOC-1. Appendix B contains a fragment of the behavior of Robox-Soar while it solves this task.

Go(LOC-8, LOC-9)
Push(BOX-1, LOC-9, LOC-1)
Open(DOOR-1, LOC-1)
PushThru(BOX-1, LOC-1, LOC-2, DOOR-1)
Push(BOX-1, LOC-2, LOC-3)
PushThru(BOX-1, LOC-3, LOC-4, DOOR-2)
Push(BOX-1, LOC-4, LOC-5)
Open(DOOR-3, LOC-5)
PushThru(BOX-1, LOC-5, LOC-6, DOOR-3)
Push(BOX-1, LOC-6, LOC-18)
Go(LOC-18, LOC-6)
GoThru(LOC-6, LOC-5, DOOR-3)
Go(LOC-5, LOC-15)
Push(BOX-2, LOC-15, LOC-4)
PushThru(BOX-2, LOC-4, LOC-3, DOOR-2)
Push(BOX-2, LOC-3, LOC-2)
PushThru(BOX-2, LOC-2, LOC-1, DOOR-1)
GoThru(LOC-1, LOC-2, DOOR-1)
Go(LOC-2, LOC-12)

Figure 9. The plan Robox-Soar generates to solve the example task with chunking activated.

The planner initially computes three differences between the current state and the goal conditions: two room differences involving the two boxes and one room difference involving the robot itself. These differences invoke two instantiations of *PushThru* and one instantiation of *GoThru*, which lead to a tie impasse. In the valuation space, set up to resolve the tie, each instantiation of *PushThru* gets an indifferent preference by the action of [4] and are both made better than *GoThru* by [5]. One *PushThru* instantiation gets also a best preference by the action of [6]. Soar then picks out the one with the best preference. In this case, it selects the *PushThru* directed at *BOX-1* to get this box into *ROOM-4*. As soon as Soar reaches an intermediate state, say *S'*, this operator gets applied. At this point, Soar "remembers" the other *PushThru* with indifferent preference, directed at *BOX-2*. Since there does not exist any production rule or a chunk to shadow this choice in the top space, the planner is "forced" to focus its "attention" on finding another state in which this operator in turn can be applied, so it fails to consider pushing *BOX-1* to its final destination while the robot is in *ROOM-4*.

If chunking is switched on, chunks get indeed built, which improves the planner's behavior considerably and as a result, as can be seen from Figure 9, only 19 operators are required instead of 26 to arrive at the specified end state.

The program needs 208 decision cycles to solve this particular task with no learning, 61 while learning at all levels, and 8 when run with chunks learned, that is, after full learning. On this task, Robox-Soar learns 36 chunks.[8] The reduction in the number of decisions to be made is largely due to macrochunks that Soar has learned in operator subgoals.

It should be noted that the planner opens a door *only when* it is appropriate to do so, which is clearly an implicit goal condition that arises during planning for other goal conditions. Linear planners like STRIPS, Prodigy, or even GPS, in contrast, would need additional effort to avoid plans with spurious steps, stemming from such implicit goal conditions.

Discussion

The results presented in this paper contribute to closing an outstanding method-implementation gap in Soar in that the architecture has been shown to accommodate means-ends analysis, a psychologically important, weak method of problem solving. The scheme likewise extends Soar's capability for planning (cf. Laird & Rosenbloom, 1990). Specifically, I have demonstrated that a difference reduction process can be interleaved with a modified version of operator subgoaling to incorporate means-ends analysis into Soar. I have shown that a small modification of the original default rules for operator subgoaling is sufficient to this end. The difference reduction process consists of selecting an operator that can reduce an extant difference, and applying it to *some state* in its domain. Operator subgoaling supports this process in finding that state if it is *not* the current state. Newell (1992) construes GPS as having two methods: means-ends analysis and operator subgoaling, apparently equating the first to the difference reduction process alone. Obviously, I do not subscribe this view (cf. Carbonell, 1983; Ernst, 1969; Newell, Shaw, & Simon, 1962; Newell & Simon, 1963, 1972; Nilsson, 1980; Sandewall, 1969). Like in Robox-Soar, means-ends analysis in GPS in fact integrates two primary processes, difference reduction and operator subgoaling, each of which can be employed, no doubt, as weak methods of problem solving. For instance, human subjects exhibit behavior on some tasks that appears to involve a form of difference reduction process rather than means-ends analysis as a whole (Atwood & Polson, 1976; Jeffries, Polson, & Razran, 1977).

Operator subgoaling has been shown to create a problem-solving structure in which the same state is shared across goals and operator actions update the shared state directly. This means that, as soon as the state is modified in a subgoal, this modified state is immediately upward visible. This upward visibility of the changing state has been observed to have two interesting consequences for the architecture. First, it enables the architecture to produce versatile and non-expensive macrochunks, two-step macro-operators that can cooperate well with each other, primitive operators on which they are based, and search. Second, it discloses a puzzling error in the Soar architecture which is seen in the operator implementation problem. When confronted with operators that start applying one after another during an elaboration phase, the architecture has been shown, in a serendipitous case, to re-apply an already applied operator on the results of its successor, thereby causing unintended results. Robox-Soar solves this problem by adding a done? attribute to all productions that concern operators. The solution effectively catches the error that derives from the way in which Soar implements and terminates operators. Without this solution, the architecture may run into the same problem in applying the macrochunks that it learns, albeit in a different guise. The operator implementation problem can be solved, however, within the architecture itself by removing a selected operator from working memory immediately after that operator is terminated.

The planner, driven by means-ends analysis, is capable of generating satisfactory plans for conjunctive sets of goal conditions in its domain of application. The results suggest that means-ends planning as developed here can be used to study planning for complex cognitive tasks in environments such as text editors or operating systems. One direction for future research is to consider extending the planner with abstraction mechanisms (Knoblock, 1989; Sacerdoti, 1974; Tenenberg, 1988; Unruh & Rosenbloom, 1989, 1990). Also, work has to be done to assess whether it can be combined with a case-based planner as discussed elsewhere (Akyürek, 1992).

The valuation process, which exploits the predefined preference primitives of Soar, is a promising research area in that as a method it can play a role in characterizing knowledge-intensive domains. Another area of research would be the extension of SoarL, which explicitly distinguish between dynamic and static facts, to cover more complex representational issues in Soar.

Acknowledgements

This work was supported in part by IBM Nederland under a Study Contract with John A. Michon and in part by a grant (Dossier No. R 57-273) from the Netherlands Organization for Scientific Research (NWO) to the author. I am indebted to John A. Michon for his support and reflections on this material. I also would like to thank Brian G. Milnes for numerous helpful discussions about Robox-Soar, GPS, and Soar.

NOTES

[1]Find-Differences followed by Identify-Operator can be said to implement an operator selection process. Laird (1984) appears to equate this process with means-ends analysis.

[2]Also, it has proven impossible to realize working programs implementing the GPS procedure as defined in Figure 3 with operators treated as goal states.

[3]This is meant to abbreviate *achieve-preconditions-of.*

[4]Another reason that makes learning macrochunks possible is that a part of the chunking mechanism—called *notifier*—has been replaced in the current Soar. Without this and the present solution to the operator implementation problem, Soar would produce productions, which, in an earlier version of this paper, were referred to as "killer chunks."

[5]It should be noted that the sample task is not an example of interacting goals of the sort observed in the Sussman Anomaly, a case of protection-violation (Sussman, 1975; Wilkins, 1988) in which a goal condition already achieved must be undone in order to achieve another from a conjunctive set of goal conditions.

[6]Including the clause `-{ (goal <g> ^applied <o>) }` in the condition side of each production that implements a task operator can also solve operator implementation problem, but chunking will not include this negated clause in the chunks that it builds. Such chunks would then fire on operators that are already implemented.

[7]This proposal is due to John E. Laird (E-mail communication, August 27, 1990).

[8]On a variety of 20 planning problems in the same domain, the planner exhibits a similar performance.

REFERENCES

Akyürek, A. (1992). On a computational model of human planning. In J. A. Michon & A. Akyürek (Eds.), *Soar: A cognitive architecture in perspective* (pp. 81-108). Dordrecht, The Netherlands: Kluwer.

Anderson, J. R. (1986). Knowledge compilation: The general learning mechanism. In R. S. Michalski, J. G. Carbonell, & T. M. Mitchell (Eds.), *Machine learning: An artificial intelligence approach* (Vol. II, pp. 289-310). Los Altos, CA: Morgan Kaufmann.

Atwood, M. E., & Polson, P. G. (1976). A process model for water jug problems. *Cognitive Psychology, 8*, 191-216.

Carbonell, J. G. (1983). Learning by analogy: Formulating and generalizing plans from past experience. In R. S. Michalski, J. G. Carbonell, & T. M. Mitchell (Eds.), *Machine learning: An artificial intelligence approach* (pp. 137-161). Los Altos, CA: Morgan Kaufmann.

Dawson, C., & Siklóssy, L. (1977). The role of preprocessing in problem solving systems. In *Proceedings of the Fifth International Joint Conference on Artificial Intelligence* (pp. 465-471). San Mateo, CA: Morgan Kaufmann.

DeJong, G., & Mooney, R. (1986). Explanation-based learning: An alternative view. *Machine Learning, 1*, 145-176.

Ernst, G. W. (1969). Sufficient conditions for the success of GPS. *Journal of the Association for Computing Machinery, 16*, 517-533.

Fikes, R. E., Hart, P. E., & Nilsson, N. J. (1972). Learning and executing generalized robot plans. *Artificial Intelligence, 3*, 251-288.

Fikes, R. E., & Nilsson, N. J. (1971). STRIPS: A new approach to the application of theorem proving to problem solving. *Artificial Intelligence, 2*, 189-208.

Hayes, P. J. (1973). The frame problem and related problems in artificial intelligence. In A. Elithorn & D. Jones (Eds.), *Artificial and human thinking* (pp. 45-59). Amsterdam: Elsevier.

Jeffries, R., Polson, P. G., & Razran, L. (1977). A process model for missionaries-cannibals and other river-crossing problems. *Cognitive Psychology, 9*, 412-440.

Korf, R. E. (1985). *Learning to solve problems by searching for macro-operators*. Boston, MA: Pitman.

Knoblock, C. A. (1989). Learning hierarchies of abstraction spaces. In *Proceedings of the Sixth International Workshop on Machine Learning* (pp. 241-245). San Mateo, CA: Morgan Kaufmann.

Laird, J. E. (1984). *Universal subgoaling* (Tech. Rep. CMU-CS-84-129). Pittsburgh, PA: Carnegie Mellon University, Department of Computer Science. [Also available as part of Laird, J., Rosenbloom, P., & Newell, A. (1986). *Universal subgoaling and chunking: The automatic generation and learning of goal hierarchies* (pp. 1-131). Boston, MA: Kluwer.]

Laird, J. E., Congdon, C. B., Altmann, E., & Swedlow, K. (1990). *Soar user's manual: Version 5.2* (Tech. Rep. CMU-CS-90-179). Pittsburgh, PA: Carnegie Mellon University, School of Computer Science.

Laird, J., & Newell, A. (1983). *A universal weak method* (Tech. Rep. CMU-CS-83-141). Pittsburgh, PA: Carnegie Mellon University, Department of Computer Science.

Laird, J. E., & Rosenbloom, P. S. (1990). Integrating execution, planning, and learning in Soar for external environments. In *Proceedings of the Eighth National Conference on Artificial Intelligence* (pp. 1022-1029). San Mateo, CA: Morgan Kaufmann.

Laird, J. E., Rosenbloom, P. S., & Newell, A. (1984). Towards chunking as a general learning mechanism. In *Proceedings of the Fourth National Conference on Artificial Intelligence* (pp. 188-192). San Mateo, CA: Morgan Kaufmann.

Laird, J. E., Rosenbloom, P. S., & Newell, A. (1986). Chunking in Soar: The anatomy of a general learning mechanism. *Machine Learning, 1,* 11-46.

Laird, J., Swedlow, K., Altmann, E., Congdon, C. B., & Wiesmeyer, M. (1989). *Soar user's manual: Version 4.5.* Pittsburgh, PA: Carnegie Mellon University, School of Computer Science.

McDermott, D. (1987). AI, logic, and the frame problem. In F. M. Brown (Ed.), *The frame problem in artificial intelligence* (pp. 105-118). Los Altos, CA: Morgan Kaufmann.

McDermott, D. (1978). Planning and acting. *Cognitive Science, 2,* 71-109).

Minton, S. (1988). *Learning search control knowledge: An explanation-based approach.* Boston, MA: Kluwer.

Minton, S., Knoblock, C. A., Kuokka, D. R., Gil, Y., Joseph, R. L., & Carbonell, J. G. (1989). *PRODIGY 2.0: The manual and tutorial* (Tech. Rep. CMU-CS-89-146). Pittsburgh, PA: Carnegie-Mellon University, School of Computer Science.

Mitchell, T. M., Keller, R. M., & Kedar-Cabelli, S. T. (1986). Explanation-based generalization: A unifying view. *Machine Learning, 1,* 47-80.

Newell, A. (1980). Reasoning, problem solving, and decision processes: The problem space as a fundamental category. In R. S. Nickerson (Ed.), *Attention and performance* (Vol. 8, pp. 693-718). Hillsdale, NJ: Erlbaum.

Newell, A. (1990). *Unified theories of cognition.* Cambridge, MA: Harvard University Press.

Newell, A. (1992). Unified theories of cognition and the role of Soar. In J. A. Michon & A. Akyürek (Eds.), *Soar: A cognitive architecture in perspective* (pp. 25-79). Dordrecht, The Netherlands: Kluwer.

Newell, A., Rosenbloom, P. S., & Laird, J. E. (1989). Symbolic architectures for cognition. In M. I. Posner (Ed.), *Foundations of cognitive science* (pp. 93-131). Cambridge, MA: MIT Press.

Newell, A., Shaw, J. C., & Simon, H. A. (1962). The processes of creative thinking. In H. E. Gruber, G. Terrell, & M. Wertheimer (Eds.), *Contemporary approaches to creative thinking* (pp. 63-119). New York: Atherton Press.

Newell, A., & Simon, H. A. (1963). GPS, a program that simulates human thought. In E. A. Feigenbaum & J. Feldman (Eds.), *Computers and thought* (pp. 279-293). New York: McGraw-Hill. (Original work published 1961)

Newell, A., & Simon, H. A. (1972). *Human problem solving*. Englewood Cliffs, NJ: Prentice-Hall.

Newell, A., Yost, G., Laird, J. E., Rosenbloom, P. S., & Altmann, E. (1990). *Formulating the problem space computational model*. Paper presented at the 25th Anniversary Symposium, School of Computer Science, Carnegie Mellon University, Pittsburgh, PA.

Nilsson, N. J. (1980). *Principles of artificial intelligence*. Los Altos, CA: Morgan Kaufmann.

Russell, S. J. (1989). Execution architectures and compilation. In *Proceedings of the Eleventh International Joint Conference on Artificial Intelligence* (pp. 15-20). San Mateo, CA: Morgan Kaufmann.

Sacerdoti, E. D. (1974). Planning in a hierarchy of abstraction spaces. *Artificial Intelligence, 5*, 115-135.

Sandewall, E. J. (1969). A planning problem solver based on look-ahead in stochastic game trees. *Journal of the Association for Computing Machinery, 16*, 364-382.

Schubert, L. (1990). Monotonic solution of the frame problem in the situation calculus: An efficient method for worlds with fully specified actions. In H. E. Kyburg, R. P. Loui, & G. N. Carlson (Eds.), *Knowledge representation and defeasible reasoning* (pp. 23-67). Dordrecht, The Netherlands: Kluwer.

Sussman, G. J. (1975). *A computer model of skill acquisition*. New York: American Elsevier.

Tambe, M., Newell, A., & Rosenbloom, P. S. (1990). The problem of expensive chunks and its solution by restricting expressiveness. *Machine Learning, 5*, 299-348.

Tenenberg, J. D. (1988). *Abstraction in planning* (Tech. Rep. No. 250). Rochester, NY: University of Rochester, Computer Science Department.

Unruh, A., & Rosenbloom, P. S. (1989). Abstraction in problem solving and learning. In *Proceedings of the Eleventh International Joint Conference on Artificial Intelligence* (pp. 681-687). San Mateo, CA: Morgan Kaufmann.

Unruh, A., & Rosenbloom, P. S. (1990). *Two new weak method increments for abstraction*. Manuscript submitted for publication.

Wilkins, D. E. (1988). *Practical planning: Extending the classical AI planning paradigm*. San Mateo, CA: Morgan Kaufmann.

Woods, W. A. (1975). What's in a link: Foundations for semantic networks. In D. G. Bobrow & A. Collins (Eds.), *Representation and understanding: Studies in cognitive science* (pp. 35-82). Orlando, FL: Academic Press.

Appendices

APPENDIX A: ROBOX-SOAR

The following is the Soar code for the planner reviewed in the body of the present paper; a soft copy along with example problems is available from the author on request.

Soar Declarations

```
(defun init-task ()
  (init-soar)
  (user-select
   (soar-menu
    "Select path"
    '(("Deterministically random" first)
      ("Random" nil))))
  (set-learning-choice))

(user-select 'first)

(multi-attributes '((state success) (state pursue)
                    (state location) (state room)
                    (state door) (state box)
                    (state holds) (room after)
                    (goal desired) (goal difference)))

(trace-attributes '((state holds) (holds robot) (holds box)
                    (holds at) (holds door) (holds status)
                    (operator name) (operator directed-at)
                    (operator from) (operator to) (operator door)))
```

Top Goal: Robox

```
(sp top-goal*elaborate*goal*robox
    (goal <g> ^object nil)
    -->
    (goal <g> ^name robox))
```

Top Goal Problem Space: Robox

```
(sp robox*propose*space*robox
    (goal <g> ^object nil ^name robox)
    -->
    (goal <g> ^problem-space <p>)
    (problem-space <p> ^name robox))
```

Robox Problem Space: Initial State and Desired State

```
(sp robox*propose*state*initial-and-desired-states
    (goal <g> ^problem-space <p> ^name robox)
    (problem-space <p> ^name robox)
    -->
    (goal <g> ^state <s>)
    (state <s> ^location <L1> + &, <L2> + &, <L3> + &, <L4> + &,
        <L5> + &, <L6> + &, <L7> + &, <L8> + &, <L9> + &, <L10> + &,
        <L11> + &, <L12> + &, <L13> + &, <L14> + &, <L15> + &,
        <L16> + &, <L17> + &, <L18> + &
        ^door <k1> + &, <k2> + &, <k3> + &
        ^room <r1> + &, <r2> + &, <r3> + &, <r4> + &
        ^box <b1> + &, <b2> + & ^robot <fred>
        ^holds <h1> + &, <h2> + &, <h3> + &, <h4> + &,
               <h5> + &, <h6> + & )
    (location <L1> ^name loc-1 ^nextto <k1> ^in <r1>)
    (location <L2> ^name loc-2 ^nextto <k1> ^in <r2>)
    (location <L3> ^name loc-3 ^nextto <k2> ^in <r2>)
    (location <L4> ^name loc-4 ^nextto <k2> ^in <r3>)
    (location <L5> ^name loc-5 ^nextto <k3> ^in <r3>)
    (location <L6> ^name loc-6 ^nextto <k3> ^in <r4>)
    (location <L7> ^name loc-7 ^in <r1>)
    (location <L8> ^name loc-8 ^in <r1>)
    (location <L9> ^name loc-9 ^in <r1>)
    (location <L10> ^name loc-10 ^in <r2>)
    (location <L11> ^name loc-11 ^in <r2>)
    (location <L12> ^name loc-12 ^in <r2>)
    (location <L13> ^name loc-13 ^in <r3>)
    (location <L14> ^name loc-14 ^in <r3>)
    (location <L15> ^name loc-15 ^in <r3>)
    (location <L16> ^name loc-16 ^in <r4>)
    (location <L17> ^name loc-17 ^in <r4>)
    (location <L18> ^name loc-18 ^in <r4>)
    (door <k1> ^type door ^name door-1 ^connects <c1>)
    (door <k2> ^type door ^name door-2 ^connects <c2>)
    (door <k3> ^type door ^name door-3 ^connects <c3>)
    (connects <c1> ^location <L1> ^to <L2>)
    (connects <c2> ^location <L3> ^to <L4>)
    (connects <c3> ^location <L5> ^to <L6>)
    (room <r1> ^name room-1 ^after <r2> + &, <r3> + &, <r4> + & )
    (room <r2> ^name room-2 ^after <r3> + &, <r4> + & )
    (room <r3> ^name room-3 ^after <r4>)
    (room <r4> ^name room-4 ^after none)
    (box <b1> ^type object ^name box-1)
    (box <b2> ^type object ^name box-2)
    (robot <fred> ^name fred)
```

```
    (holds <h1> ^robot <fred> ^at <L8>)
    (holds <h2> ^box <b1> ^at <L9>)
    (holds <h3> ^box <b2> ^at <L15>)
    (holds <h4> ^door <k1> ^status closed)
    (holds <h5> ^door <k2> ^status open)
    (holds <h6> ^door <k3> ^status closed)
    (goal <g> ^desired <d1> + &, <d2> + &, <d3> + & )
    (desired <d1> ^robot <fred> ^at <L12>)
    (desired <d2> ^box <b1> ^at <L18>)
    (desired <d3> ^box <b2> ^at <L1>))
```

Robox Problem Space Operators: Pushthru, Push, Gothru, Go, Open, and Close

```
(sp robox*propose*operator*pushthru*a
    (goal <g> ^difference <u>)
    (goal <g> ^problem-space <p> ^state <s>)
    (difference <u> ^isa box-room-difference ^involves <b>
        ^current <room-b> ^want <room>)
    (problem-space <p> ^name robox)
    (state <s> ^holds <h>)
    (room <room-b> ^after <room>)
    (holds <h> ^door <door>)
    (door <door> ^connects <c>)
    (connects <c> ^location <loc1> ^to <loc2>)
    (location <loc2> ^in <room>)
    -->
    (goal <g> ^operator <o>)
    (operator <o> ^name pushthru ^done? no ^for <u> ^door <door>
        ^directed-at <b> ^from <loc1> ^to <loc2>))

(sp robox*propose*operator*pushthru*b
    (goal <g> ^difference <u>)
    (goal <g> ^problem-space <p> ^state <s>)
    (difference <u> ^isa box-room-difference ^involves <b>
        ^current <room-b> ^want <room>)
    (problem-space <p> ^name robox)
    (state <s> ^holds <h>)
    (room <room> ^after <room-b>)
    (holds <h> ^door <door>)
    (door <door> ^connects <c>)
    (connects <c> ^location <loc1> ^to <loc2>)
    (location <loc1> ^in <room>)
    -->
    (goal <g> ^operator <o>)
    (operator <o> ^name pushthru ^done? no ^for <u> ^door <door>
        ^directed-at <b> ^from <loc2> ^to <loc1>))
```

```
(sp robox*propose*operator*push
    (goal <g> ^difference <u>)
    (goal <g> ^problem-space <p> ^state <s>)
    (difference <u> ^isa box-location-difference ^involves <b>
        ^current <loc1> ^want <loc2>)
    (problem-space <p> ^name robox)
    (location <loc1> ^in <r>)
    (location <loc2> ^in <r>)
    -->
    (goal <g> ^operator <o>)
    (operator <o> ^name push ^done? no ^for <u>
        ^directed-at <b> ^from <loc1> ^to <loc2>))

(sp robox*propose*operator*gothru*a
    (goal <g> ^difference <u>)
    (goal <g> ^problem-space <p> ^state <s>)
    (difference <u> ^isa robot-room-difference ^involves self
        ^current <room-r> ^want <room>)
    (problem-space <p> ^name robox)
    (state <s> ^holds <h>)
    (room <room-r> ^after <room>)
    (holds <h> ^door <door>)
    (door <door> ^connects <c>)
    (connects <c> ^location <loc1> ^to <loc2>)
    (location <loc2> ^in <room>)
    -->
    (goal <g> ^operator <o>)
    (operator <o> ^name gothru ^done? no ^for <u> ^door <door>
        ^directed-at self ^from <loc1> ^to <loc2>))

(sp robox*propose*operator*gothru*b
    (goal <g> ^difference <u>)
    (goal <g> ^problem-space <p> ^state <s>)
    (difference <u> ^isa robot-room-difference ^involves self
        ^current <room-r> ^want <room>)
    (problem-space <p> ^name robox)
    (state <s> ^holds <h>)
    (room <room> ^after <room-r>)
    (holds <h> ^door <door>)
    (door <door> ^connects <c>)
    (connects <c> ^location <loc1> ^to <loc2>)
    (location <loc1> ^in <room>)
    -->
    (goal <g> ^operator <o>)
    (operator <o> ^name gothru ^done? no ^for <u> ^door <door>
        ^directed-at self ^from <loc2> ^to <loc1>))
```

```
(sp robox*propose*operator*go
    (goal <g> ^difference <u>)
    (goal <g> ^problem-space <p> ^state <s>)
    (difference <u> ^isa robot-location-difference ^involves self
        ^current <loc1> ^want <loc2>)
    (problem-space <p> ^name robox)
    (location <loc1> ^in <r>)
    (location <loc2> ^in <r>)
    -->
    (goal <g> ^operator <o>)
    (operator <o> ^name go ^done? no ^for <u>
        ^directed-at self ^from <loc1> ^to <loc2>))

(sp robox*propose*operator*open*a
    (goal <g> ^difference <u>)
    (goal <g> ^problem-space <p> ^state <s>)
    (difference <u> ^isa closed->open-difference ^involves <door>)
    (problem-space <p> ^name robox)
    (state <s> ^holds <h1> <h2>)
    (holds <h1> ^door <door> ^status closed)
    (holds <h2> ^robot <rob> ^at <loc-r>)
    (location <loc-r> ^in <room-r>)
    (door <door> ^connects <c>)
    (connects <c> ^location <loc1> ^to <loc2>)
    (location <loc2> ^in <room>)
    (room <room-r> ^after <room>)
    -->
    (goal <g> ^operator <o>)
    (operator <o> ^name open ^done? no
        ^directed-at <door> ^from <loc1>))
```

```
(sp robox*propose*operator*open*b
    (goal <g> ^difference <u>)
    (goal <g> ^problem-space <p> ^state <s>)
    (difference <u> ^isa closed->open-difference ^involves <door>)
    (problem-space <p> ^name robox)
    (state <s> ^holds <h1> <h2>)
    (holds <h1> ^door <door> ^status closed)
    (holds <h2> ^robot <rob> ^at <loc-r>)
    (location <loc-r> ^in <room-r>)
    (door <door> ^connects <c>)
    (connects <c> ^location <loc1> ^to <loc2>)
    (location <loc1> ^in <room>)
    (room <room> ^after <room-r>)
    -->
    (goal <g> ^operator <o>)
    (operator <o> ^name open ^done? no
        ^directed-at <door> ^from <loc2>))

(sp robox*propose*operator*close*a
    (goal <g> ^difference <u>)
    (goal <g> ^problem-space <p> ^state <s>)
    (difference <u> ^isa open->closed-difference ^involves <door>)
    (problem-space <p> ^name robox)
    (state <s> ^holds <h1> <h2>)
    (holds <h1> ^door <door> ^status open)
    (holds <h2> ^robot <rob> ^at <loc-r>)
    (location <loc-r> ^in <room-r>)
    (door <door> ^connects <c>)
    (connects <c> ^location <loc1> ^to <loc2>)
    (location <loc2> ^in <room>)
    (room <room-r> ^after <room>)
    -->
    (goal <g> ^operator <o>)
    (operator <o> ^name close ^done? no
        ^directed-at <door> ^from <loc1>))
```

```
(sp robox*propose*operator*close*b
    (goal <g> ^difference <u>)
    (goal <g> ^problem-space <p> ^state <s>)
    (difference <u> ^isa open->closed-difference ^involves <door>)
    (problem-space <p> ^name robox)
    (state <s> ^holds <h1> <h2>)
    (holds <h1> ^door <door> ^status open)
    (holds <h2> ^robot <rob> ^at <loc-r>)
    (location <loc-r> ^in <room-r>)
    (door <door> ^connects <c>)
    (connects <c> ^location <loc1> ^to <loc2>)
    (location <loc1> ^in <room>)
    (room <room> ^after <room-r>)
    -->
    (goal <g> ^operator <o>)
    (operator <o> ^name close ^done? no
        ^directed-at <door> ^from <loc2>))
```

Robox Problem Space: Operator Implementation Rules

```
(sp implement*pushthru
    (goal <g> ^operator <o>)
    (goal <g> ^problem-space <p> ^state <s>)
    (operator <o> ^name pushthru ^done? no ^door <door>
        ^directed-at <b> ^from <floc> ^to <tloc>)
    (problem-space <p> ^name robox)
    (state <s> ^holds <h1> <h2> <h3>)
    (holds <h1> ^robot <rob> ^at <floc>)
    (holds <h2> ^box <b> ^at <floc>)
    (holds <h3> ^door <door> ^status open)
    (location <floc> ^nextto <door> ^in <r1>)
    (location <tloc> ^nextto <door> ^in <r2>)
    -->
    (holds <h1> ^at <tloc> + <floc> - )
    (holds <h2> ^at <tloc> + <floc> - )
    (operator <o> ^done? yes + no - ))
```

```
(sp implement*push
    (goal <g> ^operator <o>)
    (goal <g> ^problem-space <p> ^state <s>)
    (operator <o> ^name push ^done? no
        ^directed-at <b> ^from <floc> ^to <tloc>)
    (problem-space <p> ^name robox)
    (state <s> ^holds <h1> <h2>)
    (holds <h1> ^robot <rob> ^at <floc>)
    (holds <h2> ^box <b> ^at <floc>)
    (location <floc> ^in <r>)
    (location <tloc> ^in <r>)
    -->
    (holds <h1> ^at <tloc> + <floc> - )
    (holds <h2> ^at <tloc> + <floc> - )
    (operator <o> ^done? yes + no - ))

(sp implement*gothru
    (goal <g> ^operator <o>)
    (goal <g> ^problem-space <p> ^state <s>)
    (operator <o> ^name gothru ^done? no ^door <door>
        ^directed-at self ^from <floc> ^to <tloc>)
    (problem-space <p> ^name robox)
    (state <s> ^holds <h1> <h2>)
    (holds <h1> ^robot <rob> ^at <floc>)
    (holds <h2> ^door <door> ^status open)
    (location <floc> ^nextto <door> ^in <r1>)
    (location <tloc> ^nextto <door> ^in <r2>)
    -->
    (holds <h1> ^at <tloc> + <floc> - )
    (operator <o> ^done? yes + no - ))

(sp implement*go
    (goal <g> ^operator <o>)
    (goal <g> ^problem-space <p> ^state <s>)
    (operator <o> ^name go ^done? no
        ^directed-at self ^from <floc> ^to <tloc>)
    (problem-space <p> ^name robox)
    (state <s> ^holds <h>)
    (holds <h> ^robot <rob> ^at <floc>)
    (location <floc> ^in <r>)
    (location <tloc> ^in <r>)
    -->
    (holds <h> ^at <tloc> + <floc> - )
    (operator <o> ^done? yes + no - ))
```

```
(sp implement*open
    (goal <g> ^operator <o>)
    (goal <g> ^problem-space <p> ^state <s>)
    (operator <o> ^name open ^done? no
        ^directed-at <door> ^from <loc>)
    (problem-space <p> ^name robox)
    (state <s> ^holds <h1> <h2>)
    (holds <h1> ^robot <rob> ^at <loc>)
    (holds <h2> ^door <door> ^status closed)
    (location <loc> ^nextto <door>)
    -->
    (holds <h2> ^status open closed - )
    (operator <o> ^done? yes + no - ))

(sp implement*close
    (goal <g> ^operator <o>)
    (goal <g> ^problem-space <p> ^state <s>)
    (operator <o> ^name close ^done? no
        ^directed-at <door> ^from <loc>)
    (problem-space <p> ^name robox)
    (state <s> ^holds <h1> <h2>)
    (holds <h1> ^robot <rob> ^at <loc>)
    (holds <h2> ^door <door> ^status open)
    (location <loc> ^nextto <door>)
    -->
    (holds <h2> ^status closed open - )
    (operator <o> ^done? yes + no - ))
```

Robox Problem Space: Operator Termination Rules

```
(sp terminate*pushthru
    (goal <g> ^operator <o>)
    (operator <o> ^name pushthru ^done? yes)
    (goal <g> ^problem-space <p> ^state <s>)
    (problem-space <p> ^name robox)
    -->
    (goal <g> ^operator <o> @ ))

(sp terminate*push
    (goal <g> ^operator <o>)
    (operator <o> ^name push ^done? yes)
    (goal <g> ^problem-space <p> ^state <s>)
    (problem-space <p> ^name robox)
    -->
    (goal <g> ^operator <o> @ ))
```

```
(sp terminate*gothru
    (goal <g> ^operator <o>)
    (operator <o> ^name gothru ^done? yes)
    (goal <g> ^problem-space <p> ^state <s>)
    (problem-space <p> ^name robox)
    -->
    (goal <g> ^operator <o> @ ))

(sp terminate*go
    (goal <g> ^operator <o>)
    (operator <o> ^name go ^done? yes)
    (goal <g> ^problem-space <p> ^state <s>)
    (problem-space <p> ^name robox)
    -->
    (goal <g> ^operator <o> @ ))

(sp terminate*open
    (goal <g> ^operator <o>)
    (operator <o> ^name open ^done? yes)
    (goal <g> ^problem-space <p> ^state <s>)
    (problem-space <p> ^name robox)
    -->
    (goal <g> ^operator <o> @ ))

(sp terminate*close
    (goal <g> ^operator <o>)
    (operator <o> ^name close ^done? yes)
    (goal <g> ^problem-space <p> ^state <s>)
    (problem-space <p> ^name robox)
    -->
    (goal <g> ^operator <o> @ ))
```

Robox Problem Space: Operator Subgoaling Rules

```
(sp default*generic*opsub*elaborate*goal*desired
    (goal <g> ^problem-space <p> ^name operator-subgoal ^object <g2>)
    (goal <g2> ^operator <o>)
    -->
    (goal <g> ^achieve <o>))

(sp default*generic*select*operator*reject-desired
    (goal <g> ^name operator-subgoal ^problem-space <p> ^state <s>
        ^achieve <o>)
    -->
    (goal <g> ^operator <o> - ))
```

```
(sp default*generic*opsub*detect*state*success
    (goal <g-eval> ^problem-space <p> ^state <s> ^achieve <o>
        ^applied <o>)
    -->
    (state <s> ^success <o>))

(sp robox*subgoal-on*operator*pushthru
    (goal <g> ^achieve <o>)
    (goal <g> ^problem-space <p> ^state <s>)
    (operator <o> ^name pushthru ^done? no ^directed-at <b>
        ^door <door> ^from <floc> ^to <tloc>)
    (problem-space <p> ^name robox)
    (state <s> ^holds <h1> <h2> <h3>)
    (holds <h1> ^robot <rob> ^at <loc-r>)
    (holds <h2> ^box <b> ^at <loc-b>)
    (holds <h3> ^door <door> ^status)
    (location <floc> ^in <froom>)
    (location <tloc> ^in <troom>)
    -->
    (goal <g> ^desired <d1> + &, <d2> + &, <d3> + & )
    (desired <d1> ^door <door> ^status open)
    (desired <d2> ^box <b> ^at <floc>)
    (desired <d3> ^robot <rob> ^at <floc>))

(sp robox*subgoal-on*operator*push
    (goal <g> ^achieve <o>)
    (goal <g> ^problem-space <p> ^state <s>)
    (operator <o> ^name push ^done? no ^directed-at <b>
        ^from <loc-b> ^to <loc>)
    (problem-space <p> ^name robox)
    (state <s> ^holds <h1> <h2>)
    (holds <h1> ^robot <rob> ^at <loc-r>)
    (holds <h2> ^box <b> ^at <loc-b>)
    (location <loc-b> ^in <room>)
    (location <loc> ^in <room>)
    -->
    (goal <g> ^desired <d> + & )
    (desired <d> ^robot <rob> ^at <loc-b>))
```

```
(sp robox*subgoal-on*operator*gothru
    (goal <g> ^achieve <o>)
    (goal <g> ^problem-space <p> ^state <s>)
    (operator <o> ^name gothru ^done? no ^directed-at self
        ^door <door> ^from <floc> ^to <tloc>)
    (problem-space <p> ^name robox)
    (state <s> ^holds <h1> <h2>)
    (holds <h1> ^robot <rob> ^at <loc-r>)
    (holds <h2> ^door <door> ^status)
    (location <floc> ^in <froom>)
    (location <tloc> ^in <troom>)
    -->
    (goal <g> ^desired <d1> + &, <d2> + & )
    (desired <d1> ^door <door> ^status open)
    (desired <d2> ^robot <rob> ^at <floc>))

(sp robox*subgoal-on*operator*open
    (goal <g> ^achieve <o>)
    (goal <g> ^problem-space <p> ^state <s>)
    (operator <o> ^name open ^done? no
        ^directed-at <door> ^from <loc>)
    (problem-space <p> ^name robox)
    (state <s> ^holds <h>)
    (holds <h> ^robot <rob> ^at <loc-r>)
    (location <loc> ^nextto <door> ^in <room>)
    -->
    (goal <g> ^desired <d> + & )
    (desired <d> ^robot <rob> ^at <loc>))

(sp robox*subgoal-on*operator*close
    (goal <g> ^achieve <o>)
    (goal <g> ^problem-space <p> ^state <s>)
    (operator <o> ^name close ^done? no
        ^directed-at <door> ^from <loc>)
    (problem-space <p> ^name robox)
    (state <s> ^holds <h>)
    (holds <h> ^robot <rob> ^at <loc-r>)
    (location <loc> ^nextto <door> ^in <room>)
    -->
    (goal <g> ^desired <d> + & )
    (desired <d> ^robot <rob> ^at <loc>))
```

Subgoal Difference Computation: Compute-Diffs Problem Space

```
(sp state-no-change*propose*problem-space*compute-diffs
    (goal <g1> ^object <g> ^impasse no-change
        ^attribute state ^choices none)
    (goal <g> ^problem-space <p>)
    (problem-space <p> ^name robox)
    -->
    (goal <g1> ^problem-space <p1>)
    (problem-space <p1> ^name compute-diffs))
```

Compute-Diffs Problem Space: Initial State

```
(sp compute-diffs*propose*initial-state
    (goal <g1> ^problem-space <p1> ^object <g>)
    (problem-space <p1> ^name compute-diffs)
    (goal <g> ^state <s>)
    -->
    (goal <g1> ^state <s1>)
    (state <s1> ^current-state <s>))
(sp compute-diffs*elaborate*goal*diffs
    (goal <g> ^problem-space <p> ^state <s>)
    (problem-space <p> ^name compute-diffs)
    -->
    (goal <g> ^name diffs))
```

Compute-Diffs Problem Space: Difference Computation Rules

```
(sp compute-diffs*elaborate*state*desired-state
    (goal <g1> ^problem-space <p1> ^state <s1> ^object <g>)
    (problem-space <p1> ^name compute-diffs)
    (state <s1> ^current-state <cs>)
    (goal <g> ^desired <d>)
    -->
    (state <s1> ^desired-state <d> + & ))

(sp compute-diffs*propose*operator*differentiate
    (goal <g> ^problem-space <p> ^state <s>)
    (problem-space <p> ^name compute-diffs)
    -->
    (goal <g> ^operator <q>)
    (operator <q> ^name differentiate))
```

```
(sp implement*differentiate*box-room-difference
    (goal <g> ^operator <q> ^object <sg>)
    (goal <g> ^problem-space <p> ^state <s>)
    (operator <q> ^name differentiate)
    (problem-space <p> ^name compute-diffs)
    (state <s> ^desired-state <ds> ^current-state <cs>)
    (desired <ds> ^box <b> ^at <loc>)
    (state <cs> ^holds <h>)
    (holds <h> ^box <b> ^at <loc-b>)
    (location <loc> ^in <room>)
    (location <loc-b> ^in { <> <room> <room-b> })
    -->
    (goal <sg> ^difference <u> + & )
    (difference <u> ^isa box-room-difference ^involves <b>
        ^current <room-b> ^want <room>))

(sp implement*differentiate*box-location-difference
    (goal <g> ^operator <q> ^object <sg>)
    (goal <g> ^problem-space <p> ^state <s>)
    (operator <q> ^name differentiate)
    (problem-space <p> ^name compute-diffs)
    (state <s> ^desired-state <ds> ^current-state <cs>)
    (desired <ds> ^box <b> ^at <loc>)
    (state <cs> ^holds <h>)
    (holds <h> ^box <b> ^at { <> <loc> <loc-b> })
    (location <loc> ^in <r>)
    (location <loc-b> ^in <r>)
    -->
    (goal <sg> ^difference <u> + & )
    (difference <u> ^isa box-location-difference ^involves <b>
        ^current <loc-b> ^want <loc>))

(sp implement*differentiate*robot-room-difference
    (goal <g> ^operator <q> ^object <sg>)
    (goal <g> ^problem-space <p> ^state <s>)
    (operator <q> ^name differentiate)
    (problem-space <p> ^name compute-diffs)
    (state <s> ^desired-state <ds> ^current-state <cs>)
    (desired <ds> ^robot <rob> ^at <loc>)
    (state <cs> ^holds <h>)
    (holds <h> ^robot <rob> ^at <loc-r>)
    (location <loc> ^in <room>)
    (location <loc-r> ^in { <> <room> <room-r> })
    -->
    (goal <sg> ^difference <u> + & )
    (difference <u> ^isa robot-room-difference ^involves self
        ^current <room-r> ^want <room>))
```

```
(sp implement*differentiate*robot-location-difference
    (goal <g> ^operator <q> ^object <sg>)
    (goal <g> ^problem-space <p> ^state <s>)
    (operator <q> ^name differentiate)
    (problem-space <p> ^name compute-diffs)
    (state <s> ^desired-state <ds> ^current-state <cs>)
    (desired <ds> ^robot <rob> ^at <loc>)
    (state <cs> ^holds <h>)
    (holds <h> ^robot <rob> ^at { <> <loc> <loc-r> })
    (location <loc> ^in <r>)
    (location <loc-r> ^in <r>)
    -->
    (goal <sg> ^difference <u> + & )
    (difference <u> ^isa robot-location-difference ^involves self
        ^current <loc-r> ^want <loc>))

(sp implement*differentiate*closed->open-difference
    (goal <g> ^operator <q> ^object <sg>)
    (goal <g> ^problem-space <p> ^state <s>)
    (operator <q> ^name differentiate)
    (problem-space <p> ^name compute-diffs)
    (state <s> ^desired-state <ds> ^current-state <cs>)
    (desired <ds> ^door <door> ^status open)
    (state <cs> ^holds <h>)
    (holds <h> ^door <door> ^status closed)
    -->
    (goal <sg> ^difference <u> + & )
    (difference <u> ^isa closed->open-difference ^involves <door>))

(sp implement*differentiate*open->closed-difference
    (goal <g> ^operator <q> ^object <sg>)
    (goal <g> ^problem-space <p> ^state <s>)
    (operator <q> ^name differentiate)
    (problem-space <p> ^name compute-diffs)
    (state <s> ^desired-state <ds> ^current-state <cs>)
    (desired <ds> ^door <door> ^status closed)
    (state <cs> ^holds <h>)
    (holds <h> ^door <door> ^status open)
    -->
    (goal <sg> ^difference <u> + & )
    (difference <u> ^isa open->closed-difference ^involves <door>))
```

Subgoal Operator Valuation: Valuation Problem Space

```
(sp operator-tie*propose*problem-space*valuation
    (goal <g1> ^object <g> ^impasse tie
        ^attribute operator ^choices multiple)
    (goal <g> ^problem-space <p>)
    (problem-space <p> ^name robox)
    -->
    (goal <g1> ^problem-space <p1>)
    (problem-space <p1> ^name valuation))
```

Valuation Problem Space: Initial State

```
(sp valuation*propose*initial-state
    (goal <g1> ^problem-space <p1> ^object <g>)
    (problem-space <p1> ^name valuation)
    (goal <g> ^state <s>)
    -->
    (goal <g1> ^state <s1>)
    (state <s1> ^current-state <s>))

(sp valuation*elaborate*goal*opval
    (goal <g> ^problem-space <p> ^state <s>)
    (problem-space <p> ^name valuation)
    -->
    (goal <g> ^name opval))
```

Valuation Problem Space: Operator Valuation Rules

```
(sp valuation*propose*operator*valuate
    (goal <g> ^problem-space <p> ^state <s>)
    (problem-space <p> ^name valuation)
    -->
    (goal <g> ^operator <q>)
    (operator <q> ^name valuate))

(sp implement*valuate*door-ops*indifferent-and-worst
    "make indifferent and worst an operator that is door-directed"
    (goal <g> ^operator <q> ^object <sg>)
    (goal <g> ^problem-space <p> ^state <s> ^item <o>)
    (operator <q> ^name valuate)
    (problem-space <p> ^name valuation)
    (state <s> ^current-state <cs>)
    (state <cs> ^door <door>)
    (operator <o> ^directed-at <door>)
    -->
    (goal <sg> ^operator <o> =, <o> < ))
```

```
(sp implement*valuate*object-ops*indifferent
    "make indifferent an operator that is object-directed"
    (goal <g> ^operator <q> ^object <sg>)
    (goal <g> ^problem-space <p> ^state <s> ^item <o>)
    (operator <q> ^name valuate)
    (problem-space <p> ^name valuation)
    (state <s> ^current-state <cs>)
    (state <cs> ^<x> <z>)
    (<x> <z> ^type object)
    (operator <o> ^directed-at <z>)
     -->
    (goal <sg> ^operator <o> = ))

(sp implement*valuate*operator*push-ops*go-ops
    "box-* diff is more important than robot-* diff"
    (goal <g> ^operator <q> ^object <sg>)
    (goal <g> ^problem-space <p> ^item <o1> { <> <o1> <o2> })
    (operator <q> ^name valuate)
    (problem-space <p> ^name valuation)
    (operator <o1> ^name <n1> ^for <u>)
    (operator <o2> ^name <n2> ^for <v>)
    (difference <u> ^isa << box-room-difference
                            box-location-difference >> )
    (difference <v> ^isa << robot-location-difference
                            robot-room-difference >> )
    -->
    (goal <sg> ^operator <o1> > <o2> ))

(sp implement*valuate*least-effort*better*a
    "rule that observes least-effort principle"
    (goal <g> ^operator <q> ^object <sg>)
    (goal <g> ^problem-space <p> ^state <s> ^item <o>)
    (operator <q> ^name valuate)
    (problem-space <p> ^name valuation)
    (state <s> ^current-state <cs>)
    (state <cs> ^holds <h1> <h2>)
    (holds <h1> ^robot <rob> ^at <loc-r>)
    (holds <h2> ^{ <> robot <x> } <z> ^at <loc-z>)
    (operator <o> ^directed-at <z>)
    (location <loc-r> ^in <room-r>)
    (location <loc-z> ^in <room-r>)
    -->
    (goal <sg> ^operator <o> > ))
```

```
(sp implement*valuate*least-effort*better*b
    "rule that observes least-effort principle"
    (goal <g> ^operator <q> ^object <sg>)
    (goal <g> ^problem-space <p> ^state <s> ^item <o>)
    (operator <q> ^name valuate)
    (problem-space <p> ^name valuation)
    (state <s> ^current-state <cs>)
    (state <cs> ^holds <h1> <h2>)
    (holds <h1> ^robot <rob> ^at <loc-r>)
    (holds <h2> ^{ <> robot <x> } <z> ^<w> <loc-z>)
    (operator <o> ^directed-at <z> ^to <tloc>)
    (location <loc-r> ^in <room-r>)
    (location <loc-z> ^in <room-r>)
    (location <tloc> ^in <room-r>)
    -->
    (goal <sg> ^operator <o> > ))
```

Goal Test

```
(sp robox*mark*desired-of-robot*satisfied
    (goal <g> ^object nil ^desired <d>)
    (goal <g> ^problem-space <p> ^state <s>)
    (desired <d> ^robot <rob> ^at <loc-r>)
    (state <s> ^holds <h>)
    (holds <h> ^robot <rob> ^at <loc-r>)
    -->
    (desired <d> ^is satisfied))

(sp robox*mark*state*desired-of-box*satisfied
    (goal <g> ^object nil ^desired <d>)
    (goal <g> ^problem-space <p> ^state <s>)
    (desired <d> ^box <b> ^at <loc-b>)
    (state <s> ^holds <h>)
    (holds <h> ^box <b> ^at <loc-b>)
    -->
    (desired <d> ^is satisfied))

(sp robox*mark*state*desired-of-door*satisfied
    (goal <g> ^object nil ^desired <d>)
    (goal <g> ^problem-space <p> ^state <s>)
    (desired <d> ^door <door> ^status <status>)
    (state <s> ^holds <h>)
    (holds <h> ^door <door> ^status <status>)
    -->
    (desired <d> ^is satisfied))
```

```
(sp top-goal*mark*state*pursue
    (goal <g> ^object nil ^problem-space <p> ^state <s> ^desired <d>)
    (desired <d> -^is satisfied)
    -->
    (state <s> ^pursue <d> + & ))

(sp impasse*propose*operator*goal-test
    (goal <g1> ^problem-space <p1> ^state <s1> ^object <g>)
    (problem-space <p1> ^name <p1-name>)
    (goal <g> ^object nil ^problem-space <p> ^state <s>)
    (problem-space <p> ^name <p-name>)
    (state <s> -^pursue -^success)
    -->
    (goal <g> ^operator <q> =, <q> + )
    (operator <q> ^name goal-test))

(sp top-goal*add*desired-to-mark*goal-test
    (goal <g> ^operator <q>)
    (goal <g> ^object nil ^problem-space <p> ^state <s> ^desired <d>)
    (operator <q> ^name goal-test -^desired-to-mark <d>)
    (state <s> -^pursue -^success <d>)
    (desired <d> ^is satisfied)
    -->
    (operator <q> ^desired-to-mark <d> + & ))

(sp implement*goal-test
    (goal <g> ^operator <q>)
    (goal <g> ^problem-space <p> ^state <s>)
    (operator <q> ^name goal-test ^desired-to-mark <d>)
    (state <s> -^pursue -^success <d>)
    (desired <d> ^is satisfied)
    -->
    (state <s> ^success <d> + & ))

(sp terminate*goal-test
    (goal <g> ^operator <q>)
    (goal <g> ^object nil ^problem-space <p> ^state <s> ^desired <d>)
    (operator <q> ^name goal-test ^desired-to-mark <d>)
    (problem-space <p> ^name <name>)
    (state <s> -^pursue ^success <d>)
    (desired <d> ^is satisfied)
    -->
    (goal <g> ^operator <q> @ ))
```

State Monitor

```
(sp robox*monitor*predicate*desired*a
    (goal <g> ^problem-space <p> ^state <s> ^object nil ^desired <d>)
    (problem-space <p> ^name robox)
    (desired <d> ^<ob> <obval> ^{ <> <ob> <rel> } <relval>)
    (<ob> <obval> ^name <n1>)
    (<class> <relval> ^name <n2>)
    -->
    (tabstop <tab>)
    (write2 (crlf) (tabto <tab>) "  DESIRED " <d> " ^" <ob>
        " " <n1> " ^" <rel> " " <n2>))

(sp robox*monitor*predicate*desired*b
    (goal <g> ^problem-space <p> ^state <s> ^object nil ^desired <d>)
    (problem-space <p> ^name robox)
    (desired <d> ^<ob> <obval> ^status <status>)
    (<ob> <obval> ^name <n>)
    -->
    (tabstop <tab>)
    (write2 (crlf) (tabto <tab>) "  DESIRED " <d> " ^" <ob>
        " " <n> " ^STATUS " <status>))

(sp robox*monitor*predicate*holds*a
    (goal <g> ^problem-space <p> ^state <s> ^object nil)
    (problem-space <p> ^name robox)
    (state <s> ^<ob> <obval> ^holds <h>)
    (holds <h> ^<ob> <obval> ^{ <> <ob> <rel> } <relval>)
    (<ob> <obval> ^name <n1>)
    (<class> <relval> ^name <n2>)
    -->
    (tabstop <tab>)
    (write2 (crlf) (tabto <tab>) "  HOLDS " <h> " ^" <ob>
        " " <n1> " ^" <rel> " " <n2>))

(sp robox*monitor*predicate*holds*b
    (goal <g> ^problem-space <p> ^state <s> ^object nil)
    (problem-space <p> ^name robox)
    (state <s> ^<ob> <obval> ^holds <h>)
    (holds <h> ^<ob> <obval> ^status <status>)
    (<ob> <obval> ^name <n>)
    -->
    (tabstop <tab>)
    (write2 (crlf) (tabto <tab>) "  HOLDS " <h> " ^" <ob>
        " " <n> " ^STATUS " <status>))
```

APPENDIX B: A SAMPLE TRACE

The trace below is a fragment of the behavior of Robox-Soar on an example task, without chunking being activated.

```
;Loading "Robox-Soar"...

? (d)

0    G: G1
1    P: P2 (ROBOX)
2    S: S3 (((DOOR-3) CLOSED) ((DOOR-2) OPEN) ((DOOR-1) CLOSED)
           ((BOX-2) (LOC-15)) ((BOX-1) (LOC-9)) ((FRED) (LOC-8)))
     DESIRED D43 ^BOX BOX-2 ^AT LOC-1
     DESIRED D42 ^BOX BOX-1 ^AT LOC-18
     DESIRED D41 ^ROBOT FRED ^AT LOC-12
```

Each DESIRED points to a goal condition.

```
     HOLDS H32 ^ROBOT FRED ^AT LOC-8
     HOLDS H34 ^BOX BOX-2 ^AT LOC-15
     HOLDS H33 ^BOX BOX-1 ^AT LOC-9
     HOLDS H37 ^DOOR DOOR-3 ^STATUS CLOSED
     HOLDS H36 ^DOOR DOOR-2 ^STATUS OPEN
     HOLDS H35 ^DOOR DOOR-1 ^STATUS CLOSED
```

Each HOLDS points to a dynamic fact in the current state.

```
3    ==>G: G45 (STATE NO-CHANGE)
4       P: P46 (COMPUTE-DIFFS)
5       S: S47
6       O: Q48 (DIFFERENTIATE)
7    ==>G: G58 (OPERATOR TIE)
8       P: P60 (VALUATION)
9       S: S61
10      O: Q62 (VALUATE)
11   O: O56 ((BOX-1) (LOC-5) (LOC-6) (DOOR-3) PUSHTHRU)
```

A PushThru is selected to get BOX-1 in ROOM-4.

```
12   ==>G: G68 (OPERATOR NO-CHANGE)
13      P: P2 (ROBOX)
14      S: S3 (((DOOR-3) CLOSED) ((DOOR-2) OPEN) ((DOOR-1) CLOSED)
              ((BOX-2) (LOC-15)) ((BOX-1) (LOC-9)) ((FRED) (LOC-8)))
```

Robox-Soar subgoals on PushThru (o56).

```
15      ==>G: G72 (STATE NO-CHANGE)
16         P: P73 (COMPUTE-DIFFS)
17         S: S74
18         O: Q75 (DIFFERENTIATE)
19      ==>G: G85 (OPERATOR TIE)
20         P: P87 (VALUATION)
21         S: S88
```

```
22        O: Q89 (VALUATE)
23      O: O82 ((BOX-1) (LOC-3) (LOC-4) (DOOR-2) PUSHTHRU)
```

A PushThru is selected to get BOX-1 in ROOM-3

```
24      ==>G: G94 (OPERATOR NO-CHANGE)
25        P: P2 (ROBOX)
26        S: S3 (((DOOR-3) CLOSED) ((DOOR-2) OPEN) ((DOOR-1) CLOSED)
               ((BOX-2) (LOC-15)) ((BOX-1) (LOC-9))
               ((FRED) (LOC-8)))
```

Robox-Soar subgoals on PushThru (o82).

```
27        ==>G: G98 (STATE NO-CHANGE)
28          P: P99 (COMPUTE-DIFFS)
29          S: S100
30          O: Q101 (DIFFERENTIATE)
31        ==>G: G108 (OPERATOR TIE)
32          P: P110 (VALUATION)
33          S: S111
34          O: Q112 (VALUATE)
35        O: O106 ((BOX-1) (LOC-1) (LOC-2) (DOOR-1) PUSHTHRU)
```

A PushThru is selected to get BOX-1 in ROOM-2

```
36        ==>G: G116 (OPERATOR NO-CHANGE)
37          P: P2 (ROBOX)
38          S: S3 (((DOOR-3) CLOSED) ((DOOR-2) OPEN)
                 ((DOOR-1) CLOSED) ((BOX-2) (LOC-15))
                 ((BOX-1) (LOC-9)) ((FRED) (LOC-8)))
```

Robox-Soar subgoals on PushThru (o106).

```
39          ==>G: G120 (STATE NO-CHANGE)
40            P: P121 (COMPUTE-DIFFS)
41            S: S122
42            O: Q123 (DIFFERENTIATE)
43          ==>G: G133 (OPERATOR TIE)
44            P: P135 (VALUATION)
45            S: S136
46            O: Q137 (VALUATE)
47          O: O130 ((BOX-1) (LOC-9) (LOC-1) PUSH)
```

A Push is selected to get BOX-1 in front of DOOR-1.

```
48          ==>G: G143 (OPERATOR NO-CHANGE)
49            P: P2 (ROBOX)
50            S: S3 (((DOOR-3) CLOSED) ((DOOR-2) OPEN)
                   ((DOOR-1) CLOSED) ((BOX-2) (LOC-15))
                   ((BOX-1) (LOC-9)) ((FRED) (LOC-8)))
```

Robox-Soar subgoals on Push (o130).

```
51            ==>G: G145 (STATE NO-CHANGE)
52              P: P146 (COMPUTE-DIFFS)
53              S: S147
54              O: Q148 (DIFFERENTIATE)
55            O: O151 (SELF (LOC-8) (LOC-9) GO)
```

```
                HOLDS H32 ^ROBOT FRED ^AT LOC-9
```

A Go is selected to get FRED next to BOX-1 and applied.

```
                HOLDS H32 ^ROBOT FRED ^AT LOC-1
                HOLDS H33 ^BOX BOX-1 ^AT LOC-1
```

Push (o130) is applied.

```
56            ==>G: G179 (STATE NO-CHANGE)
57                P: P180 (COMPUTE-DIFFS)
58                S: S181
59                O: Q182 (DIFFERENTIATE)
60            O: O184 ((DOOR-1) (LOC-1) OPEN)
              HOLDS H35 ^DOOR DOOR-1 ^STATUS OPEN
```

An Open is selected to open DOOR-1 and applied.

```
              HOLDS H32 ^ROBOT FRED ^AT LOC-2
              HOLDS H33 ^BOX BOX-1 ^AT LOC-2
```

PushThru (o106) is applied.

APPENDIX C: LEARNING IN ROBOX-SOAR

Macrochunks have been discussed in the main body of the paper (see section on *Operator Subgoaling*).

Difference Computation Chunks

```
(SP P50
   (GOAL <G1> ^STATE <S1> ^PROBLEM-SPACE <P1> ^DESIRED <D1>)
   (PROBLEM-SPACE <P1> ^NAME ROBOX)
   (DESIRED <D1> ^ROBOT <F1> ^AT <L2>)
   (STATE <S1> ^HOLDS <H1>)
   (HOLDS <H1> ^ROBOT <F1> ^AT <L1>)
   (LOCATION <L1> ^IN <R1>)
   (LOCATION <L2> ^IN { <> <R1> <R2> })
   -->
   (GOAL <G1> ^DIFFERENCE <U1> + <U1> & )
   (DIFFERENCE <U1> ^WANT <R2> + <R2> + ^CURRENT <R1> + <R1> +
       ^INVOLVES SELF + SELF +
       ^ISA ROBOT-ROOM-DIFFERENCE + ROBOT-ROOM-DIFFERENCE + ))
```

```
(SP P52
    (GOAL <G1> ^STATE <S1> ^PROBLEM-SPACE <P1> ^DESIRED <D1>)
    (PROBLEM-SPACE <P1> ^NAME ROBOX)
    (DESIRED <D1> ^BOX <B1> ^AT <L2>)
    (STATE <S1> ^HOLDS <H1>)
    (HOLDS <H1> ^BOX <B1> ^AT <L1>)
    (LOCATION <L1> ^IN <R1>)
    (LOCATION <L2> ^IN { <> <R1> <R2> })
    -->
    (GOAL <G1> ^DIFFERENCE <U1> + <U1> & )
    (DIFFERENCE <U1> ^WANT <R2> + <R2> + ^CURRENT <R1> + <R1> +
        ^INVOLVES <B1> + <B1> +
        ^ISA BOX-ROOM-DIFFERENCE + BOX-ROOM-DIFFERENCE + ))
```

Search-Control (Valuation) Chunks

```
(SP P64
    (GOAL <G1> ^OPERATOR <O1> + { <> <O1> <O2> } + ^STATE <S1>
        ^PROBLEM-SPACE <P1>)
    (OPERATOR <O1> ^NAME GOTHRU ^FOR <U1>)
    (OPERATOR <O2> ^NAME PUSHTHRU ^FOR <U2>)
    (PROBLEM-SPACE <P1> ^NAME ROBOX)
    (DIFFERENCE <U2> ^ISA BOX-ROOM-DIFFERENCE)
    (DIFFERENCE <U1> ^ISA ROBOT-ROOM-DIFFERENCE)
    -->
    (GOAL <G1> ^OPERATOR <O2> > <O1>))

(SP P65
    (GOAL <G1> ^STATE <S1> ^OPERATOR <O1> + ^PROBLEM-SPACE <P1>)
    (PROBLEM-SPACE <P1> ^NAME ROBOX)
    (OPERATOR <O1> ^DIRECTED-AT <B1>)
    (STATE <S1> ^HOLDS <H2> <H1>)
    (HOLDS <H2> ^BOX <B1> ^AT <L2>)
    (LOCATION <L2> ^IN <R1>)
    (HOLDS <H1> ^AT <L1> ^ROBOT <F1>)
    (LOCATION <L1> ^IN <R1>)
    -->
    (GOAL <G1> ^OPERATOR <O1> > ))
```

Macrochunks

```
(SP P107
    (GOAL <G1> ^STATE <S1> ^PROBLEM-SPACE <P1> ^OPERATOR <O1>)
    (PROBLEM-SPACE <P1> ^NAME ROBOX)
    (OPERATOR <O1> ^NAME PUSH ^DONE? NO ^DIRECTED-AT <B1> ^FROM <L3>
        ^TO <L1>)
    (LOCATION <L3> ^IN <R1>)
    (LOCATION <L1> ^IN <R1>)
    (STATE <S1> ^HOLDS <H1> <H2>)
    (HOLDS <H1> ^BOX <B1> ^AT <L3>)
    (HOLDS <H2> ^AT { <> <L3> <L2> } ^ROBOT <F1>)
    (LOCATION <L2> ^IN <R1>)
    -->
    (HOLDS <H2> ^AT <L2> - <L3> + ))

(SP P108
    (GOAL <G1> ^PROBLEM-SPACE <P1> ^STATE <S1> ^OPERATOR <O1>)
    (PROBLEM-SPACE <P1> ^NAME ROBOX)
    (OPERATOR <O1> ^NAME PUSHTHRU ^DONE? NO ^DIRECTED-AT <B1>
        ^DOOR <K1> ^FROM <L2> ^TO <L1>)
    (LOCATION <L2> ^IN <R2>)
    (STATE <S1> ^HOLDS <H1> <H2> <H3>)
    (HOLDS <H1> ^STATUS CLOSED ^DOOR <K1>)
    (HOLDS <H2> ^BOX <B1> ^AT { <> <L2> <L4> })
    (LOCATION <L4> ^IN <R2>)
    (HOLDS <H3> ^AT { <> <L4> <L3> } ^ROBOT <F1>)
    (LOCATION <L3> ^IN <R2>)
    (LOCATION <L1> ^IN <R1>)
    -->
    (HOLDS <H3> ^AT <L3> - <L4> + ))
```

```
(SP P109
    (GOAL <G1> ^STATE <S1> ^PROBLEM-SPACE <P1> ^OPERATOR <O1>)
    (PROBLEM-SPACE <P1> ^NAME ROBOX)
    (OPERATOR <O1> ^NAME PUSHTHRU ^DONE? NO ^DIRECTED-AT <B1>
        ^DOOR <K1> ^FROM <L2> ^TO <L1>)
    (LOCATION <L2> ^IN <R2>)
    (STATE <S1> ^HOLDS <H2> <H1> <H3> <H4>)
    (HOLDS <H2> ^STATUS CLOSED ^DOOR <K2>)
    (DOOR <K2> ^CONNECTS <C1>)
    (CONNECTS <C1> ^TO <L3> ^LOCATION <L4>)
    (LOCATION <L3> ^IN <R2>)
    (LOCATION <L4> ^IN { <> <R2> <R3> })
    (ROOM <R3> ^AFTER <R2>)
    (HOLDS <H1> ^STATUS OPEN ^DOOR <K1>)
    (HOLDS <H3> ^BOX <B1> ^AT { <> <L4> <L6> })
    (LOCATION <L6> ^IN <R3>)
    (HOLDS <H4> ^AT { <> <L6> <L5> } ^ROBOT <F1>)
    (LOCATION <L5> ^IN <R3>)
    (LOCATION <L1> ^IN <R1>)
    -->
    (HOLDS <H4> ^AT <L5> - <L6> + ))

(SP P209
    (GOAL <G1> ^STATE <S1> ^PROBLEM-SPACE <P1> ^OPERATOR <O1>)
    (PROBLEM-SPACE <P1> ^NAME ROBOX)
    (OPERATOR <O1> ^NAME PUSHTHRU ^DONE? NO ^DIRECTED-AT <B1>
        ^DOOR <K1> ^FROM <L3> ^TO <L1>)
    (LOCATION <L3> ^IN <R2>)
    (STATE <S1> ^HOLDS <H1> <H3> <H2>)
    (HOLDS <H1> ^STATUS OPEN ^DOOR <K1>)
    (HOLDS <H3> ^BOX <B1> ^AT { <> <L3> <L2> })
    (LOCATION <L2> ^IN <R2>)
    (HOLDS <H2> ^AT <L2> ^ROBOT <F1>)
    (LOCATION <L1> ^IN <R1>)
    -->
    (HOLDS <H2> ^AT <L3> + <L2> - )
    (HOLDS <H3> ^AT <L2> - <L3> + ))
```

```
(SP P304
    (GOAL <G1> ^PROBLEM-SPACE <P1> ^STATE <S1> ^OPERATOR <O1>)
    (PROBLEM-SPACE <P1> ^NAME ROBOX)
    (OPERATOR <O1> ^NAME PUSH ^DONE? NO ^DIRECTED-AT <B1> ^FROM <L2>
        ^TO <L1>)
    (LOCATION <L2> ^IN <R1>)
    (LOCATION <L1> ^IN <R1>)
    (STATE <S1> ^HOLDS <H2> <H1> <H3>)
    (HOLDS <H2> ^STATUS OPEN ^DOOR <K1>)
    (DOOR <K1> ^CONNECTS <C1>)
    (CONNECTS <C1> ^LOCATION <L3> ^TO <L5>)
    (LOCATION <L3> ^IN <R1>)
    (LOCATION <L5> ^IN { <> <R1> <R2> })
    (ROOM <R1> ^AFTER <R2>)
    (HOLDS <H1> ^BOX <B1> ^AT <L2>)
    (HOLDS <H3> ^AT { <> <L5> <L4> } ^ROBOT <F1>)
    (LOCATION <L4> ^IN <R2>)
    -->
    (HOLDS <H3> ^AT <L4> - <L5> + ))

(SP P421
    (GOAL <G1> ^STATE <S1> ^PROBLEM-SPACE <P1> ^OPERATOR <O1>)
    (PROBLEM-SPACE <P1> ^NAME ROBOX)
    (OPERATOR <O1> ^NAME PUSHTHRU ^DONE? NO ^DIRECTED-AT <B1>
        ^DOOR <K1> ^FROM <L2> ^TO <L1>)
    (LOCATION <L2> ^IN <R2>)
    (STATE <S1> ^HOLDS <H4> <H1> <H2> <H3>)
    (HOLDS <H4> ^STATUS OPEN ^DOOR <K2>)
    (DOOR <K2> ^CONNECTS <C1>)
    (CONNECTS <C1> ^LOCATION <L3> ^TO <L4>)
    (LOCATION <L3> ^NEXTTO <K2> ^IN { <> <R2> <R3> })
    (LOCATION <L4> ^NEXTTO <K2> ^IN <R2>)
    (ROOM <R3> ^AFTER <R2>)
    (HOLDS <H1> ^STATUS OPEN ^DOOR <K1>)
    (HOLDS <H2> ^AT <L3> ^ROBOT <F1>)
    (HOLDS <H3> ^BOX <B1> ^AT <L3>)
    (LOCATION <L1> ^IN <R1>)
    -->
    (HOLDS <H2> ^AT <L4> + <L3> - )
    (HOLDS <H3> ^AT <L3> - <L4> + ))
```

MULTITASKING IN DRIVING

JANS AASMAN
Traffic Research Center, University of Groningen
Haren, The Netherlands

AND

JOHN A. MICHON
Department of Psychology and Traffic Research Center
University of Groningen, Groningen, The Netherlands

ABSTRACT. Driving an automobile is a highly complex task requiring concurrent execution of a number of subtasks. This paper reviews part of a cognitive model of driver behavior that focuses on the multitasking nature of the driving task. The approach adopted here is not to describe this model in detail, but to show the implications that the multitasking features of the model have for an implementation in Soar.

Introduction

Driving is a well practiced and comparatively well studied example of complex dynamic performance in which an operator is required to cope with several tasks at once. The set of driver subtasks appears to be structured as a functional hierarchy in which conventionally three performance levels are distinguished (Michon, 1976, 1985): long term, strategic tasks, involving route planning and navigation; tactical or maneuvering tasks which comprise the various real time interactions with objects in the traffic environment, including other road users; and finally, short term operational tasks which include the basic handling and control tasks that are required to operate the vehicle in a proper fashion. A second way of looking at the driving task takes the driver's cognitive functioning as its vantage point. Rasmussen (1985,

J. A. Michon and A. Akyürek (eds.), Soar: A Cognitive Architecture in Perspective, 169–198.

1987) and Reason (1987) in particular, have conveniently introduced the distinction between knowledge-based, rule-based, and skill-based performance to describe operator activities in complex tasks. Since these two perspectives are more or less orthogonal, one may classify various driver subtasks as in Table 1 (see Hale, Stoop, & Hommels, 1990, p. 1383).

Table 1. *Matrix of Tasks*

	Planning	Maneuvering	Control
Knowledge	navigating in unfamiliar town	controlling a skid on icy roads	learner on first lesson
Rule	choice between familiar routes	passing other cars	driving an unfamiliar car
Skill	commuter travel	negotiating familiar junctions	road following around corners

Task elements from different levels frequently need to be performed simultaneously. Drivers must be able to handle both speed and heading, while, at the same time they are trying to survey the trajectories of other cars and the intentions of their operators, and to plan their own route towards their destination. An experienced driver is capable of integrating these tasks seemingly without effort, whereas learner drivers may show high levels of stress in their effort to coordinate the various driver subtasks. Descriptions of the driver's capability of simultaneously performing multiple tasks often refer to the distinction between automatic and controlled, or to the distinction between conceptually driven (or top-down) processing and data-driven processing (Norman & Bobrow, 1975). The distinction between *automatic* and *controlled* behavior was first described systematically by Shiffrin and Schneider (1977). Automatic behavior is characterized by its parallel nature. Such behavior cannot be inhibited, it is fast, independent of workload, and people are unaware of any processing going on. For an expert the basic control tasks of operating the vehicle seem to fall under this type of behavior (see, for instance, the lower right cell in Table 1). In contrast, controlled behavior is characterized by its serial nature. People can inhibit this type of behavior, it is slow, workload-dependent and there is awareness of the processing. Navigational tasks and the tasks that comprise the real time interactions with objects in the traffic environment seem to fall for a considerable part under this regime (covering, in fact, the upper left cells in Table 1). Effortless simultaneous execution of multiple 'controlled behavior' tasks in driving requires a long learning period to allow some driving subtasks to become really automatic (vehicle control) and to achieve coordination between other driving subtasks that cannot be made automatic. De Velde Harsenhorst and Lourens (1987, 1988) have given, by means of error analysis, a detailed account of this learning process in a learner driver.

The second distinction is that between *top-down* controlled and *data-driven* behavior. In driving, there is ample evidence for top-down control—sometimes also referred to as conceptually driven or goal-oriented. Drivers do apply fixed plans and use simple, overlearned strategies in their driving. Aasman and Lourens (1991) describe such relatively fixed strategies (in terms of speed control, car control, and visual orientation) as a function of the type of intersection and the intended maneuver at the intersection. The data-driven nature of at least part of the driving task is evident too. Thus, for instance, an ongoing maneuver may be interrupted by critical events in the outside world (e.g., children dashing out in front of the car). In the second place, driver goals appear to be determined by local circumstances, also causing driving to be partly data-driven.

USING SOAR IN MODELING MULTITASKING DRIVER BEHAVIOR

The aim of this study is to review a number of aspects of a cognitive model of multitasking in driving. Multitasking should eventually be a crucial feature of a comprehensive model that is able to function as an autonomous agent in a complex dynamic environment. The model to be discussed in this paper takes into account the distinctions between automatic and controlled, as well as between top-down and data-driven task performance. Soar (Laird, Newell, & Rosenbloom, 1987) has been chosen as the medium for implementing the model as a computational system. One important reason for this choice is that the Soar architecture directly supports both the distinction between automatic and controlled processing, and that between goal-directed and data-driven behavior (Newell, 1990). This choice determines our definition of task and multiple task performance to a significant extent.

In Soar all activity is described as the application of operators to states, within a problem space. A goal, in this context, is some desired situation, states are data structures that define possible states of progress in the problem. Operators transform a state through some action. A problem space is a collection of states and operators for achieving the goal. Executing a task or, what amounts to the same, solving a problem is the process of moving from a given initial state in the problem space, through intermediate states generated by operators, and reaching a desired state representing the goal. Solving a problem or performing a task is essentially a sequential activity since at any one time only one operator can be active.

Pursuing multiple goals is obviously of the essence of any multitasking theory. Less clear, on closer inspection, appears to be the nature of the goals that an autonomous agent in a dynamic environment might pursue. The above description which closely follows the Soar manual (Laird, Congdon, Altmann, & Swedlow, 1990) is not sufficiently detailed to reflect the diversity of goals that autonomous systems may pursue. Covrigaru (1990), for instance, has identified several types of goals that characterize systems that can survive in a dynamic world and that, therefore, qualify as autonomous. Five distinguishing characteristics of goals appear to be important from our point of view.

The first is that between *achievable* and *homeostatic* goals. Achievable goals have a well defined set of initial and final states in a state space, and activity will stop once the goal has indeed been achieved. Such goals are common in AI systems. Planning a route before one actually goes behind the wheel is a task involving this type of goal. Homeostatic goals, in contrast, are pursued and 'achieved' continuously. Activity does not cease when the system is in one of its final states because the world will keep changing and sustained control activity is required to remain in the desired state or to reach it again. Lane keeping and speed control are examples of tasks aiming for homeostatic goals.

The second distinction is that between *exogenous* and *endogenous* goals. Exogenous goals are set by the external environment. As soon as a driver perceives she is approaching an intersection she will set up a goal to deal with that intersection; that at least, is what happens in our driver model. Endogenous goals, in contrast, are generated within the system. Searching for the presence of a parking place may be considered an endogenous goal.

A third distinction is that between *top-level* goals and *subgoals*. The existence of top goals and subgoals is obvious in a goal-directed architecture like Soar. The main activity in Soar's subgoals is directed at solving impasses occurring at the top level. In general this amounts either to directly selecting a particular operator from the available set at the top level, or solving the problem and learning how to apply operators at the top level.

The fourth distinction is that between *long term* and *short term* goals. The importance to our present concern is that the lifetime of goals should be an obvious determinant of the performance of an autonomous system.

The final distinction is directly relevant to our multitasking theory. It distinguishes between *multiple top-level* and *single top-level* goals. As stated at the outset, the need for multiple top goals is obvious in a task such as driving. The driver model discussed in this paper is capable of controlling course and speed, and navigating at the same time.[1]

The goals pursued by the driver model presented in this paper can be characterized in terms of these five polarities. Thus, for instance, some of the goals in the driving task may be considered homeostatic whilst others are achievable. Most of the goals pursued in driving are endogenous, although the environment can set goals too.

Multiple top-level goals have become a research issue in the Soar community quite recently (Covrigaru, 1990; Hucka, 1991). The present paper is the first report on a series of studies which essentially date back to the beginning of our involvement with Soar. It deals with one specific option of handling multiple goals at the top level. It uses the general idea of goals and tasks in Soar as the context of discourse in which to describe the multitasking features of complex task performance. In its bare essence this amounts to the following, quite simple and straightforward position. In Soar only one task can be active at any one time, that is, a single operator implementing a task or a step in a task. Given this constraint, multitasking must be defined as some form of *switching between subtasks.*

The driver model, to be discussed in detail in the next section, is capable of handling a set of active top goals or tasks within an environment that represents a simple four-way intersection. The tasks in the model are speed control, course control, and navigation. A goal for a particular task is achieved by applying a sequence of internal and external operators. An internal operator makes a change to an internal representation of the world, as does for instance, the look-ahead operator in navigation. In contrast an external operator, for instance a change of speed, will attempt a change in the real world. Only one operator may be selected and applied at any one time. Multitasking is achieved by a uniform mechanism that allows for task switching and task resumption. Task switching in this case refers to the switching of control between different subtasks and basically amounts to interleaving operators from different tasks.

INTERRUPTION AND TASKING AT THE TOP LEVEL A CONSTRAINT FROM SOAR AS UTC

The choice of Soar as the medium for modeling the multitasking aspects of the driving task was at least partly based on Newell's claim that Soar qualifies as a *unified theory of cognition* (UTC). This claim extends to the so-called implementation claim: Newell (1990) has argued that since productions are ultimately implemented at the neural level, estimates for the execution times of elaboration phases, decision phases, and applications of operators can be derived from what we know about the central nervous system. This leads directly to an explicit description of the classic recognize-decide-act cycle, the minimal scheme for immediate responses. Using this scheme in combination with the estimated execution times for elaboration cycles, decision cycles, and operators, one should be able to predict the execution times of simple tasks conceived as sequences of applied operators.

One important part of this claim, and in fact the part upon which this study rests, is that attention—in Soar the *attend* operator—and the setting of new tasks—the *tasking* operator—reside in the *base level problem space*, the highest goal context in the goal stack. This claim is the single most important constraint on our model. The attend operator functions as an interrupt, halting all ongoing activity and focusing the system on other tasks (Newell, 1990, p. 262). The essential consequence of the claim that interrupt operators are applied in the base level space is that the interrupt operator has the power to break the goal hierarchy and to terminate all ongoing activity.

The Model

In this section we will describe the multitasking driver model, the perception of the driver, and the simulated environment in which we test the model.

Starting with the latter, the model is tested in a small, simulated traffic environment. This allows us to provide our model with real time input that simulates some aspects of the dynamic traffic environment. The implementation of a small world and its usage as a testbed for intelligent architectures has been described by several authors (e.g., Aasman, 1988; Reece & Shafer, 1988; Wierda & Aasman, 1988). Basically a small world simulation comprises a number of intelligent agents (drivers, cyclists, and other road users) moving around in a network of streets and intersections. The term intelligent in this case refers to the fact that each agent has the ability to perceive the environment, including the other agents, and a set of decision rules to interpret these perceptions in order to produce an optimal speed and course decision. Two aspects characterize the present implementation. First, it is intelligent in a distinctly non-psychological sense: perception is perfect, in this case with a 360 degrees visual field, control of speed is immediate rather than by way of motor commands, and the agents have no limits on their working memory. Second, the implementation is interactive, agents basing their behavior, in real time, on their own goals, as well as on the goals and behavior of other agents. This property distinguishes the present implementation from the traffic flow models conventionally used in traffic engineering. The resulting interactive behavior of agents in this small world turns out to be amazingly 'natural,' that is, close to expectation if we assume the agents to behave rationally. Altogether, this need not come as a surprise if one considers that the important speed-control and risk parameter estimates that have been used to calibrate the model were derived from empirical observations. Note also that the driver model to be tested in this simulated environment is the only entity in the small world endowed thus far with a Soar intelligence; all other agents use the perfect non-psychological perception and decision mechanisms mentioned above.

PERCEPTION AND INTERNAL REPRESENTATION OF THE WORLD

The simulated driver, as one of the agents in the simulated traffic world, is able to perceive both the road environment and the other traffic agents. Perception in humans is presumably a massively parallel, continuous, and asynchronous process, and this is in a very primitive way reflected by the perception unit in the model. In terms of Soar a continuous stream of inputs enters the system and is added to the top state, the highest state in the goal stack. These inputs will be referred to as *perceptual objects.* The perception unit is currently realized as a Lisp program, simulating a transducer process that can translate properties of objects and relations between objects in the small world into Soar data structures. These Soar structures constitute the internal representation of the world (see Figure 1).

Perceptual objects are elaborated to the degree that Soar knows their type—*automobile, bicycle, pedestrian,* or *intersection.* Every object is assigned an identity (a unique name in Soar's internal model). A moving object is represented as a sequence of objects with the same identity. The principal properties of every moving object are its position, direction, speed, and the required time to reach the intersection. The main spatial and temporal relations between objects are the relative position of objects (where an object can be of any type) and collision course information. Time is represented as a list of so-called *event objects.* During the decision cycle such an event object is generated and linked to both the state and the previous event object. All perceptual objects that enter in the same decision phase are linked to appropriate perceptual object. This mechanism enables the model to distinguish between newly observed objects and less recently perceived objects.[2]

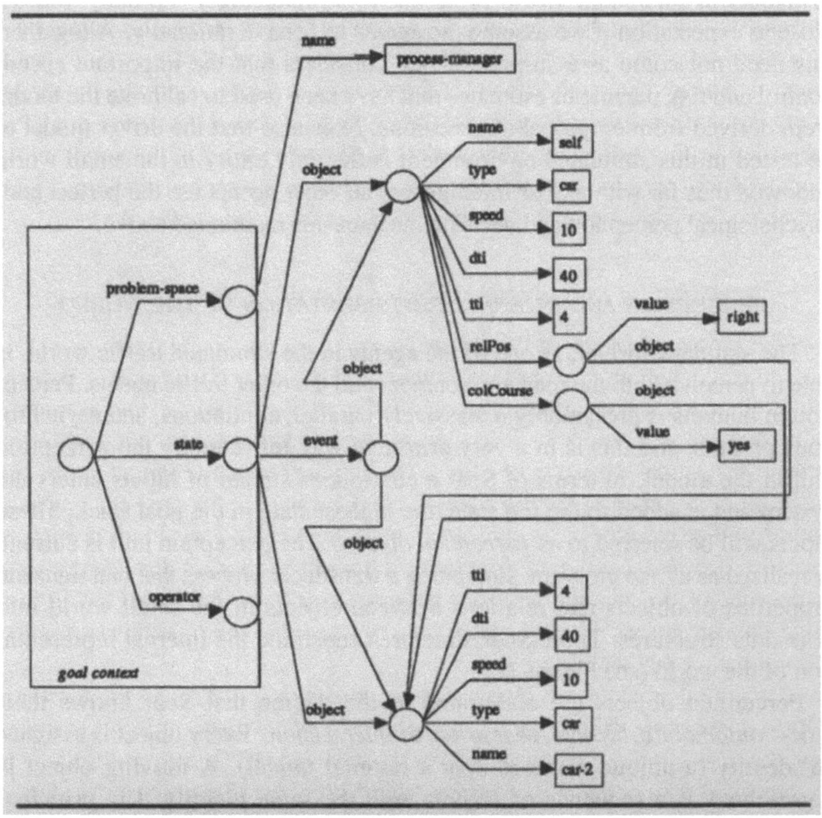

Figure 1. A graphical representation of the contents of Soar's working memory, showing two cars approaching an intersection. The upper object represents the modeled driver, here referred to as the 'self.' The lower object is the representation of the other car. Note how relations between objects require special relation objects: car-2 is coming from the right and is on a collision course from the point of view of the 'self.' Event objects represent time; dti is distance to intersection, and tti is time to intersection, that is, dti/speed. All objects seen in the most recent decision cycle are attached to the event generated in this decision cycle.

It may be argued that there is too much intelligence in the perceptual unit. In the first place, relating the various dynamic objects may require the help of higher processes in cognition. At least some of these relations will be inferred at a high level, the detection of a collision course being a likely candidate. In the second place, we totally ignore low-level manifestations of selective attention. Thirdly, we are making no difference between foveal and peripheral vision. Still other, equally critical problems include the representation of quantities, such as the distance to intersection, speed, and the spatio-temporal relations between objects. In the current version of the model real numbers are used to represent these variables.

Table 2. *Goals Subsumed Under the Process Manager Space*

Control Speed	
task:	keep the speed within a given range
type:	homeostatic, long term, high priority, operational, interrupt-driven
action:	change-speed (external operator)
Control Course	
task:	keep the car within lanes (with a certain tolerance)
type:	homeostatic, long term, high priority, operational, interrupt-driven
action:	change-course (external operator)
Negotiate Intersection	
task:	deal with intersection and traffic on intersection
type:	achievable/homeostatic, short term, high priority, tactical, both interrupt-driven and top-down
action:	choose correct acceleration and set speed parameters (to be dealt with by control-speed)
Find Destination	
task:	find a route from origin to destination
type:	achievable, middle long term, lower priority, strategic runs in the slack time of other goals
action:	choices at nodes in network

MULTITASKING: MANAGING MULTIPLE TASKS IN THE PROCESS MANAGER SPACE

The essence of the multitasking theory set forth in this paper is that the management of multiple, concurrent goals is represented as a problem that, like any other problem can be solved by Soar in an appropriate problem space. The problem space in this case will be referred to as the *process manager space* (PMS). The purpose of the PMS is to select the right subgoal to be performed at the right moment since only one subtask can be active at any one moment. The subtasks—also called goals in Soar, or processes in other AI contexts—that this space has to manage and that we use as an example in our model are shown in Table 2. The table describes the four subtasks to be managed by the PMS in terms of task, goal type, and action proposed.

PROCESS OBJECTS REPRESENT GOALS PROCESS OPERATORS IMPLEMENT TASKS

Goals or subtasks are represented as *process objects* on the top state. A goal is conventionally represented as a name and a desired on the goal object. However, in our multitasking theory it is the task of the PMS to manipulate goals as normal objects. This justifies our choice of representing goals on the top state—quite apart from the fact that in Soar it would be impossible to manipulate multiple goals through a single desired on the goal object. A process object has three basic properties: the name of the process that it stands for, the priority of this process, and the type. The use of these properties will be elucidated in the following sections. Figure 2 shows the representation of the control-speed, control-course, and find-destination processes. These examples reveal that, apart from the basic properties, objects may carry additional information such as, for instance, a range in the case of control-speed, or a current value in the case of the find-destination process.

Processes are implemented in lower level problem spaces. The name of such a space is by default the name of the process object. The model arrives in such a space through a so-called *process operator*. This type of operator has two basic properties, the name of and a pointer to the process it intends to implement. The application of a process operator will lead to a no-change impasse and a default multitasking rule will select a problem space with the name of the process. The resolution of impasses in a lower-level space can, in principle, lead to application chunks that avoid going into lower levels in the future. We will discuss these chunks later.

INTERRUPT OBJECTS SIGNAL POSSIBLE CHANGE OF PROCESS

Switching between processes is initiated by interrupts. In this case an interrupt object is generated for an process object on the top state. It is, however, possible that an interrupt is generated for a process that is not yet available at the top state. Interrupt objects have three basic properties: a name for the process for which they are generated, priority information, and the current event object. Remember that these event objects were generated at each wave of perceptual objects entering cognition. Figure 3 shows a few examples of interrupt objects.

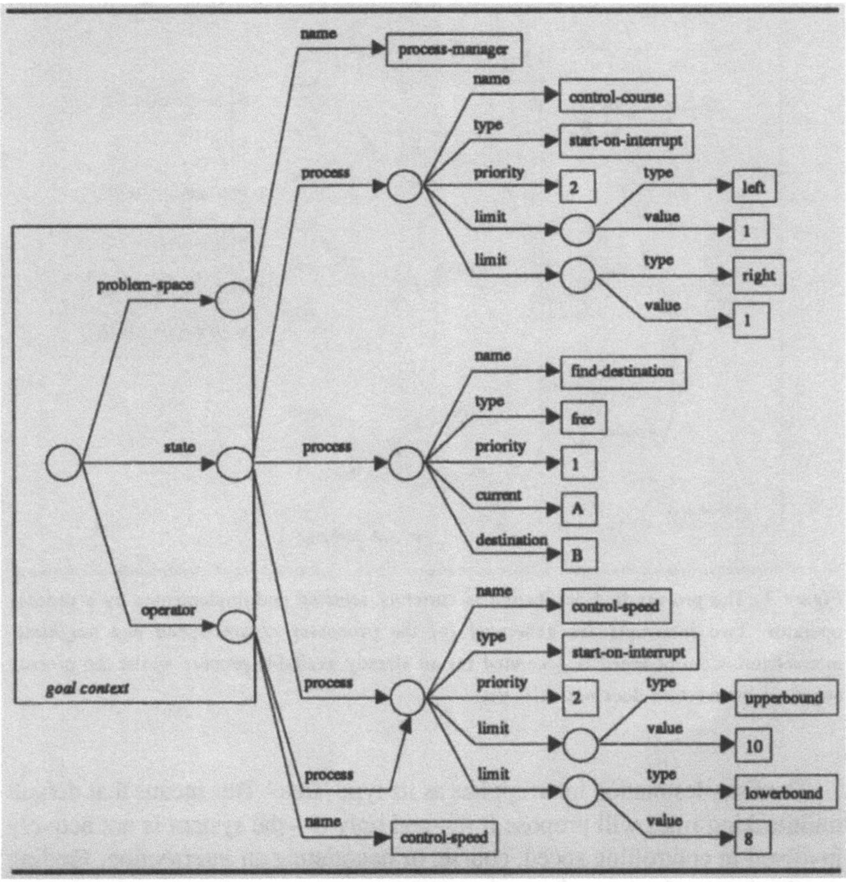

Figure 2. The process objects that exist in the top state. Control-speed is currently selected and implemented in a subgoal (not shown) by a process operator that has the name control-speed and a pointer to the control-speed object.

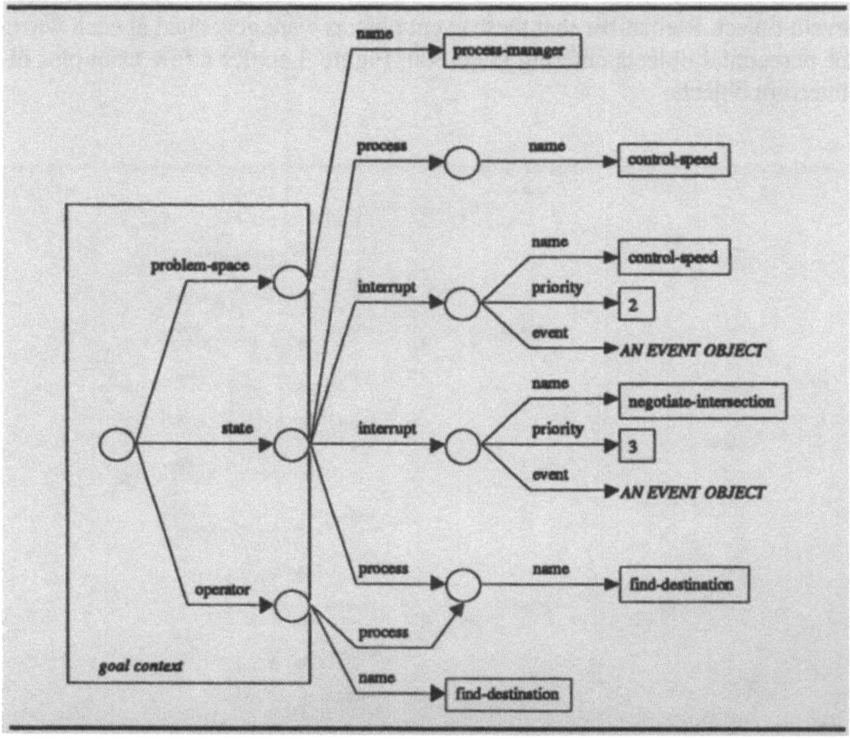

Figure 3. The process find-destination is currently selected and implemented by a process operator. Two interrupts are generated for the processes control-speed and negotiate-intersection. Control-speed is generated for an already available process whilst the process negotiate-intersection does not exist yet.

The find-destination interrupt has as its type 'free.' This means that default multitasking rules will propose it if—and only if—the system is not actively involved in controlling speed, course, or negotiating an intersection. Finding the destination is thus a low priority process, compared to the more urgent driving tasks. The interrupt negotiate-intersection is added to the top state whenever a driving related rule notices that there is an intersection less than 100 meters away. Note that this is an interrupt for an process that is not yet available on the top state: the process object for negotiating intersections will only become active (i.e., become available on the top state) when the process is actually relevant. Interrupts for the negotiate-intersection process may also be generated when this process is already active. This happens for example when rules related to driving notice that a car is coming from the right and is on collision course. The control-speed interrupt is generated by a rule that constantly monitors both the bounds on the control-speed object and the current speed. The rules that generate interrupts for processes which start-on-interrupt can be functionally described as 'monitors.' Monitor rules respond to perceptual information and process information on the top state independently of other goal-directed activity. The following structure shows a monitor production in Soar format (in Soar4, with comments added).

```
(sp  drive*check&mark-on-upper-speed-limit
     (goal <g> ^problem-space <p> ^state <s>
            -^supergoal)
If goal is top goal and
     (state <s> ^process <pr> ^object <o>)
     (process <pr> ^name control-speed ^limit <limit>)
there is a process with name control-speed
     (limit <limit> ^upperbound ^value <limitvalue>)
and an upperbound limit on speed
     (object <o> ^name self -^next
              ^speed { > <limitvalue> })
and self has higher value,
     -->
     (state <s> ^interrupt <intr>)
     (interrupt <intr> ^priority 2 ^name control-speed))
then add interrupt for control-speed to state.
```

CHANGE-PROCESS OPERATORS SHIFT PROCESSES

For each interrupt that is added to the top state a change-process operator is generated. Figure 4 shows the basic properties of such an operator. The interrupt on the operator is essentially the one for which the operator was generated, whilst the allow feature carries the name of the process that is to be installed. This name is the same as that on the interrupt that generated the operator (see preceding section). The identifier, finally, is the event object that we already mentioned in the section about perception. This allows the process manager to know the most recent interrupts in the system.

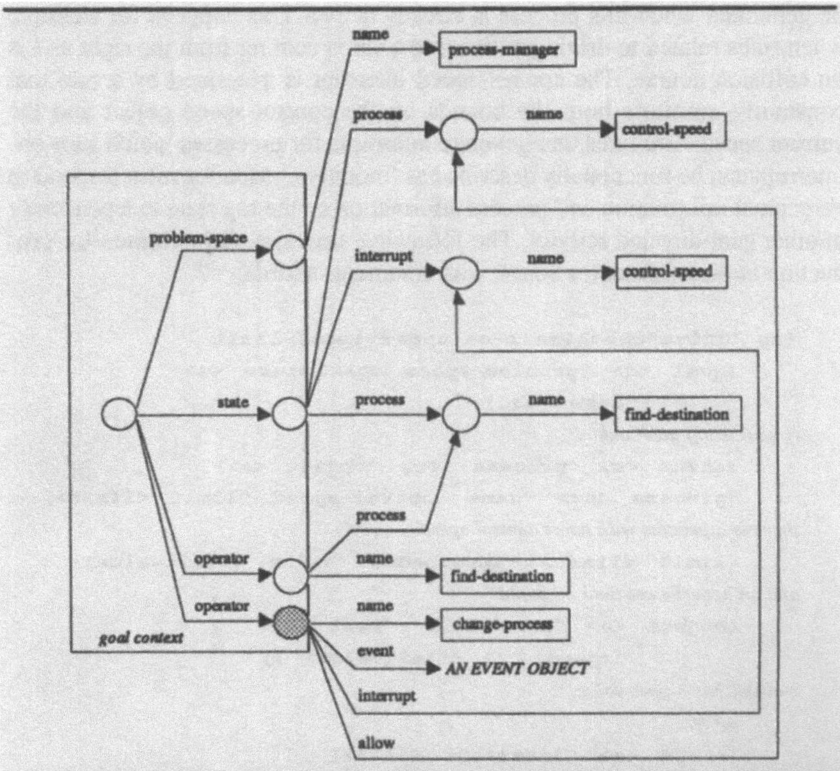

Figure 4. The process find-destination is currently selected and implemented by a find-destination process operator. An interrupt was generated for control-speed. A change-process operator is proposed for this interrupt.

Choosing Between Change-Process Operators

Whenever an interrupt occurs and the corresponding change-process operator is generated, this new operator will compete with the current process operator for the operator slot in the PMS. It is even possible that there are multiple interrupts in the PMS so that there are multiple change-process operators competing for the operator slot. If the competition is not resolved within the current decision cycle, a tie impasse will arise and the current subtask is interrupted. In the following cases this tie impasse will not arise: (1) a change-process operator for a process that is already active will be rejected; (2) as in most modern operating systems, interrupts in our multitasking model may be disabled in some time-critical task. For instance, in the current version of the model interrupts are disabled when there is already a tie impasse for conflicting change-process operators. When interrupts are disabled, no new change-process operators for an interrupt will be generated; (3) there are chunks that deal with a particular type of conflict and that 'know' how to choose between operators; (4) a change-process operator has a lower priority than the current task or a competing change-process operator, and can thus be rejected. In all other cases a tie will arise that is handled in the *interrupt handler space*, to be discussed in the next section.

Choosing Between Change-Process Operators in the Interrupt Handler Space

The interrupt handler space replaces the so-called selection space, Soar's normal space for dealing with ties. The main reason for this replacement is that the original selection space is intended for choosing between tied operators by employing look-ahead search and not for dealing with evaluations of external operators in time-critical situations. We must be able to account, however, for the fact that there is simply no time in critical situations to evaluate all the change-process operators in the selection space by applying all the operators to copies of the top state, quite apart from the fact that some change-process operators can only be evaluated after they have been applied in the real world. Soar's normal default rules for deciding between two unevaluated operators requires at least 15 decision cycles. Using Newell's estimate of 100 ms per decision cycle in humans, this would require at least 1.5 seconds. Approximate as these calculations may be, we see that in situations generating many interrupts the system would quickly grind to a halt if it were to use the normal Soar default rules for deciding between competing change-process operators (see Aasman & Akyürek, 1992, for an alternative to Soar's default rules).

In the present version of the model not much knowledge is available to the interrupt handler space. The only rule that is implemented states that during driving any driving-related process is more important than any process that is not related to the driving task.

Applying the Change-Process Operator

If the change-process operator is preferred over the current process operator the change-process operator is eventually applied and this will result in a new top state in the PMS with the new process allowed. For this new allowed process an operator is generated that has both the name of the new allowed process plus a pointer to that process (see Figure 2). If no application chunk is available the operator will lead to a no-change impasse and start the process in a subspace in which the processes that implement process objects and process operators do apply (see the discussion in the preceding section).

The multitasking mechanisms discussed so far do not alter the ways tasks are normally coped with in Soar. One way of looking at what is achieved by these mechanisms is that they act like a shell in which Soar proceeds in an entirely normal fashion with its problem solving activity. The exclusive function of this shell is to determine the next process to be initialized.

Summary of Multitasking Mechanism

The following points summarize the multitasking mechanisms discussed so far: (1) Process objects (declarative structures) on the top state represent multiple goals. (2) Only one process is active at any one time. A process operator initializes a process in a subgoal via a no-change impasse. (3) Events in the external world as well as internal events may lead to interrupts on the top state. (4) Interrupts lead to change-process operators: (a) In some cases knowledge is available to reject the new change-process operator and the current process can proceed; (b) In some cases knowledge is available to directly choose the new change-process operator and a new task can be installed; (c) If no knowledge is available to reject the new change-process operators then an operator tie arises between the current process operator and these new operators. This tie is resolved in the interrupt handler space. (5) Application of change-process leads to a new 'allowed' process on the state and a process operator to implement the task.

Driving Tasks

In this section we will discuss in greater detail the specific driving tasks that are managed by the model's top level process manager.

THE CONTROL-SPEED AND CONTROL-COURSE SPACES

Some of the functionality of the control-speed space has already been discussed. In the preceding section it was explained how interrupts for this space are created by a monitor rule whenever the speed of the car exceeds one of the limits defined in the control-speed process object on the top state. This makes speed-control a purely reactive process. In a more advanced model, however, the driver should be able to actively search for speed information, for example, by looking at the speedometer. Presently speed is controlled by simply decelerating when the speed is too high and by accelerating when speed is too low. The acceleration and deceleration commands are given directly to the Lisp motor function from within the control-speed space. In a later version of the model the change in speed will be effected by means of motor commands that translate into vehicle control actions which, in turn, will be transformed, into speed commands.

The control-course space resembles the control-speed space in many respects: it too features a passive strategy for controlling course, and course commands are directly given in Lisp. That is, whenever the car swerves out of bounds the system will react by installing the control-course space and correcting the course.

THE NEGOTIATE-INTERSECTION SPACE

The negotiate-intersection space is proposed when an interrupt signals an approaching intersection. Whereas control-speed and control-course are continually active homeostatic goals, the process negotiate-intersection is set by the environment and remains active for the short period during which the intersection that triggered the process is a relevant feature of the environment. Two basic actions can be proposed in this space. The first is simply to reduce speed whenever the approach to an intersection is noticed. In the present model this is done without regard for the type of intersection, the intended maneuver at the intersection, or the visibility at the intersection. In a later version these important factors will play a role. Speed is reduced by changing the limits on the process object for control-speed. The second action in the negotiate-intersection space is to reduce speed whenever a car from the right is found to be on a collision course. Whenever a monitor rule notices that a car is approaching from the right on a collision course, an interrupt for the negotiate-intersection space will be generated. A high priority is assigned to this space and accordingly will be selected with very high probability. Within the space, speed limits on the control-speed process object will be reduced to avoid a collision. Once these limits are set, the negotiate-intersection space can be left.

THE FIND-DESTINATION SPACE

The third task under concern is the navigation or find-destination task. Navigation is a subtask that is handled by drivers at a different performance level than are speed and course control. Coping with a navigation task while driving involves a heavy use of the goal stack and a good deal of multitasking, that is, task interruption and task resumption. The navigation task, performed by our model, referred to as find-destination task, consists of finding a path through a directed graph, representing a road network map. A detailed description of this task can be found in van Berkum (1988). The nodes in this graph are states in the find-destination task. Move operators in the task are the direction choices at each node. Available search control knowledge classifies operators as 'good,' 'medium,' or 'bad' by comparing the directions of the destination and the current move operator. Problem solving here is a simple hill-climbing search where states in the goal stack indicate the path followed so far. The main chunks learned in the problem solving process are evaluation chunks that avoid dead branches in future search.

The interesting aspect of this task is not in the first place that the model will eventually reach its destination or learn the network; in this respect it is actually little else than a simplified version of the real task. The real interest lies in the process of interrupting and resuming such a task. Whenever the search for the destination is interrupted by one of the other tasks, for example, control-speed, the whole goal stack within the find-destination space will be lost in principle. This derives from our decision to have the interrupts and change-process operators at the top level. The consequence is that when later there is slack time again to do the find-destination task, the whole goal stack must be rebuilt before the model can proceed from the node where search was initially interrupted.

This leads to the basic question in task interruption and resumption: *What is it that needs to be remembered about the interrupted task in order to enable one to resume it efficiently at a later instant?* One answer is to store the entire search tree on the process object generated up to the time of the interruption. In this case a residue of all the intermediate states is stored onto the process operator so that in the resumption of the task this information may be used to rebuild the goal stack fast and efficiently. For at least two reasons this procedure seems unattractive. First, it is psychologically implausible that subjects will store extremely large data structures in working memory about one (inactive task) while executing another task, even if the two tasks do not interfere. A second, quite mundane reason is that the administration of states and operators applied is almost impossible in the Soar version we initially used. The current version (i.e., Soar5) can indeed destructively modify data structures, making this administrative problem somewhat more tractable.

In our model we have used a much less extreme and more plausible way of storing state information to allow task resumption. This procedure retains the basic network map on the process object, thus creating an analogy with the concept of mental map (Pailhous, 1970). Searching this map for the destination, evaluations of operators are stored in chunks, whilst the nodes that are 'visited' are indeed marked as such, both on the network map and in the chunks that are being built. If search is interrupted and the goal stack is lost, only the basic network remains on the process object. After resumption both the visit-marks, visit-chunks, and the operator evaluation chunks will guide the search very quickly and efficiently to the point where the search was interrupted. The visit-marks and visit-chunks force Soar to explore trodden paths, while the evaluation chunks (both rejections and better preferences) keep the search from going into wrong directions.

Visit-chunks may seem redundant when there are visit-marks on the network map. However, it is conceivable that somehow the find-destination process is lost from the top state and thereby also losing the map's visit-marks. In these cases the visit-chunks will take over by quickly restoring all the visit-marks on the network map.

Although this procedure is very efficient, it is still lacking in psychological plausibility, since human subjects—unlike certain species of animals—will resume a search task from some landmark in their mental map rather than reconstruct their entire trip from their point of departure, however efficiently and effectively they may be able to do this.

Multitasking Driver Model At Work

The following is a brief "artist's impression" of the model at work in a prototypical situation that it can (learn to) cope with. The Appendix contains a summary Soar trace of this scenario. Initially, the model only uses the processes of controlling speed and course since these have a higher priority than navigation. If, however, no attention to speed and course is required the system will be able to engage in solving the navigation task, that is, in finding its preset destination. While at the navigation task, the system will notice that an intersection is less than 150 meters ahead. An interrupt operator for negotiate-intersection is proposed which will replace the navigation operator. In case the system does not have the knowledge that negotiate-intersection has a higher priority than the find-destination task it will drop into the interrupt handler space where it finds the general rule that "driving-related tasks are more important than non-driving-related tasks." This will generate a chunk that will give preference to the negotiate-intersection process operator and break the tie. The next time around the navigation task will automatically be replaced by the negotiate-intersection process. In the negotiate-intersection space the limits on the control-speed process are lowered. This will immediately generate an interrupt for the control-speed process. Once in the control-speed problem space speed will be reduced simply by lowering acceleration and the control-speed problem space is terminated. After giving the reduce-speed command the system will engage in navigation again. A short while later the system observes a car, a perceptual object designating a car is added to the top state. Another interrupt is generated, this time in the intersection problem space where knowledge resides about how to deal with cars at an intersection. Again speed is reduced upon the observation that the car comes from the right. Finally the system can finish its navigation task.

Discussion and Evaluation of the Model

MAPPING PROCESSING TYPES ONTO THE DRIVER MODEL

Our aim in this study is to present a cognitive model of multitasking in driving that can take into account the distinctions between automatic and controlled on the one hand, and between data-driven and top-down processing on the other. It was claimed in the introduction that Soar does support these various types of processing but thus far we have not really justified this statement. Having discussed our model of multitasking in driving, however, we are now in a position to discuss the relation between types of processing in this driver model.

The mapping of automatic and controlled behavior on Soar and our driver model is fairly straightforward. Soar is a parallel production system where productions are matched and fire in parallel. The seriality in the Soar is forced by the goal stack—the goal hierarchy—because at any one time only one operator can occupy the operator slot in a goal context. Thus, executing a sequence of operators and solving impasses in subgoals translates directly into controlled processing; selecting and applying operators in sequence is a slow process, requiring a minimum of 100 ms per operator in humans, which can be interrupted at will. The parallel activity in the elaboration phases, involving the generation of operators and their preferences and the application of operators to states is automatic because it is fast and cannot be interrupted.[3]

The serial activity in the multitasking activity of the driver model is clear. At the top level we observe a continuous stream of process and change-process operators. Switching between processes is for the greater part a serial, controlled process.

Prominent automatic and parallel behavior in the driver model is found in the perceptual unit of the model, in the productions that generate interrupts and in the automatic resolution of multiple interrupts. The productions that handle perception and the automatic updating of the world are clearly autonomous, that is, independent of the activity in the goal stack. This activity will therefore proceed irrespective of whatever else is happening on the goal stack. A second, more interesting form of automatic behavior lies in the generation of interrupts. The model contains several types of 'monitor' productions (Kuokka, 1990) that allow the system to remain reactive independent of its current focus of activity. We have already discussed a production that will generate an interrupt whenever the speed exceeds one of the speed limits. There are similar types of monitor functions for course control and for noticing the presence of traffic objects, especially those on a collision course. These productions too are independent of activity in the goal stack: they will only react to process objects on the top state and to perceptual objects on the top state. The third form of automatic behavior, finally, lies in the automatic resolution of change-process operator ties. In some cases the system has knowledge to automatically select or reject new change-process operators.

Mapping the distinction between top-down and data-driven behavior onto Soar and onto the driver model is also fairly straightforward. Soar is a goal-oriented system, making it, predominantly, a top-down control system; nearly all actions in the system are performed in order to serve goals. The driver model is facing the problem of integrating multiple tasks. Solving this problem is certainly a goal-directed process: given a set of tasks, that is, a set of goals in this environment, to find the optimal ordering of operators that comprise these tasks. If the driver model has the knowledge that in this particular situation it is best to switch operators in a certain order, we may speak of *top-down-controlled switching*. Soar, like other production systems, can also be data- or interrupt-driven: activity within elaboration cycles cannot be stopped by external or internal interrupts. However, the decision procedure allows for the interruption of a string of operators and the temporary insertion of other operators. The essence of data-driven or interrupt-driven processing is that a string of operators working on a main task can, at any time, be interrupted by another, secondary and maybe temporary task, for instance if the model perceives an unexpected situation and is required to set a new goal in order to deal with this new situation. In order to enable interrupt-driven switching between tasks the model has several important features. First, it has the capability of perceiving more than is strictly required for the current task; thus, for example, while approaching the intersection the system must be able to perceive that the car phone is beginning to ring, or that a child is dashing out into the street. In the second place there is a way to interrupt the current task in order to install operators that will address the critical event.

EVALUATION AND SUGGESTIONS FOR FUTURE RESEARCH

The remainder of this paper will be devoted to a discussion of some specific features of our model and the direction in which the next steps towards a more detailed model are taking us. First some issues concerning multitasking will be dealt with. Next some implications for driver task descriptions will be discussed, and finally we will make a few remarks about the Soar version used to implement the model.

Process objects. The process objects in the current model have priorities and types that are entirely built in by the designer. By and large, these prevent ties between process operators and change-process operators. However, there are problems associated with the use of these priorities and types. In the first place, the priorities and types are absolute in the sense that presently they are not context-dependent. Whether, for instance, navigation, that is, thinking about the route, is a free process or not should eventually depend on the current task being executed. Another shortcoming facing the present approach to process objects is that the priorities and types should, in fact, be learnable. Programming them in advance prevents the program from learning these priorities. A third issue, the difference between types and priorities has come up in hindsight but the issue is not a serious one. One can, of course, replace a type by a very low priority, making the type obsolete. The fourth issue, finally, is that priorities are a kind of indirect preference mechanism; one might therefore conceivably use Soar's inherent preference mechanism to order priorities. The reason for using the indirect mechanism is that in Soar it is possible to reason about priorities but not about preferences.

Interrupt objects. It is a meaningful question to ask why interrupts are generated as data structures on the top state rather than directly as change-process operators. The principal reason for employing an indirect mechanism in this case is that it is more convenient to work with data structures on the top state than having operators dangling somewhere in memory. It would have been possible, however, to directly generate operators instead of interrupt objects.

Rules learned in multitasking. Multitasking was described earlier as the ability to integrate several tasks or to switch between them in real time. Whilst our first concern was to realize a model of multitasking, the second was to study the role of learning within the mechanism of multitasking. In order to be able to study learning we had to slightly modify the model discussed so far. In the modified version the command for changing speed is not directly given within the control-speed problem space, but as a declarative structure on the top state where default multitasking rules interpret this command. Two types of chunks are learned in this case. The first type implements a task and is, in Soar terms, an operator application chunk. The second type is search control knowledge that affects the choice between change-process operators. An example of each type follows.

```
If    a process operator for control-speed is selected,
      and the upperbound limit is 10,
      and the current speed of self is 11
Then  modify acceleration <-0.5>.

If    there is an acceptable preference for an operator
          that will invoke find-destination process,
      and there is an acceptable preference for an
          operator that will invoke
          negotiate-intersection process
Then  create a better preference for the second
          operator, over the first.
```

The main conclusion regarding these chunks is that they are not well-behaved. They are either too specific (the first example) or overly general (the second example). Suppose that the driver model is in the interrupt handler space and is required to choose between two change-process operators; one for a control-speed interrupt and the other for a negotiate-intersection interrupt because a car is perceived to be on a collision course. If the default multitasking rules test for entire interrupts in the interrupt handler space, the resulting chunks will contain overly specific knowledge as in the first example. This would also happen in the control-speed problem space The reason is that traffic objects are represented here using real numbers. These values will therefore appear in the chunks that are learned, making them too specific. When, for example, will a driver at 15.3 m from an intersection and advancing at a speed of 16.3 m/s encounter a car approaching from the right at a speed of 12.7 m/s?

On the other hand, we obtain overly general chunks, as in the second example above, if we test only on the names of the interrupts pertaining to the change-process operators. Such chunks will be context-independent and consequently fire far too often and, as a result, disrupt the program that implements the model. In a future version of the model the problems of specific and overly general chunks should be remedied by a form of reasoning about interrupts, and by addressing the problem of quantitative code in Soar (Newell, 1988), that is, by replacing numbers for speed and distance by symbols such as close, medium, and far, perhaps in a fuzzy fashion.

Multitasking as integrating problem spaces. A further general observation is that the model provides, in Soar terms, a problem space switching mechanism. One way to avoid the overhead of switching between problem spaces or tasks is by integrating them into one larger task (e.g., driving as such) and execute this task at the top level. Integration can be achieved by the two types of chunks discussed above. This is essentially what is required in the modified version of the model in the learning mode. The first type of chunk will avoid going into the control-speed space and directly implement a desired amount of acceleration. This chunk features, in a sense, a generic 'drive' operator at the top level. The second type will avoid going into tie impasses and automatically select the right task at the top level. A process manager space that has such chunks would behave as the drive task space. The issue of task integration and incremental problem space expansion is a current research topic in the Soar community. Covrigaru (1990), for instance, deals with the issue of merging interrelated tasks in Soar by proposing an explicit mechanism to intentionally create a new problem space from other problem spaces. Laird (1989) has proposed to discard the problem space as the first class object in the goal context and make it a 'replaceable' feature of the goal instead. This would make it possible to add multiple problem spaces (as features) to the top goal or even replace problem spaces at the top level and thus simplify task switching considerably.

Task resumption. As mentioned earlier, task interruption and task resumption have recently become research topics in Soar (Hucka, 1989, 1991; Laird, in press; Laird & Rosenbloom, 1990). Hucka (1989) proposes to deal with interrupts at the deepest level space in the goal stack, thus making it possible to keep the goal stack intact while processing them. On the other hand, the principle of top level interrupt operators implies that the goal stack is lost after an interrupt. As we have seen, the consequence is that rebuilding the whole stack may take a considerable amount of time, proportional to the depth of the goal stack. However, the model presented in this paper demonstrates that there is no need for a special task resumption mechanism to support rebuilding. Task resumption is made possible by keeping a minimal amount of task information about the interrupted task on the top state, whilst the chunks learned before the interrupt do guide the search back to the point where processing was interrupted. If the model in its present form must cope with too many interrupts, the result is that there never will be time to solve the navigation task. Aasman and Akyürek (1992) propose several variations on Soar's default rules (for look-ahead search) to decrease the time required to rebuild the goal stack by making the goal stack flatter. The most drastic of these proposals is the destructive look-ahead. This variation has become feasible because of the destructive state modification that is available in Soar5.

The driver tasks. The model in its present form succeeds in handling tasks at the strategic, tactical, and operational levels of driving performance. However, all of the driver tasks in the current version are rather knowledge-lean. Control-speed, control-course, and negotiate-intersection have only the barest minimum of the knowledge required to get safely across the intersection. Two issues came up in the discussion of the driver problem spaces. First, it was noted that these spaces are too reactive; there is, for example, no 'active search' for speed or course deviations. We rely on the 'monitor' rules to signal that speed is too low or high. This is what makes the system almost entirely data-driven. In future versions we shall employ more active, and primarily visual strategies (including eye and head movement) in order to get information from the environment. The second issue was that commands to correct speed and course were given directly in the subspaces and directly to a transducer routine implemented in Lisp. In the forthcoming version of the model we will account for the manual control of the vehicle, following Newell's base level theory, by giving the motor commands at the top level.

Visual strategies and motor behavior. The current model lacks both perceptual and action strategies. A future perceptual unit will have to have foveal as well as peripheral vision, and perceptual objects will be more or less elaborate, depending on the part of the visual field in which they originate. Decision making about where to look next, involving eye movements and head movements as well as operators within the functional field (Wiesmeyer & Laird, 1990), will constitute an important extension in the enhanced model. A second addition is the development of motor control. A Soar model of vehicle handling by actively controlling the extremities will be integrated into the available multitasking structure, and speed will be controlled by active manipulation of the car rather than direct value settings set up through Lisp commands.

Limitations of Soar4. One conclusion from the attempt to use Soar in modeling multitasking behavior is that Soar4, the Soar version that was initially used to implement the model discussed in the present paper, is not an entirely adequate vehicle for this endeavor. The most serious limitation was that, in Soar4, data structures in working memory cannot be modified destructively: in principle, data can only be added. Yet, the deletion of data can be achieved in Soar4 in two ways. The first, conventional way, is to replace a state by a new state and to copy only part of the contents of the old state, thereby indirectly achieving deletion. The second way of deleting, used heavily in the present model, is to simulate deletion by invalidating data structures. Invalidation is achieved by explicitly marking data structures as 'old' or 'nonexistent.' However, this procedure slows down Soar's matcher considerably when an increasing number of objects is made invalid. The main reason for having deletion at the top level is to allow both (parallel) perception and (parallel) interrupts at the top level without interrupting the activity in the goal stack. This, however, requires some very complicated bookkeeping of interrupts and perceptual objects at the top level. With each new perceptual object coming in, old objects have to be marked as 'old' and a link between the new object and the old one must be established. When processing in the goal stack (while doing the navigation task) proceeds for some protracted period of time the list of objects at the top level becomes intolerably long, bringing Soar almost to a halt. Only after an interrupt most of the perceptual objects and the old interrupts at the top level can be removed.

The revised model of multitasking behavior in traffic will adopt Soar5, not simply because it is the present standard, but rather because it supports both destructive state modification and a truth maintenance system (see Laird et al, 1990), thus removing, or at least reducing, some serious but essentially logistic problems.

NOTES

[1]One could conceivably use a single goal representation by defining *drive* as the top goal that includes all other goals related to the driving task. However, since people are apparently capable of engaging in other tasks while driving, the single goal would be self-defeating.

[2]Representing moving objects as a sequence of objects with the same identity is one of the drawbacks in Soar4 that was eliminated when Soar5 was introduced. The reason is that, in Soar5, it is possible to destructively modify data structures. As a result, the properties of an object and its relations to other objects may now change without affecting its identity.

[3]One difficulty that we have with the mapping of automatic and controlled processing onto Soar is that a string of operators might be so well learned that no subgoals are required to solve the ordering between operators. This state of affairs has been identified by some authors as "veiled processing," different from automatic processing in the proper sense.

REFERENCES

Aasman, J. (1988). Implementations of car driver behaviour and psychological risk models. In J. A. Rothengatter & R. A. de Bruin (Eds.), *Road user behaviour: Theory and research* (pp. 106–117). Assen, The Netherlands: Van Gorcum.

Aasman, J., & Akyürek, A. (1992). Flattening goal hierarchies. In J. A. Michon & A. Akyürek (Eds.), *Soar: A cognitive architecture in perspective* (pp. 199-217). Dordrecht, The Netherlands: Kluwer.

Aasman, J., & Lourens, P. F. (1991). *Timing of basic driver operations in the negotiation of general rule intersections*. Unpublished manuscript, University of Groningen, Traffic Research Center, Haren, The Netherlands.

Covrigaru, A. (1989). *The goals of autonomous systems*. Unpublished manuscript, University of Michigan, Electrical Engineering and Computer Science Department, Ann Arbor.

Covrigaru, A. (1990, October). *Merging interrelated tasks*. Paper presented at the Eighth Soar Workshop, Information Sciences Institute, University of Southern California, Los Angeles, CA.

de Velde Harsenhorst, J. J., & Lourens, P. F. (1987). *Classificatie van rijtaakfouten en analyse van rijtaakverrichtingsparameters* (Tech. Rep. VK 87-17) [Classification of driving errors and analysis of driving performance parameters]. Haren, The Netherlands: University of Groningen, Traffic Research Center.

de Velde Harsenhorst, J. J., & Lourens, P. F. (1988). *Het onderwijs leerproces bij een leerlingautomobiliste en specifieke rijgedrag van jonge automobilisten* (Tech. Rep. VK 88–25) [The educational learning process of a novice driver and specific driving behavior of young automobile operators]. Haren, The Netherlands: University of Groningen, Traffic Research Center.

Hale, A. R., Stoop, J., & Hommels, J. (1990). Human error models as predictors of accident scenarios for designers in road transport systems. *Ergonomics, 33*, 1377-1387.

Hucka, M. (1989). *Planning, interruptability, and learning in Soar.* Unpublished manuscript, University of Michigan, Electrical Engineering and Computer Science Department, Ann Arbor.

Hucka, M. (1991). *Interruption and resumption in integrated intelligent agents.* Unpublished manuscript, University of Michigan, Electrical Engineering and Computer Science Department, Ann Arbor.

Kuokka, D. R. (1990). *The deliberative integration of planning, execution, and learning* (Tech. Rep. CMU-CS-90-135). Pittsburgh, PA: Carnegie Mellon University, School of Computer Science.

Laird, J. E. (1989, May). *Why we don't need P in GPSO.* Paper presented at the Sixth Soar Workshop, University of Michigan, Ann Arbor, MI.

Laird, J. E. (1990). *Integrating planning and execution in Soar.* Manuscript submitted for publication.

Laird, J. E., Congdon, C. B., Altmann, E., & Swedlow, K. (1990). *Soar user's manual: Version 5.2* (Tech. Rep. CMU-CS-90-179). Pittsburgh, PA: Carnegie Mellon University, School of Computer Science.

Laird, J. E., Newell, A., & Rosenbloom, P. S. (1987). SOAR: An architecture for general intelligence. *Artificial Intelligence, 33,* 1-64.

Laird, J. E., & Rosenbloom, P. S. (1990). Integrating execution, planning, and learning in Soar for external environments. In *Proceedings of the Eighth National Conference on Artificial Intelligence* (pp. 1022-1029). San Mateo, CA: Morgan Kaufmann.

Michon, J. A. (1976). The mutual impacts of transportation and human behavior. In P. Stringer & H. Wenzel (Eds.), *Transportation planning for a better environment* (pp. 221-235). New York: Plenum Press.

Michon, J. A. (1985). A critical review of driver behavior models: What do we know, what should we do? In L. A. Evans & R. C. Schwing (Eds.), *Human behavior and traffic safety* (pp. 487-525). New York: Plenum Press.

Newell, A. (1988, September). *The basic quantitative code.* Paper presented at the Fifth Soar Workshop, Carnegie Mellon University, Pittsburgh, PA.

Newell, A. (1990). *Unified theories of cognition.* Cambridge, MA: Harvard University Press.

Norman, D. A., & Bobrow, D. G. (1975). On data limited and resource limited processes. *Cognitive Psychology, 7,* 44-64.

Pailhous, J. (1970). *La représentation de l'espace urbain* [The representation of urban space]. Paris: Presses Universitaires de France.

Rasmussen, J. (1985). Trends in human reliability analysis. *Ergonomics, 28,* 1185-1195.

Rasmussen, J. (1987). The definition of human error and a taxonomy for technical system design. In J. Rasmussen, K. Duncan, & J. Leplat (Eds.), *New technology and human error* (pp. 23-31). New York: Wiley.

Reason, J. (1987). Generic error-modelling system (GEMS): A cognitive framework for locating common human error forms. In J. Rasmussen, K. Duncan, & J. Leplat (Eds.), *New technology and human error* (pp. 63-85). New York: Wiley.

Reece, D., & Shafer, S. (1988). An overview of the Pharos traffic simulator. In J. A. Rothengatter & R. A. de Bruin (Eds.), *Road user behaviour: Theory and research* (pp. 285-293). Assen, The Netherlands: Van Gorcum.

Shiffrin, R. M., & Schneider, W. (1977). Controlled and automatic human information processing: II. Perceptual learning, automatic attending, and a general theory. *Psychological Review, 84,* 127-190.

van Berkum, J. A. (1988). *Cognitive modelling in Soar* (WR 88-01). Haren, The Netherlands: University of Groningen, Traffic Research Center.

Wierda, M., & Aasman J. (1988). *Expertsystemen en computers in verkeersopvoeding in het voortgezet onderwijs* (Tech. Rep. VK 88-24) [Expert systems and computers in traffic education in secondary schools]. Haren, The Netherlands: University of Groningen, Traffic Research Center.

Wiesmeyer, M., & Laird, J. (1990). A computer model of 2D visual attention. In *Proceedings of the Twelfth Annual Conference of the Cognitive Science Society* (pp. 582-589). Hillsdale, NJ: Erlbaum.

Appendix

The following is a commented segment of the trace of the model at work with learning disabled.

```
0    G: G1
1    P: P3 PROCESS-MANAGER-SPACE
2    S: S4
```
The initial state that s4 points to contains process objects find-destination, control-speed and control-course.
```
3    O: O13 FIND-DESTINATION
```
A process operator for find-destination activates find-destination process.
```
4    ==>G: G14 (FIND-DESTINATION OPERATOR NO-CHANGE)
5       P: P16 FIND-DESTINATION
6       S: S17 X=>A
```
As a result, a search is started to reach the destination during which an interrupt arrives
```
7    O: O41 CHANGE-PROCESS
```
for negotiate-intersection.
```
8    S: S42
```
The new state will now allow process negotiate-intersection
```
9    O: O43 NEGOTIATE-INTERSECTION
```
and an operator activates it.

```
10  ==>G: G44 (NEGOTIATE-INTERSECTION OPERATOR NO-CHANGE)
11      P: P46 NEGOTIATE-INTERSECTION
12      S: S47
```

Interrupt handler space changes limits on control-speed process

```
13  ==>G: G68 (UNDECIDED OPERATOR TIE)
```

which immediately generates interrupt for control-speed.

```
14      P: P69 INTERRUPT-HANDLER-SPACE
```

This causes a tie to occur between negotiate-intersection and control-speed,

```
15      S: S70
```

which is won by control-speed.

```
16  O: O67 CHANGE-PROCESS
```

So a change-process operator for control-speed is installed

```
17  S: S84
18  O: O85 CONTROL-SPEED
19  ==>G: G86 (CONTROL-SPEED OPERATOR NO-CHANGE)
20      P: P88 CONTROL-SPEED
```

A set of operator applications bring speed down to the new desired value after which

```
21      S: S89
22      O: O103
23      S: S104
24      O: O117
25      S: S118
26      O: O131
27      S: S132
28      O: O145
29      S: S146
30      O: O159
31      S: S160
32  O: O173 CHANGE-PROCESS
```

there is again time for find-destination ...

```
33  S: S174
34  O: O175 FIND-DESTINATION
...
```

FLATTENING GOAL HIERARCHIES[1]

JANS AASMAN
Traffic Research Center, University of Groningen
Haren, The Netherlands

AND

ALADIN AKYÜREK
Department of Psychology, University of Groningen
Groningen, The Netherlands

ABSTRACT. Current default rules for operator tie impasses in Soar are examined in relation to known constraints on human memory and real-time requirements imposed on human behavior in dynamic environments. The analysis shows that an alternative approach is required for resolving such impasses, which does not ignore these constraints. As such, this objective is not new. Newell (1990) advocated that the "single state principle" be used in all impasse handling to reduce the "computational cost" associated with it. While the current version of Soar is based on this principle, the default rules for ties still do not satisfy the constraints in question. This paper explores alternative sets of rules that appear promising in meeting them.

Introduction

The growing body of Soar literature shows that both artificial intelligence (AI) researchers and cognitive psychologists do benefit from using the Soar system in their research (e.g., Steier et al., 1987; Lewis et al., 1990). Soar is considered an AI architecture for general intelligence (e.g., Laird, Newell, & Rosenbloom, 1987; Laird, Rosenbloom, & Newell, 1986; Rosenbloom, Laird, Newell, & McCarl, 1991) as well as an architecture for cognition (Newell, Rosenbloom, & Laird, 1989), and is said to instantiate a unified theory of cognition (Newell, 1990). The notion of architecture is taken here to

J. A. Michon and A. Akyürek (eds.), Soar: A Cognitive Architecture in Perspective, 199–217.

mean "the fixed system of mechanisms that underlies and produces cognitive behavior" (Newell, Rosenbloom, & Laird, 1989, p. 94). The claim that Soar is an AI architecture for general intelligence is not at stake here. The real concern of this paper is Soar as a unified theory of cognition (UTC). Some properties of Soar as a system for general intelligence appear to weaken the Soar theory as a candidate UTC, that is, they make the system too powerful as a theory of human cognition. One of the strongest points of Soar is its combination of the basically 'chaotic' nature of a parallel production system with the tight administrative powers of a *goal stack* and the simplicity of an efficient chunking mechanism. Another is the set of default rules that supports the problem-solving behavior of Soar as a weak method problem solver.

But, why would psychologists worry about such a powerful combination? The problem is that Soar seems to deviate from human cognition in significant ways: (a) the size of working memory is virtually unbounded; (b) learning that occurs in a single problem solving episode is too fast; (c) backtracking to previous problem states and noticing duplicate problem states during search are virtually effortless; and (d) as a real-time system Soar does not seem to adequately match the interrupt-driven character of human behavior. It is the contention of the present paper that these issues arise in large part from the behavior of the current default rules that involve operator tie impasses. The following section briefly describes the key concepts involved, the current default mechanism, and their relationship to the above issues. The *interrupt* issue will be dealt with in a section of its own.

The Default Mechanism for Operator Tie Impasses

A goal (or context) stack is a temporary data structure in working memory that links together the *goal contexts*, each of which is composed of a goal (G), together with slots for the current problem space (P), state (S), and operator (O). A goal context is frequently referred to, in an abbreviated form, as context or simply goal. Any context slot is allowed only a single value at a time. The desired state[2] that Soar is set to achieve is usually specified through a slot of G, called *desired*. The first element of the stack is called the top level goal or just top goal for the obvious reasons. All other goals below it are subgoals, created in response to impasses in problem solving. Hence, a goal stack represents a *goal hierarchy*. An *operator tie* impasse occurs when two or more operators are proposed while none of these has a better preference than the others. An operator tie impasse can be resolved when additional preferences are created that prefer one option over others, eliminate alternatives, or make all of the operators indifferent (Laird, Congdon, Altmann, & Swedlow, 1990).

In Soar, a subset of default rules implements a mechanism in order to decide operator tie impasses. This mechanism works as follows. Given a task, task rules will select a problem space within which to attempt the task. In this problem space, an initial state is selected and problem solving proceeds by repetitively proposing, selecting, and applying task operators to the state. In response to an operator tie impasse Soar itself sets up a subgoal. The goal context of a tie impasse is also called a *tie-context*. Default rules that are responsive to the tie impasse propose the *selection problem space* in the associated subgoal. If no competing problem spaces exist, the selection problem space gets selected. An empty initial state is then created, where evaluations are posted as soon as they become available. The *evaluation* operators of this space evaluate the tied task operators, a process that allows preferences to be created for the latter. To compute an evaluation, an *evaluation operator* is proposed for each of the tied task operators. The evaluation operators are mutually indifferent, so Soar can select one at random. Since this is an abstract operator in an abstract space, an *operator no-change* impasse arises. As a result a further subgoal is created, known as the *evaluation subgoal*.

There exist default rules that are sensitive to the evaluation subgoal and they propose the problem space of the tie-context, that is, the one above the selection problem space. If this problem space gets selected, these rules also propose a new state and upon its selection, they copy down relevant information from the state of the tie-context to the new state. The principle behind this is that Soar will try to assess the ramifications of the task operators without actually modifying the original task state. Technically, the system is said to engage in a *look-ahead search*. Thus, the operator that is linked to the evaluation operator is selected in the evaluation subgoal and applied to the *copy* of the task state, leading to one of the following results.

Case 1: Another operator is selected. The modified state does not match the desired state, and there is only one operator available or the preferences favor a single operator. This operator then gets applied to the current state without further subgoaling.

Case 2: Another operator tie impasse occurs. The modified state does not match the desired state, and there is a set of instantiated task operators to select from. This will cause additional levels of subgoaling.

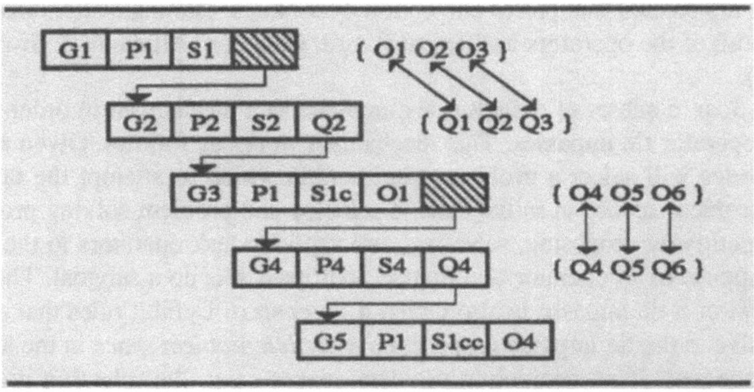

Figure 1. Soar's default mechanism for operator tie impasses. Shaded areas indicate tie-contexts where an operator tie impasse occurs. G1 is the top-level goal: P1 is the task problem space. S1 the task state, and {O1 O2 O3} the set of tied task operators. G2 is the subgoal generated because of the tie impasse: P2 is the selection space and S2 will contain the evaluations for O1 to O3 when they become available. {Q1 Q2 Q3} is the set of evaluation operators for {O1 O2 O3}. G3 (i.e., the evaluation subgoal) is the result of the operator no-change impasse associated with Q2: It shares P1 with G1 and its state, S1c, is a copy of the task state S1. It can be seen that O1 is tried on S1c. Again an operator tie impasse occurs, followed by another instantiation of the selection space, and so on.

Case 3: An evaluation is computed. The modified state does not match the desired state, but a symbolic or numeric evaluation exists for the modified state. Task specific rules put this evaluation into a slot of the state of the selection problem space as the result of the evaluation operator. Default rules that are sensitive to this slot will then terminate the current evaluation operator and proceed to the selection of another evaluation operator. When eventually enough evaluations have been computed so that the operators in the tie set can be compared, default rules convert them into preferences that break the tie in the original task space. Of course, if success is detected—that is, the desired state has been attained in the evaluation subgoal—a best preference will immediately resolve the tie. This eliminates the need to apply the rest of evaluation operators. Figure 1 summarizes the whole process described so far in a schematic way. When an evaluation is computed, two chunks are learned: one pertaining to the selection problem space, the other to the problem space of the tie-context. In the process, it is possible and, in fact, fairly common that the whole solution path, the operator sequence that achieves the desired state, is learned at once.

Issues

MEMORY

Current default rules behave such that the goal stack can grow to arbitrary depths. As a result, they impose an unrealistic load on the working memory. Newell signaled this issue and its psychological implications with respect to Soar4, and discussed the *single-state principle* as a potential answer (Newell, 1990). Soar5, the current version of the Soar system, does indeed employ this principle according to which Soar should keep only a single state in working memory when doing search in a problem space. Whilst copying states within goals is reduced to some extent in Soar5, between goals it is still very much present. This is due to the fact that default rules do not obey the single-state principle when they implement look-ahead search to determine the relevance of tying operators. As described in the preceding section, their effects are simulated on *copies* of the superstates. Since the goal stack is unbounded, the number of intermediate state copies that need to be held in working memory is in principle also unbounded.

It is fairly trivial to show that the look-ahead search these rules implement cannot be the scheme that humans use. With just the rules of chess at its disposal, the default rules would allow Soar, unlike humans, to traverse a search tree of, say, 20 levels deep in a game without using, for example, an *external* chessboard for guidance. Improbable for humans but quite possible for Soar is that, while 20 levels down in the search tree, it can decide on rejecting, say, a move at level 8, go back to that level, and consider a different move.

Human working memory may normally contain up to seven or eight chunks of items at a time. Making this constraint a built-in feature of Soar by *fixing* the size of its working memory will not help, because memory-hungry processing mechanisms like the current look-ahead would immediately break down. It is rather more likely that the processing mechanisms themselves are adapted to this feature of working memory, that is, the size of their output is inherently constrained (cf. Bobrow & Norman, 1975; Elgot-Drapkin, Miller, & Perlis, 1987). This point will be treated here as a requirement.

SEARCH

One issue related to search is that in Soar the goal stack allows for virtually effortless backtracking, that is, branching back to a previous problem state to consider alternatives without this incurring any cognitive or computational cost. This is presumably a desirable property for an AI system, but it does not quite mimic human problem solving where one may occasionally hear: "OK, this is all wrong, but how did I get here in the first place?" The default rules make it possible to maintain a large search tree in the goal stack with relevant intermediate states available at each branch. Evaluation operators that are not in the operator slot will stay around in memory and remain 'visible' to productions. This enables Soar—to return for a moment to the chess example—to see at level 20 that an operator at level 8 is 'wrong,' then backtrack to that level and continue the search from there. However, a closer examination of the problem solving protocols and their analysis provided in Newell and Simon (1972) makes it convincingly clear that backtracking is never this simple. Most of the time it requires an operator or a set of productions. If humans jump back to a previous state, they will nearly always jump back to the initial state, or to a stable intermediate state—often using external memory to find such a state. In any case it is much less automatic than is currently in Soar. One partial way out of this problem is progressive deepening. Newell and Simon (1972) have claimed that this is the strategy humans appear to use most in their problem solving. Although progressive deepening has been attempted in Soar, it has always been implemented, like most other weak methods, as a method increment to the selection problem space and evaluation subgoaling (see Laird, 1984). Such an implementation imparts of course processing characteristics similar to the current look-ahead method.

An ancillary issue is the relative ease of detecting duplicate states. Because copies of problem states are available throughout the goal stack, it is very simple for Soar to detect recurring problem states. Humans too are capable of noticing such duplicate states: "Hey, I was here a few steps before, what did I do wrong?" But the question is, if they cannot apparently hold extended records of their problem solving in their working memories, how do they succeed in noticing such states?

A requirement that derives from the discussion above is the following: the process that investigates the effects of a candidate set of task operators must be organized in a such way that it does not capitalize on deep goal stacks, while known weak methods of problem solving (e.g., see Laird & Newell, 1983; Laird, 1984; Nilsson, 1971; Rich, 1983) can be based on it.

LEARNING

Currently, in look-ahead search, learning comes at almost no cost. Operators are applied to copies of higher states, and the resulting evaluations passed up to the operators in the original space. Because an evaluation is dependent on the changed copy of a superstate and a superoperator, the resulting chunk will contain appropriate state and operator conditions so that a correct evaluation chunk is learned. As such, this is a very useful mechanism to have. However, in combination with a deep goal stack it may lead to curious phenomena such as learning an entire solution path as soon as success is detected while looking ahead. If one accepts that ten seconds per chunk is a serious estimate for the speed of learning (Newell & Simon, 1972, p. 793), then it is a bit odd to observe that Soar should be capable of learning, say, 40 chunks in just a few simulated seconds.

There is also sufficient evidence that learning can increase the computational cost of processes that underlie problem solving (Minton, 1988; Tambe & Newell, 1988; Tambe & Rosenbloom, 1989). The chunks that are learned may have, for example, low utility and/or high matching cost. A contributing factor no doubt is the number of chunks learned, that is, how efficiently the acquired knowledge is stored. A requirement that follows from these observations is that default rules should not cause learning more chunks than are needed for efficient problem solving.

Alternative Approaches to Deal With Ties

As was pointed out before, an operator tie impasse is currently resolved in the selection problem space. As can be seen from Figure 1, the knowledge needed for distinguishing a single choice among the operators of a tie-context is often secured in the evaluation subgoals below a selection problem space. Evidently, the selection problem space adds to the depth of the goal stack that obtains during the look-ahead search. Since the Soar architecture creates a chunk for each result obtained in a subgoal, many chunks will be included into its production memory, ensuing from both the selection and evaluation subgoals. As will be shown below, it appears that the selection problem space is not really needed to generate the knowledge required for deciding among alternatives. In fact, several sets of rules can be conceived that do not call for it.

ALTERNATIVE 1 — ELIMINATING THE SELECTION PROBLEM SPACE

In the first scheme to be considered, following an operator tie impasse the problem space of the tie-context is selected, and a new state is created in the associated subgoal for every tying task operator (see Figure 2). These states are given indifferent preferences and one is chosen at random. From this point on, the problem solving that takes place is analogous to that of the current default rules when they attempt to evaluate task operators. Thus, the super-operator is installed in the subgoal, while the relevant aspects of the task state are copied to the state specific to that operator. This operator is then applied to the copied state.

If no evaluation is available, problem solving continues, possibly with a new set of instantiated task operators. If a numeric evaluation is available, this evaluation is stored on the operator, another operator from the tie set is selected, and again the superstate is copied down to the state created for it. When the tie set is exhausted, available evaluations are converted into preferences, breaking the tie, upon which the winning operator is selected in the supergoal and applied. If success is detected before the tie set is exhausted, the subgoal terminates instantly, and the operator responsible for success is directly selected and applied in the supergoal. If a failure is detected, the operator gets a reject preference, and problem solving continues with another operator from the tie set. Note that all problem solving in this scheme is carried out in the original task problem space.

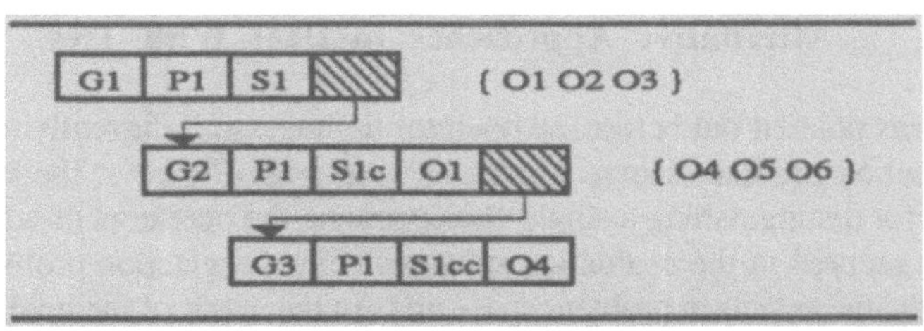

Figure 2. An alternative default mechanism for operator tie impasses that eliminates the selection problem space. The shaded areas indicate tie-contexts. In this scheme, an operator tie impasse may also occur following an operator application in the same subgoal, set up to resolve an earlier tie impasse. G1 is the top-level goal: P1 is the task problem space. S1 the task state, and {O1 O2 O3} the set of tied task operators. G2 is the subgoal generated as a result of the tie impasse: it has the same problem space as the supergoal, that is, the task problem space P1. Its state is a copy of the task state, and it is created to evaluate a specific task operator. Thus S1c is a copy of task state from the supergoal on which O1 is tried out. As soon as O1 has been applied another tie impasse arises, consisting of {O4 O5 O6}. This causes Soar to set up another subgoal, G3, whose state S1cc is a copy of the superstate, created to try out O4 in turn.

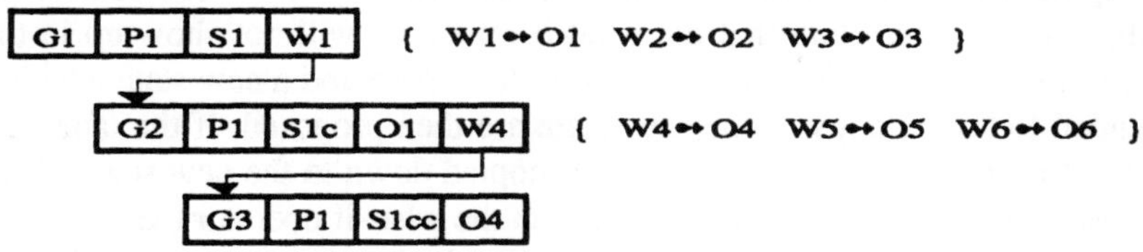

Figure 3. An alternative default mechanism for look-ahead search in which operator tie impasses will not occur, for each task operator instantiation is assigned a *what-if* operator with an indifferent preference. G1 is the top-level goal: P1 is the task problem space. S1 the task state, and {W1 W2 W3} is the set of what-if operators whose every element is paired with an element of {O1 O2 O3}, the set of instantiated task operators. G2 is the subgoal generated because of the operator no-change impasse, associated with W1: the subgoal has the same problem space as the supergoal, that is, the task problem space P1. Its state is a copy of the task state, and it is created to evaluate a specific task operator. Thus S1c is a copy of the task state from the supergoal on which O1 is tried out. As soon as O1 has been applied, other task operators {O4 O5 O6} are instantiated, which leads to the creation of corresponding what-if operators {W4 W5 W6}. This causes Soar to set up another subgoal, G3, whose state S1cc is a copy of the superstate S1c, created to try out O4 in turn.

Compared with Soar's current default mechanism, the scheme outlined above (a) requires fewer default rules, (b) produces a smaller goal stack, (c) reduces the number of chunks learned by one half—due to the absence of the selection problem space, and (d) induces faster performance, both during learning and after learning. Moreover, its rules are much simpler to understand. However, the processing that this scheme instantiates still does not constrain the size of the goal stack, and the state copying that it needs for evaluating candidate task operators is identical to that of the current Soar scheme.

ALTERNATIVE 2 — AVOIDING TIES

In the second scheme, to which we turn now, ties do not arise. The idea is that if a task operator is proposed that does not have an evaluation attribute, the operator may be conjoined with a *what-if operator* (see Figure 3). Instantiations of the latter are made better than the task operators, and are also made indifferent to one another so that one of them will be selected immediately at random. And, as soon as Soar enters an operator no-change subgoal, a default rule will bring down all of the superoperators to the new context *without testing the what-if operator in the supergoal's operator slot*. The reason for doing this is to ascertain that the what-if operators will not show up in the chunks that are built. The supergoal's problem space and a new state which is intended to hold a copy of the superstate are then proposed. If the latter are selected in the subgoal, the superstate is copied down to the new state. Next, the task operator which was conjoined with the what-if operator that occupies the supergoal's operator slot is selected and applied to the state in the subgoal.

If no evaluation is available, problem solving will continue, possibly with a fresh set of instantiated task operators. If a numeric evaluation is available, however, that evaluation is passed up to the supergoal. The associated what-if operator retracts, and as a result, the current subgoal will be terminated. Next, another what-if operator gets selected, and again Soar enters a no-change subgoal. This process is repeated until all task operators have their evaluations computed. When the set of what-if operators is exhausted, the available evaluations are converted into preferences so that a choice decision can be made in the supergoal. The winning operator is subsequently selected in the supergoal and applied. If success is detected, the current subgoal is terminated and the operator responsible for success is given a require preference upon which this operator is selected immediately in the supergoal, and applied to the state of that goal. All remaining what-if operators are then rejected, eliminating the need to evaluate the task operators with which they are paired. If a failure is detected, the task operator gets a 'failure' preference, the associated subgoal terminates due to the retraction of the what-if operator in the supergoal, and problem solving proceeds with another what-if operator from the extant set.

Like in the first alternative, all problem solving is again carried out in the original task problem space. Also, it should be noted that in the present scheme—as well as in the next alternative—a particular preference language is used on top of the one provided in Soar. The reason for introducing such a language is to guarantee that every production that creates a preference will participate in backtracing during chunking process.

The present alternative, however, forces Soar to enter into a no-change subgoal even if there exists only one instantiated task operator. Note that this can be avoided by having rules that determine the number of the instantiated task operators, $n(O)$, and create what-if operators only when $n(O) > 1$. It compares nevertheless to Soar's current default mechanism as favorably as the first alternative above. The next alternative addresses the issue of state copying by introducing destructive look-ahead.

ALTERNATIVE 3 — ELIMINATING STATE COPYING

It is also possible to shadow operator tie impasses, as in Alternative 2, and use the task state for operator evaluations instead of copies of the superstate. This scheme runs as follows. All task operators are by default indifferent, that is, they are proposed with indifferent preferences. Soar will select one at random and apply it, thereby directly modifying the task state. As such, this scheme differs from the previous ones and from Soar's current scheme in that it implements a destructive look-ahead search: whenever an operator is selected, the actual task state is changed, instead of a copy of that state. A record is kept, however, of the operators that have been applied (see below).

If a failure is detected, a *reversal operator* is applied to the result state, say S', to restore the state S that prevailed prior to the failed operator. It should be clear that returning to the previous state leads to new operators being proposed, identical to those proposed earlier. One of them is of course a new instantiation of the operator that led to failure. Two approaches can be taken from here to prevent the latter operator from being reselected and applied again. The first is to let a default rule compare each operator to the most recent operator that failed and give it a reject preference if their descriptions match. The second is to *explicitly* learn that the failed operator is wrong. The second approach seems more appropriate, for it is in accordance with the psychological observation that failure is often a trigger for deliberate behavior. Thus, having reinstated the original state after an operator which is evaluated to failure, default rules install a *learn-reject operator* with the failed operator as its argument. Using common data chunking procedures, a chunk is learned to the effect that if task description = x and operator = y then y will be rejected. After rejecting this operator, other task operators get a chance. The processing just outlined can also be used for other symbolic evaluations such as success as well as numerical evaluations. This has not been tried out thus far, but no difficulties are expected.

Whereas it is important that destructive look-ahead search does not require a goal stack due to the absence of selection problem space and state copying, it does have a number of drawbacks. In the first place, the capability for backtracking is lost and, consequently, effort must be invested in storing the applied task operators. Effort is also required for creating and applying reversal operators—partly in order to regain a *non-automatic* capability to enable backtracking. In the second place, *explicit* learning is needed to control problem solving. And, finally, duplicate states become difficult to detect.

In non-destructive look-ahead search, the goal stack 'remembers,' as it were, choice points in the state space, that is, points where to backtrack. In destructive look-ahead search, on the other hand, it is necessary to take explicit action in order to return to previous states. This requires recalling at least the last operator that was applied so that Soar can go back at least one step and learn an evaluation for that operator. It is obvious that search efficiency will improve as the number of recalled operators increases. Also, Soar must be provided knowledge about how to create reversal operators and when to install them. The latter requirement is not too severe considering current Soar programming practice, because most Soar programs already contain productions that reject an inverse operator. Thus, for instance, after a $Move(x, L_1, L_2)$ has taken effect, $Move(x, L_2, L_1)$ is rejected as the next action. With the present scheme it must be enforced that they are generated. These inverse operators should not be rejected but just made worse and *marked* as reversal to the effect that they can be recognized when needed.

Reversal operators are, as argued above, also associated with the problem of finding a place to return to in the state space when it is or seems appropriate to do so. Note that automatic backtracking is one of the issues that the present scheme is meant to address. A phenomenological description of this situation is that occasionally we seem not to remember how we got into a certain state, that is, we do not know which operator or operator sequence will bring us back to some previous state. One reason may be that reversing a partial operator path leads to a state were no reversal operators can be recognized or created because there is no path information available. There are basically three options a search-based problem solver can adopt after reaching a state that does not contain reversal information. The first option is to continue with the current state and hope that eventually a solution will be found. The second is to jump back to the initial state. This is probably the simplest strategy a problem solver can use, also because the initial state often can be delivered by perception. The third option is to jump back to a stable intermediate state, which is only possible if the problem solver invests sufficient effort in 'remembering' important, or promising intermediate states it encounters.

As was pointed out earlier, with Soar's current default rules which arrange for look-ahead search, learning comes at almost no cost. When an operator is applied to a copy of a higher state and leads to an evaluation, this evaluation is translated into an appropriate preference for the operator. Since such an evaluation depends on the changed copy and the operator, and the copy in turn depends on the superstate, the resulting chunk will contain the appropriate state and operator conditions so that a correct evaluation chunk is learned. When, however, the goal stack is not used directly to select from a set of candidate operators, learning must be *deliberate*. It is indicated that we design a mechanism which guides building a chunk that references the appropriate state and operator in its condition side while its action side can add the relevant evaluation to the operator. To this end, we first explain how, in the destructive look-ahead scheme under discussion, explicit rejections are learned. Proposing and selecting a *learn-reject* operator has been explained previously. The recipe for implementing this operator consists of the following seven steps: (1) Operator *learn-reject* is installed, with as argument the operator to be rejected; (2) In every no-change subgoal that occurs the problem space "learn-reject" is proposed; (3) This particular problem space is preferred over all others whenever a *learn-reject* operator is detected in the operator slot of the supergoal: This problem space is now independent of the superoperator because the chunking mechanism does not backtrace through desirability preferences; (4) All superoperators are proposed; (5) The operator linked to the *learn-reject* operator as its argument is made best and installed in the operator slot of the subgoal; (6) Two productions *recognize* the top state and the operator in the slot, each adding a unique symbol to the state; And, (7) a default production looks for these two unique symbols and rejects the superoperator that should be rejected. This results in a chunk that is exactly the same as a chunk which gets built during Soar's current look-ahead search. It should be noted that this recipe can be used for explicit learning of all evaluations.

Having the reject action built into the right hand side of the chunk is the easiest part: it is just a consequence of the fact that a reject evaluation is the only 'result' that can obtain in the learn-reject problem space, once it is selected. The hard part is getting conditions on the left hand side right. For simple tasks it is easy to test for all aspects of the task representation and get the task representation as a whole into the condition part of the rule. However, this approach sometimes turns up overly specific chunks. Also, the recognition production is committed to test for all aspects of the task, whereas only a few of them may be needed. In the farmer puzzle, for instance, it will do no harm to test for the whole state, though the resulting chunks will be quite large, and probably expensive (Tambe & Newell, 1988). A further point is that a recognition production has to be written for every task, and this could be difficult if a task's representation tends to change during problem solving. One solution is to have a general *recognize operator* that checks the problem space symbol for the name of the relevant task class so that only the task-relevant information is recognized. Unfortunately, we will still get the whole task representation into the chunk and, consequently, the recognition process will be very slow. Another solution is to remember all the task objects that were modified, added, or deleted while applying an operator. When we backtrack by applying a reversal operator and want to have an evaluation chunk built for the companion task operator, we would need to recognize only the objects that have changed.[3] This solution is actually a syntactic one; it might be far better to rely on a semantic recognizer which can use the available task knowledge to investigate the relation between the operator to apply and the task objects.

A last point to consider is the detection of duplicate states. State-space search must also deal with the occurrence of cycles or duplicate states. Although it is undecidable whether a state higher up in the goal hierarchy and the current state that is a duplicate of the former can be said to serve the same function, it is nevertheless a good heuristic to avoid duplicate states. Using Soar's current default rules, for most tasks a production can be written that creates a reject preference for the current state when it is the same as a state higher in the context stack. Likewise, the present scheme needs a way to tell duplicate states apart and to act accordingly. It is obvious that dealing with such states has now become much more complex: how can a (current) state be compared with a previous state when the latter is nowhere around? If a state does not have a recognizer chunk, a *recognize-state operator* will build one for that state. A recognizer chunk will test for relevant aspects of the task state for which it was built and add a unique recognition symbol to it. The recognition symbol will disappear from a state if the state changes. Whenever an attempt is made to install the *recognize-state* operator for recognizing a given state and that state has already a unique symbol added to it, this should warn for the fact that the current state might be a duplicate of some previous state. This, of course, presupposes that one knows in advance that the state representation will never change.

A crucial advantage of the alternative just reviewed is that it potentially meets all requirements imposed by the various issues related to memory, search, and learning. As will become clear in the next section, it also provides a better ground for dealing with interrupts.

It should be noted that some attractive variations to Alternatives 1 and 2 can be constructed, for example by allowing only a single copy in the look-ahead search that they implement and then applying the ideas developed under Alternative 3. This suggestion implies that the goal stack can expand at most one level or, in other words, it can have just a top state and one substate, where the substate is a copy of the top state.

The Interrupt Issue and Its Relation to Default Behavior

Previous sections have dealt with memory, search, and learning issues engendered by a subset of Soar's default rules that organize problem solving in terms of the selection problem space, and alternative sets of rules that did not use this problem space at all. In this section we discuss the processing of interrupts which, in our opinion, must be taken as a basic, real-time operating characteristic of human behavior. For this reason, it constitutes an additional constraint on the "natural modes of operation" of problem solvers, human or artificial. Default behavior is of course one such mode.

If you are interrupted by the phone that starts ringing while in the midst of figuring out an algebra problem, you normally stop what you were doing, attend to the phone, and later return to the algebra problem. Or, while you are driving, you engage, still driving, in a conversation to settle a financial matter with a friend in the back seat. Since such examples can be multiplied indefinitely, it should be obvious that human behavior is strongly "interrupt-driven" (e.g., Reitman, 1965). Does Soar behave in the same way? Newell (1990) argues that it does. Soar is in principle capable of multitasking, of doing several tasks simultaneously (see Aasman & Michon, 1992). But, the fact is that the processing of interrupts doesn't mesh well with the basic "cognitive mode of operation" that current default rules implement.

Building the goal stack during tie handling is a process that takes a certain amount of time. Independent of the tie processing related to a task *A*, an interrupt cue may penetrate into the system (e.g., a ringing phone), or operators may be created at the top level for a different task (e.g, a conversation). These "interrupt" operators have in principle the capability to destroy the entire goal stack. Technically speaking, such operators (generated at the top level) may displace the original tied operators. As a result, the goal stack will be lost and needs to be rebuilt afterwards. The real-time constraint that this process imposes on the default rules is obvious: since the depth of a goal stack determines the time to rebuild the stack, it is more efficient to have flatter stacks. As was shown, this objective can be achieved by eliminating the selection problem space and/or state copying. It must be noted that there are alternatives to the view that the goal stack is lost. One is to include, like in older versions of Soar, a 'suspension' mechanism that restores the complete goal stack after an interrupt. Another is to insert interrupt operators in the most recent goal context (Hucka, 1989). The former requires extra space, and so aggravates the memory issue. The latter appears to be at variance with the principle that interrupts should be processed in the base-level problem space (Newell, 1990).

Table 1. *Rebuild Times For Different Rule Sets (Learning Mode On)*

Rules Involved	1st Operator	2nd Operator
Current default rules	20	34
Alternative 1	11	18
Alternative 2	13	26
Alternative 3	3	9

Adopting a set of default rules obviously determines to a great extent the temporal unfolding of behavior. Table 1 shows stack rebuild times that different sets of default rules require in terms of number of production cycles. Its first column indicates how long it takes to select and apply the first of the tied operators in look-ahead.

It is obvious that Soar's standard default rules take more cycles than any of the other approaches discussed in this paper. We first have to go through a selection problem space before we can apply an operator in look-ahead. Note that we have gained nine cycles by eliminating the selection problem space (Alternative 1). If we use the what-if approach (Alternative 2), the gain is slightly less but still impressive. Alternative 3, which implements destructive look-ahead, clearly wins. Measuring the rebuild time (in number of production cycles) by looking only at the first operator does not show the efficiency of the approach. We therefore included in the last column the time to reject the first operator, and then to select and try another operator. Here we observe that the elimination of the selection problem space is a real time saver; the overhead per operator is only seven cycles. It should be noted that the table includes numbers for Alternative 3 when no explicit learning is done. When learning is deliberate (see p. 201), Alternative 3 needs 20 cycles to reject the first operator, and then to select and try the second operator. This overhead is rather large, but for small *n* this alternative set of rules is still more efficient than Soar's current set of default rules.

Concluding Remarks

In this paper we have presented the results of a "breadth-first" effort to find suitable alternative sets of rules, similar in function to the current default rules, but satisfying an important set of requirements. The alternatives that have been considered have one property in common. They do not use the selection problem space which is essential to Soar's current default rules. If the selection problem space is eliminated, the goal stack flattens considerably. Alternative 3 is probably the most attractive one in that it adheres most strongly to the single state principle and obeys known constraints most closely. Also, it probably makes interaction with the external world as tractable as a recent scheme, based on the means-ends heuristic, that operates directly on the original task state (Akyürek, 1992). Some real problems seem to be raised by Alternative 3, and these will have to be addressed, but the approach successfully avoids serious issues related to memory, search, learning, and interaction with dynamic environments. Psychologists therefore should not be weary to use the destructive look-ahead search that it implements. With some effort, its current implementation can be changed so that it will allow the full functionality of the current default rules.

Acknowledgements

This work was supported by the Dienst Verkeerskunde van Rijkswaterstaat (Netherlands Ministry of Transport) under project number TO 8562, by IBM Nederland under a Study Contract with John A. Michon, and also in part by a grant (Dossier No. R 57-273) from the Netherlands Organization for Scientific Research (NWO) to the second author.

NOTES

[1] An earlier version of this paper was presented at the Seventh Soar Workshop, February 1990, Carnegie Mellon University, Pittsburgh, PA.

[2] Also known as "goal state" in artificial intelligence.

[3] This option has not been implemented.

REFERENCES

Aasman, J., & Michon, J. A. (1992). Multitasking in driving. In J. A. Michon & A. Akyürek (Eds.), *Soar: A cognitive architecture in perspective* (pp. 169-198). Dordrecht, The Netherlands: Kluwer.

Akyürek, A. (1992). Means-ends planning: An example Soar system. In J. A. Michon & A. Akyürek (Eds.), *Soar: A cognitive architecture in perspective* (pp. 109-167). Dordrecht, The Netherlands: Kluwer.

Bobrow, D. G., & Norman, D. A. (1975). Some principles of memory schemata. In D. G. Bobrow & A. Collins (Eds.), *Representation and understanding: Studies in cognitive science* (pp. 131-149). Orlando, FL: Academic Press.

Elgot-Drapkin, J., Miller, M., & Perlis, D. (1987). Life on a desert island: Ongoing work on real-time reasoning. In F. M. Brown (Ed.), *The frame problem in artificial intelligence* (pp. 349-357). Los Altos, CA: Morgan Kaufmann.

Hucka, M. (1989). *Planning, interruptability, and learning in Soar.* Unpublished manuscript, University of Michigan, Electrical Engineering and Computer Science De-partment, Ann Arbor.

Laird, J. E. (1984). *Universal subgoaling* (Tech. Rep. CMU-CS-84-129). Pittsburgh, PA: Carnegie Mellon University, Department of Computer Science. [Also available as part of Laird, J., Rosenbloom, P., & Newell, A. (1986). *Universal subgoaling and chunking: The automatic generation and learning of goal hierarchies* (pp. 1-131). Boston, MA: Kluwer.]

Laird, J. E., Congdon, C. B., Altmann, E., & Swedlow, K. (1990). *Soar user's manual: Version 5.2* (Tech. Rep. CMU-CS-90-179). Pittsburgh, PA: Carnegie Mellon University, School of Computer Science.

Laird, J. E., Newell, A., & Rosenbloom, P. S. (1987). SOAR: An architecture for general intelligence. *Artificial Intelligence, 33,* 1-64.

Laird, J., & Newell, A. (1983). *A universal weak method* (Tech. Rep. CMU-CS-83-141). Pittsburgh, PA: Carnegie Mellon University, Department of Computer Science.

Laird, J., Rosenbloom, P., & Newell, A. (1986). *Universal subgoaling and chunking: The automatic generation and learning of goal hierarchies.* Boston, MA: Kluwer.

Lewis, R. L., Huffman, S. B., John, B. E., Laird, J. E., Lehman, J. F., Newell, A., Rosenbloom, P. S., Simon, T., & Tessler, S. G. (1990). Soar as a unified theory of cognition: Spring 1990. In *Proceedings of the Twelfth Annual Conference of the Cognitive Sci-ence Society* (pp. 1035-1042). Hillsdale, NJ: Erlbaum.

Minton, S. (1988). *Learning search control knowledge: An explanation-based approach.* Boston, MA: Kluwer.

Newell, A. (1990). *Unified theories of cognition.* Cambridge, MA: Harvard University Press.

Newell, A., Rosenbloom, P. S., & Laird, J. E. (1989). Symbolic architectures for cognition. In M. I. Posner (Ed.), *Foundations of cognitive science* (pp. 93-131). Cambridge, MA: MIT Press.

Newell, A., & Simon, H. A. (1972). *Human problem solving.* Englewood Cliffs, NJ: Prentice-Hall.

Nilsson, N. J. (1971). *Problem-solving methods in artificial intelligence.* New York: McGraw-Hill.

Reitman, W. R. (1965). *Cognition and thought: An information-processing approach.* New York: Wiley.

Rich, E. (1983). *Artificial intelligence.* New York: McGraw-Hill.

Rosenbloom, P. S., Laird, J. E., Newell, A., & McCarl, R. (1991). A preliminary analysis of the Soar architecture as a basis for general intelligence. *Artificial Intelligence, 47,* 289-325.

Steier, D. M., Laird, J. E., Newell, A., Rosenbloom, P. S., Flynn, R. A., Golding, A., Polk, T. A., Shivers, O. G., Unruh, A., & Yost, G. R. (1987). Varieties of learning in Soar: 1987. In *Proceedings of the Fourth International Workshop on Machine Learning* (pp. 300-311). San Mateo, CA: Morgan Kaufmann.

Tambe, M., & Newell, A. (1988). Some chunks are expensive. In *Proceedings of the Fifth International Workshop on Machine Learning* (pp. 451-458). San Mateo, CA: Morgan Kaufmann.

Tambe, M., & Rosenbloom, P. S. (1989). Eliminating expensive chunks by restricting expressiveness. In *Proceedings of the Eleventh International Joint Conference on Artificial Intelligence* (pp. 731-737). San Mateo, CA: Morgan Kaufmann.

KNOWLEDGE LEVEL AND INDUCTIVE USES OF CHUNKING (EBL)

PAUL S. ROSENBLOOM
Information Sciences Institute, University of Southern California
Marina del Rey, California

AND

JANS AASMAN
Traffic Research Center, University of Groningen
Haren, The Netherlands

ABSTRACT. When explanation-based learning (EBL) is used for knowledge level learning (KLL), training examples are essential, and EBL is not simply reducible to partial evaluation. A key enabling factor in this behavior is the use of domain theories in which not every element is believed a priori. When used with such domain theories EBL provides a basis for rote learning (deductive KLL) and induction from multiple examples (nondeductive KLL). This article lays the groundwork for using EBL in KLL, by describing how EBL can lead to increased belief, and describes new results from using Soar's chunking mechanism—a variation on EBL—as the basis for a task-independent rote learning capability and a version-space-based inductive capability. This latter provides a compelling demonstration of nondeductive KLL in Soar, and provides the basis for an integration of conventional EBL with induction. However, it also reveals how one of Soar's key assumptions—the ***non-penetrable memory assumption***—makes this more complicated than it would otherwise be. This complexity may turn out to be appropriate, or it may point to where modifications of Soar are needed.

Introduction

Recent analytical papers on explanation-based learning (EBL) (DeJong & Mooney, 1986; Mitchell, Keller, & Kedar-Cabelli, 1986) comment on how training examples are not logically necessary for EBL (Prieditis, 1988; van

J. A. Michon and A. Akyürek (eds.), Soar: A Cognitive Architecture in Perspective, 219–234.

Harmelen & Bundy, 1988). Their point is that a training example may serve a useful search control function in EBL—guiding the learner to regions of performance which it would be useful to operationalize—but that the resulting operationalized rule is just a specialization, in the general case, of what a partial evaluation (PE) mechanism could achieve without the training example. This is an important point which reveals a previously submerged connection between learning and program transformation. However, it is flawed by its neglect of the use of EBL in knowledge level learning (KLL) (Flann & Dietterich, 1989; Rosenbloom, Laird, & Newell, 1987); that is, for the acquisition of knowledge not implied by what is already known (Dietterich, 1986). In such situations, the combination of the training example and goal concept—an *instance*—plays an essential role; one that is quite comparable to the role of instances in classic inductive concept learning systems.

The first task of this article is to lay necessary groundwork for the use of EBL in KLL. The key idea is to explain—actually, to *rationalize*—instances via a low-belief domain theory, and then to use EBL to acquire a high-belief rule from the rationalization. Unlike in PE, the instances play a crucial role here in determining what is rationalized, and thus what becomes believed. We then build on this foundation in the context of Soar (Laird, Newell, & Rosenbloom, 1987; Rosenbloom, Laird, Newell, & McCarl, 1991)—whose learning mechanism, chunking, is a variation on EBL (Rosenbloom & Laird, 1986) in which new rules are acquired from a dependency analysis of the traces of rules that fire during subgoal-based problem solving—to take several steps towards the realization of the *integrated-learning hypothesis* (Rosenbloom, 1988). This hypothesis states that "Rote learning, empirical generalization, and explanation-based learning arise as variations in the knowledge-reconstruction process," where "knowledge-reconstruction" should be read as "rationalization." Traditional explanation-based learning differs from rote memorization and induction in that the former uses only high-belief rationalizations while the latter two necessitate aspects that are initially low in belief. Rote memorization differs from induction in that the latter utilizes additional knowledge to affect rationalization.

The subsequent sections introduce a new task-independent, rote-memorization capability in Soar; extend this to induction from multiple examples, providing a compelling example of nondeductive knowledge level learning (NKLL) (Dietterich, 1986) in Soar, and introducing a complication caused by Soar's inability to directly examine its own rules; cover the third leg of the integrated-learning hypothesis, explanation-based learning, and its use in induction; and conclude.

EBL and KLL

EBL can be applied over many types of domain theories—the only requirement being the provision by the domain theory of a way to generate a (possibly generalized) dependency structure for the instance that relates the training example to the goal concept. In a classical EBL domain theory, all of the elements—e.g., facts and rules—are ascribed a uniform high level of belief. In such a domain theory, EBL performs symbol level learning by explicitly storing knowledge that is already implicit in this domain theory. However, it does not alter levels of belief—they are all already as high as they can get. For knowledge level learning, the domain theory needs to include low-belief elements. With such a theory, EBL can lead to knowledge level learning by increasing the level of belief in selected elements of the theory.

Consider the example of a system with a domain theory that allows it to abductively generate rationalizations—that is, plausible explanations—for what it sees (or hears). One of the key ways in which a rationalization differs from a simple deductive proof—as used in EBG (Mitchell, Keller, & Kedar-Cabelli, 1986), for example—is that the facts and rules utilized in a rationalization need not be completely believed in order to be used. It is in fact essential to the rationalization process that the system be able to derive from its domain theory not just facts that are known to be true, but also ones which are not yet believed. For example, suppose the instance consists of telling the system that "Fred, a dolphin, is warm blooded"—"Fred is a dolphin" is the training example, and "Fred is warm blooded" is the goal concept. To rationalize this knowledge it might use that "dolphins are mammals" and "mammals are warm blooded," even if its a priori belief is that dolphins are fish rather than mammals. This explanation could have been created in the absence of the instance, but it would have little a priori believability. It is the existence of the instance that provides grounds for increasing the believability of the explanation.

When this example is extended to the EBL/PE situation, it becomes clear that arbitrary rules created by partially evaluating this domain theory would have low believability, while comparable rules created by EBL for specific instances could have much higher believability. The instances allow EBL to increase the scope of what is believed, thus enabling knowledge level learning. In the extreme it is possible to start with a theory consisting of a generator able to produce data structures representing all possible pieces of knowledge, all with zero belief. Such a theory has all possible knowledge implicit in it, but none of it initially believed. EBL, in conjunction with appropriate instances, can then be used selectively to learn anything, by increasing the level of belief in the appropriate, possibly implicit, knowledge structures.

One way to view this process is as explicit belief propagation, where there are belief-propagation rules that are used to compute a level of belief for an explanation—and thus for the rules learned via EBL from the explanation—as a function of the believability of the individual domain theory elements and the instance. An alternative view of this process, and the one that guides the research reported here, is that the instance acts as a filter, letting through only those explanations which should be believed. Learning then only occurs for these believed explanations.

To support this type of processing, *plausible* domain theories—that is, theories in which only plausible explanations can be generated for conclusions—are required. Such a theory can potentially explain things that aren't true—necessitating the use of instances as filters—but what is true is explained in a plausible manner. As long as a domain theory meets this condition, the a priori believability of the individual elements of the theory can be zero without affecting the believability of what is learned. At the extreme end, the domain theory could contain elements which are not representational in the domain, such as the letter "d"—or which are representational but do not have belief values, such as "dolphin"—but which can be combined syntactically to generate elements which do have belief values.

Given EBL and plausible low-belief domain theories, the one missing component is what makes the newly learned rule believed. A variety of approaches are possible, including ones that augment the EBL mechanism to generate explicit belief values, and ones that partition learned rules—which automatically receive high belief—from domain theory rules. In Soar a variation on this latter approach is used. The domain theory corresponds to the problem space used in a subgoal (Rosenbloom & Laird, 1986)—in our case, this might be a *generation* problem space, where all possible structures are generatable, but none are believed. However, the learned rule is always created for the problem space in the parent goal; perhaps a *fact* problem space, in which all retrievable structures are believed. If restrictions are then placed on which problem spaces are utilized at any point in time, it is possible to know what level of belief—0 or 1—to assign to the retrieved knowledge. This point is related to the one recently made in Flann and Dietterich (1989). They focus on how EBL can perform KLL if an explanation that is generated for one concept is used to define a second concept that is a specialization of the first one. In our work, EBL performs KLL by transferring (possibly implicit) structures from an unbelieved domain theory to a believed domain theory that contains a subset of the structures in the original theory. Despite the differences, what both have in common—in fact, what every use of EBL for KLL must have in common—is that the learned knowledge is used differently than would be the domain theory from which it is learned. It can be used at a different belief level (as here), for a different goal concept (Flann & Dietterich, 1989), or even as evidence that a particular episode occurred (in which the rule was learned) (Rosenbloom, Newell, & Laird, in press).

Rote Memorization

In previous work this general approach to knowledge level learning has been employed to perform several simple rote memorization tasks—recognition, recall, cued recall, and paired-associate recall—for hierarchical letter strings and for objects that are described by attributes with values (Rosenbloom, Laird, & Newell, 1987; Rosenbloom, Laird, & Newell, 1989, Rosenbloom, Newell, & Laird, in press). This work also provided solutions for two additional problems that arise when rules are to be learned that recall new structure: (1) the *data chunking problem*—how to enable the retrieval of new information without its already being present—and (2) the *selective retrieval problem*—how to avoid retrieving everything ever learned. The data chunking problem is solved by reconstructing new knowledge from what is already known—that is, the domain theory—rather than directly rationalizing the input structures representing the new knowledge. Since this reconstruction process is not dependent on the input structures, tests of the input do not appear in the conditions of the learned rules. The selective retrieval problem is solved by selectively acquiring retrieval cues as conditions of learned rules.

Recently, this earlier work has been extended with the development of a general, task-independent rote-memorization operator. This is a normal Soar operator that uses problem solving in a subgoal to implement solutions to the data chunking and selective retrieval problems. The operator takes two arbitrary graphs of Soar working memory elements as inputs—the first is the training example, and the second is the goal concept. The result of memorizing the pair is the acquisition of a rule that tests for the existence of the first graph (the *cue graph*) and if the test succeeds, retrieves the second graph (the *recalled graph*) into working memory. To do this, the memorization operator reconstructs the recalled graph by assembling primitive domain-theory elements into a copy of the graph (solving the data chunking problem), and then makes this copy dependent on the structure of the cue graph (solving the selective retrieval problem). Figure 1 shows such a chunk, schematized as a pair of graph structures. The cue and recalled graphs are attached to the memorization operator in the rule's conditions and actions, respectively.

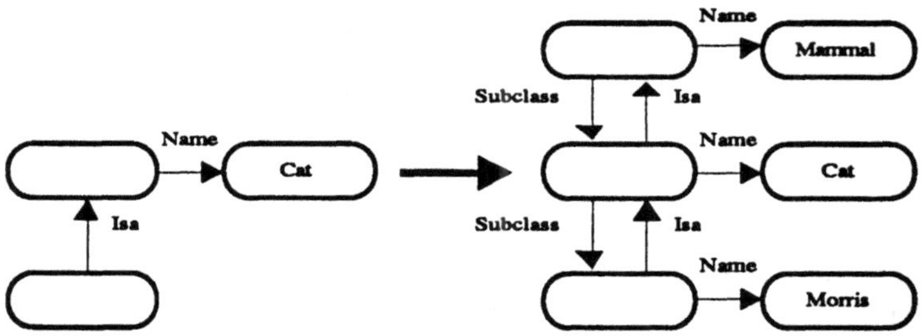

Figure 1. Chunk learned from memorizing a pair of graph structures.

Multi-Example Induction

When the contents of the initial domain theory are restricted to only elements that are completely believed, it is not possible for the domain theory itself to perform inductive leaps. If a system containing such a domain theory is to perform inductive generalization, it must be done outside the domain theory—in the EBL mechanism, for example. The most common approach is to augment EBL's standard explanation processing with some form of inductive postprocessing of either the entire explanation, or just its operational components (Flann & Dietterich, 1989; Hirsh, 1989; Sarrett & Pazzani, 1989).

If, on the other hand, the contents of the initial domain theory can include unbelieved elements, the option opens up of doing induction directly in the domain theory, and leaving explanation processing unaltered. This was proposed in Rosenbloom (1988) as part of the integrated-learning hypothesis, and is the approach taken here.[1] The domain theory includes knowledge about how to reconstruct presented objects (a stripped-down version of the task-independent memorization operator), generalization hierarchies (the basis of the concept language), rules which perform inductive leaps, and rules learned from prior instances. When a new instance is perceived, this domain theory is used to determine what is to be rationalized—it may be a generalization of the instance, rather than the instance itself—as well as how it should be rationalized.

One decision that must be made at this point is the orientation of the rule to be learned—whether the concept's name should be in the actions and its definition in the conditions, or vice versa. In EBL (and chunking), the concept definition appears in the conditions because that is where EBL has its primary generalization effect, and also where the definition can act as a recognizer of instances of the concept. However, to go beyond simple concept recognition—to retrieval and modification of the concept definition as further instances are processed—requires a fuller declarative access to the definition. Such access is not available in Soar if the definition is stored in the conditions because Soar's rule memory is *non-penetrable*—rules can be executed (forward), but can not be directly examined. Non-penetrability arises because the rules are compiled procedures that can be executed but not examined. In psychological terms, they represent *automatized* behavior (e.g., Shiffrin & Schneider, 1977). A consequence of non-penetrability is that, to access the concept definition explicitly, it must be stored in the rule's actions, where it can be retrieved by rule execution. Once retrieved, the concept definition can be used to influence what is learned for new instances, and to interpretively recognize instances of the concept (concept recognition rules, in which the definition is in the conditions, can be learned by chunking this interpretation process). As discussed later, the downside of this decision is that the generality of the concept definition is affected only by the decision of what to rationalize, and not by the rationalization process or the chunking/EBL mechanism.

The domain theory that has been implemented within Soar utilizes a variant of the Focussing algorithm (Young, Plotkin, & Linz, 1977; Bundy, Silver, & Plummer, 1985). This is a version space algorithm that works for spaces describable by a conjunction of attributes, where each attribute is defined by a tree-structured generalization hierarchy. The key ideas underlying the implemented algorithm are that: (1) the version space is kept factored—bounds are maintained independently for each attribute (Subramanian & Feigenbaum, 1986); (2) only near-miss negatives (Winston, 1975) are processed (the *zero option*)[2] to guarantee that the boundary sets will not fragment; and (3) once the first positive example is processed, the entire factored version space is explicitly represented, rather than just the boundary sets (at worst this requires space proportional to the number of attributes times the maximum depth of the generalization hierarchies).

Suppose that the task is to learn that the definition of (GOOD=TRUE) is (MOBILITY=MOBILE, SHAPE=ANY, SIZE=ANY). The algorithm starts with the goal concept, (GOOD=TRUE), and a positive example, such as (MOBILITY=WHEELED, SHAPE=SQUARE, SIZE=LARGE).[3] It then uses the generalization hierarchies in the domain theory to elaborate the example with all of the superclasses of its attributes' values, yielding for this case (MOBILITY={ANY, MOBILE, WHEELED}, SHAPE={ANY, POLYGON, REGULAR, SQUARE}, SIZE={ANY, LARGE}). This elaborated example is then memorized as the initial version space, with the retrieval cue being the goal concept:

(GOOD=TRUE) →
    (MOBILITY={ANY, MOBILE, WHEELED},
    SHAPE={ANY, POLYGON, REGULAR, SQUARE},
    SIZE={ANY, LARGE})

The memorization operator succeeds here only because the initial domain theory implicitly contains within itself every possible version space that could be generated for (GOOD=TRUE), all initially unbelieved. The example then determines which of these version spaces is explicitly stored, and thus believed.

When a succeeding positive example of this same goal concept is encountered, processing again begins by elaborating it with its values' superclasses. The current version space for the concept is then retrieved and compared to the elaborated example. All value classes in the concept version space that are not also in the elaborated example are then rejected from the version space (a form of incremental version space merging (Hirsh, 1989)). Chunking over this rejection process yields rules which, in the future, reject the inappropriate segments of the old version space. This rejection process is itself reconstructive so that the updated version space can later be retrieved without the presence of the positive example.

As an example, suppose that the next example for this goal concept is (MOBILITY=TRACKED, SHAPE=ELLIPSE, SIZE=LARGE), which when elaborated becomes (MOBILITY={ANY, MOBILE, TRACKED}, SHAPE={ANY, CONIC, ELLIPSE}, SIZE={ANY, LARGE}). From this example, the following rejection rules are learned:

(GOOD=TRUE, MOBILITY=WHEELED) →
    (MOBILITY=WHEELED) -
(GOOD=TRUE, SHAPE=POLYGON) → (SHAPE=POLYGON) -
(GOOD=TRUE, SHAPE=REGULAR) → (SHAPE=REGULAR) -
(GOOD=TRUE, SHAPE=SQUARE) → (SHAPE=SQUARE) -

The next time the same goal concept is seen, all five learned rules fire, yielding the following updated version space: (MOBILITY={ANY, MOBILE},

SHAPE=ANY, SIZE={ANY, LARGE}).

Learning from negative examples introduces an additional issue: because all of the knowledge learned from positive examples is cued off of (GOOD=TRUE), it will not be retrieved automatically for a negative example, where (GOOD=FALSE) (the converse is also true). The solution to this is to transiently cue with both TRUE and FALSE, thus retrieving all of the knowledge so far learned about the concept, and then to proceed to process the example while maintaining only the correct value (FALSE, in this case). Then, if the example is a near-miss—that is, if it mismatches in at most one attribute—those classes of the mismatched attribute that match are rejected from the version space. If the example is a far miss, it is ignored.

As an illustration, suppose the third example is the negative example (MOBILITY=STATIONARY, SHAPE=RECTANGLE, SIZE=LARGE). This example is elaborated with superclass information to become (MOBILITY={ANY, STATIONARY}, SHAPE={ANY, POLYGON, IRREGULAR, RECTANGLE}, SIZE={ANY, LARGE}), and then the existing information about the concept definition is retrieved. The mismatched attribute is MOBILITY, and the class that matches for that attribute is ANY. The rule learned for rejecting this class is:

(GOOD=FALSE, MOBILITY=ANY) → (MOBILITY=ANY) -

The resulting concept version space is (MOBILITY=MOBILE, SHAPE=ANY, SIZE={ANY, LARGE}).

These examples demonstrate that Soar can be used not only as the basis for rote memorization (deductive KLL), but also for induction (nondeductive KLL). Inductive augmentations of the EBL mechanism are not required, because the induction occurs directly in using the domain theory. As suggested by the integrated-learning hypothesis, rote learning and induction are distinguished by differences in the rationalization process. However, contrary to the intent of the hypothesis, the difference is in terms of what is rationalized rather than how it is rationalized (forced by the decision to store the concept definition in actions rather than conditions). In the induction case, rather than directly rationalizing the concept name in terms of the training example, it is rationalized in terms of the version space (or changes to it). This choice of what to rationalize is essentially a choice of what to learn. Here, this choice was based on the instance, the generalization hierarchies, the previous version space, and knowledge about how to induce. Bringing other knowledge to bear should allow additional useful variations on this choice.

Explanation-Based Learning

Using the chunking/EBL mechanism to perform explanation-based learning —that is, the standard form of symbol level learning—supports the third, and final leg of the integrated learning hypothesis. However, this needs no explicit demonstration here, as it is the foundational result of EBL. Instead, what is of interest here is the extent to which, in practice, this use of EBL can be integrated with the induction process described in the previous section. In this section we examine three successively weaker versions of this question. The first version is whether the direct use of EBL in induction, as described in the previous section, provides the requisite form of symbol level learning—that is, is EBL itself performing significant acts of "justifiable" generalization during induction? The answer, upon inspection, is "no." EBL is storing the results of inductive processing, but it is not itself contributing to their level of generalization. This is forced by the decision to store the concept definition in rule actions.

The second version is whether the standard use of EBL to perform symbol level learning—that is, with a classical believed domain theory—can help the inductive process described in the previous section (which is independently using EBL). The answer to this version of the question is once again "no." To see this, consider a domain theory with the following two believed rules.

(MOBILITY=WHEELED) → (FAST=TRUE)
(FAST=TRUE, SHAPE=CONIC) → (GOOD=TRUE)

If these rules are used to relate the training example to the goal concept, the following rule is learned.

(MOBILITY=WHEELED, SHAPE=CONIC) → (GOOD=TRUE)

This is exactly what EBL should learn. However, it is difficult to use in the induction process described in the previous section because the generalized example is in the conditions of the rule—thus the rule retrieves the goal concept when a matched training example is present, rather than retrieving the generalized example when the goal concept is present. This failure is disturbing because this is the type of gain achieved by other hybrid approaches, such as Flann and Dietterich (1989), Hirsh (1989), and Sarrett and Pazzani (1989). In these other approaches, this problem is solved by enabling the induction process to directly access the explanation, its operational fringe, or the resulting rule. In the present approach, the rule can be fired, but neither it nor any part of the explanation can be directly examined.

The third version is whether some form of explanation-based learning can lead to generalizations that are useful in the induction process described in the previous section. The answer here is finally "yes." However, it requires augmenting the domain theory itself with the ability to interpret rules and to generate and process explanations. These rules are not Soar's native rules, but declarative structures of limited expressibility that are stored in the actions of Soar's rules. These rules are retrieved as needed to support a backward-chaining process that starts with the goal concept and ends when it grounds out in attribute-value pairs contained in the elaborated example (the operational predicates). The operational fringe of the explanation derived from this process is a generalization of the example. Based on the approach in Hirsh (1989), this generalized example is used in induction by converting it into an explicit, factored version space—by assigning values to unmentioned attributes ({ANY} for positive examples, and the values in the concept version space for negative examples) and then elaborating it with superclasses—and then merging it with the current concept version space.

As illustration, consider the positive example (MOBILITY=WHEELED, SHAPE=CIRCLE, SIZE=SMALL), which becomes upon elaboration (MOBILITY={ANY, MOBILE, WHEELED}, SHAPE={ANY, CONIC, CIRCLE}, SIZE={ANY, SMALL}). If the domain theory consists of the two rules above, backward chaining yields an operational fringe of (MOBILITY=WHEELED, SHAPE=CONIC), which is more general than the original example because it ignores SIZE, and generalizes SHAPE from CIRCLE to CONIC. When this generalized example is extended to cover the unmentioned attributes, and elaborated, it becomes (MOBILITY={ANY, MOBILE, WHEELED}, SHAPE={ANY, CONIC}, SIZE=ANY). When this description is then merged with the concept version space, the result is (MOBILITY=MOBILE, SHAPE=ANY, SIZE=ANY). The rule learned from this processing is:

(GOOD=TRUE) → (SIZE=LARGE) -

This same general approach can be used to incorporate other forms of knowledge into the induction process. So far, we have partial implementations of the use of irrelevance knowledge (Subramanian & Genesereth, 1987) and determinations (Davis & Russell, 1987; Mahadevan, 1989; Russell, 1988; Widmer, 1989) in the induction process.

When taken together, the answers to the three versions of the question reveal that explanations can be effectively combined with induction in this approach, but that this is achieved only by building additional declarative rule interpretation and EBL mechanisms into the domain theory. The native mechanisms are not usable because there is no way to access the rules (or explanations) they create as declarative structures, as required by the induction process.

The question this raises is whether this is evidence that the Soar architecture needs to be changed or is evidence that some of our preconceived notions about induction, and its interaction with chunking/EBL, need to be changed. While the former is a distinct possibility, the utility of architectures as theories of intelligence stems in large part from their ability to predict unexpected but important phenomena. If the architecture is changed whenever one of its consequences violates preconceived notions, this benefit is lost. Also potentially lost are the positive consequences of the way the changed component currently works. The component is usually the way it is for good reason, which in this case is the ability to model basic aspects of human memory. Thus it is useful, before jumping in and changing the architecture, to first consider the possibility that Soar is revealing something important here. When this is done, at least one intriguing speculation arises—that chunking and EBL, though quite similar in mechanism (both compile dependency structures), are really distinct capabilities. Chunking is an automatic architectural process (it learns for every result of every subgoal, and does not compete for cognitive resources with performance), of fixed capability (how it works is not affected by what the system knows), which compiles recognition-driven procedures (productions) from experience. It is an appropriate, and effective, generalized long-term caching mechanism; but it really is a low-level mechanism that is in some ways more analogous to neural-network learning algorithms than to EBL. However, an intelligent system also needs to be able to deliberately create and utilize declarative explanations of new phenomena. This is where EBL, as used here in concept learning, comes in. It is a deliberate cognitive process, of open capability, which processes and creates declarative structures that can be used in induction, and which can also yield behavior, but only indirectly, through interpretation.

Conclusions

By making a distinction between what is in the domain theory (either implicitly or explicitly) and what is believed, it is possible to distinguish the symbol level and knowledge level uses of EBL—symbol level uses make implicit knowledge explicit, while knowledge level uses make unbelieved knowledge believed. This idea has been explored here as the foundation for chunking (EBL)-based rote memorization (deductive KLL) and induction (non-deductive KLL) capabilities. Utilizing unbelieved knowledge enables induction to be performed in the domain theory itself, rather than as a post hoc process. Chunking is used in this induction process to store the initial version space, and to record modifications to it that are required by new instances of the concept. These capabilities demonstrate why EBL is not simply reducible to partial evaluation—the training examples are essential.

When combined with the standard use of EBL for symbol level learning, these capabilities provide the three legs of support required by the integrated learning hypothesis. However, the support is weakened by the difference between rote learning and induction arising from differences in what is rationalized rather than how it is rationalized. Further weakening is engendered by the difficulty in using EBL to generalize instances for use by induction. This has been accomplished, but only by implementing an additional declarative EBL mechanism in the domain theory. Both of these weaknesses occur because of the choice to store the inductive concept definition in the actions of learned rules (rather than in the conditions), which is itself forced by the non-penetrability of Soar's rules, and the resulting difficulty in determining the contents of rule conditions. As discussed in the previous section, this may actually turn out to be appropriate, or it may reveal an aspect of Soar that should be altered.[4]

Acknowledgements

This research was sponsored by the National Aeronautics and Space Administration under cooperative agreement number NCC 2-538, and by the Defense Advanced Research Projects Agency (DOD) under contract number N00039-86C-0033 (via subcontract from the Knowledge Systems Laboratory, Stanford University). We would like to thank Yoram Reich, Haym Hirsh, Craig Miller, Peter Pirolli, and John Laird for their helpful comments.

NOTES

[1]Widmer recently proposed a similar "Explain and Compile" approach to using EBL over an expanded range of domain theories (Widmer, 1989). Anderson has also used knowledge compilation, a form of EBL, over analogical and discriminative theories (Anderson,1986).

[2]With a suitable training order, far misses are not needed for convergence (Bundy, Silver, & Plummer, 1985).

[3]This example, and all later ones have been implemented in Soar (Version 5.0.2), and verified to run correctly.

[4]*Editorial note*. Both reference citations in text and reference list have been adapted to the APA style used in this book.

REFERENCES

Anderson, J. R. (1986). Knowledge compilation: The general learning mechanism. In R. S. Michalski, J. G. Carbonell, & T. M. Mitchell (Eds.), *Machine learning: An artificial intelligence approach* (Vol. II, pp. 289-310). Los Altos, CA: Morgan Kaufmann.

Bundy, A., Silver, B., & Plummer, D. (1985). An analytical comparison of some rule-learning programs. *Artificial Intelligence*, *27*, 137-181.

Davies, T. R., & Russell, S. J. (1987). A logical approach to reasoning by analogy. In *Proceedings of the Tenth International Joint Conference on Artificial Intelligence* (pp. 264-270). San Mateo, CA: Morgan Kaufmann.

DeJong, G., & Mooney, R. J. (1986). Explanation-based learning: An alternative view. *Machine Learning*, *1*, 145-176.

Dietterich, T. G. (1986). Learning at the knowledge level. *Machine Learning*, *1*, 287-315.

Flann, N. S., & Dietterich, T. G. (1989). A study of explanation-based methods for inductive learning. *Machine Learning*, *4*, 187-226.

Hirsh, H. (1989). Combining empirical and analytical learning with version spaces. In *Proceedings of the Sixth International Workshop on Machine Learning* (pp. 29-33). San Mateo, CA: Morgan Kaufmann.

Laird, J. E., Newell, A., & Rosenbloom, P. S. (1987). SOAR: An architecture for general intelligence. *Artificial Intelligence*, *33*, 1-64.

Mahadevan, S. (1989). Using determinations in EBL: A solution to the incomplete theory problem. In *Proceedings of the Sixth International Workshop on Machine Learning* (pp. 320-325). San Mateo, CA: Morgan Kaufmann.

Mitchell, T. M., Keller, R. M., & Kedar-Cabelli, S. T. (1986). Explanation-based generalization: A unifying view. *Machine Learning*, *1*, 47-80.

Prieditis, A. E. (1988). Environment-guided program transformation. G. F. DeJong (Ed.), *Proceedings of the AAAI Symposium on Explanation-Based Learning* (pp. 201-209). Stanford, CA: American Association for Artificial Intelligence.

Rosenbloom, P. S. (1988). Beyond generalization as search: Towards a unified framework for the acquisition of new knowledge. G. F. DeJong (Ed.), *Proceedings of the AAAI Symposium on Explanation-Based Learning* (pp. 17-21). Stanford, CA: American Association for Artificial Intelligence.

Rosenbloom, P. S., & Laird, J. E. (1986). Mapping explanation-based generalization onto Soar. In *Proceedings of the Fifth National Conference on Artificial Intelligence* (pp. 561-567). San Mateo, CA: Morgan Kaufmann.

Rosenbloom, P. S., Laird, J. E., & Newell, A. (1987). Knowledge level learning in Soar. In *Proceedings of the Sixth National Conference on Artificial Intelligence* (pp. 499-504). San Mateo, CA: Morgan Kaufmann.

Rosenbloom, P. S., Laird, J. E., Newell, A. (1989). The chunking of skill and knowledge. In B. A. G. Elsendoorn & H. Bouma (Eds.), *Working models of human perception* (pp. 391-410). London: Academic Press.

Rosenbloom, P. S., Laird, J. E., Newell, A., & McCarl, R. (1991). A preliminary analysis of the Soar architecture as a basis for general intelligence. *Artificial Intelligence, 47,* 289-325.

Rosenbloom, P. S., Newell, A., & Laird, J. E. (in press). Towards the knowledge level in Soar: The role of the architecture in the use of knowledge. In K. VanLehn (Ed.), *Architectures for intelligence*. Hillsdale, NJ: Erlbaum.

Russell, S. J. (1988). Tree-structured bias. In *Proceedings of the Seventh National Conference on Artificial Intelligence* (pp. 641-645). San Mateo, CA: Morgan Kaufmann.

Sarrett, W. E., & Pazzani, M. J. (1989). One-sided algorithms for integrating empirical and explanation-based learning. In *Proceedings of the Sixth International Workshop on Machine Learning* (pp. 26-28). San Mateo, CA: Morgan Kaufmann.

Shiffrin, R. M., & Schneider, W. (1977). Controlled and automatic human information processing: II. Perceptual learning, automatic attending, and a general theory. *Psychological Review, 84,* 127-190.

Subramanian, D., & Feigenbaum, J. (1986). Factorization in experiment generation. In *Proceedings of the Fifth National Conference on Artificial Intelligence* (pp. 518-522). San Mateo, CA: Morgan Kaufmann.

Subramanian, D., & Genesereth, M. R. (1987). The relevance of irrelevance. In *Proceedings of the Tenth International Joint Conference on Artificial Intelligence* (pp. 416-422). San Mateo, CA: Morgan Kaufmann.

van Harmelen, F., & Bundy, A. (1988). Explanation-based generalization = partial evaluation. *Artificial Intelligence, 36*, 401-412.

Widmer, G. (1989). A tight integration of deductive and inductive learning. In *Proceedings of the Sixth International Workshop on Machine Learning* (pp. 11-13). San Mateo, CA: Morgan Kaufmann.

Winston, P. H. (1975). Learning structural descriptions from examples. In P. H. Winston, (Ed.), *The psychology of computer vision* (pp. 157-209). New York: McGraw-Hill.

Young, R. M., Plotkin, G. D., & Linz, R. F. (1977). Analysis of an extended concept-learning task. In *Proceedings of the Fifth International Joint Conference on Artificial Intelligence* (p. 285). San Mateo, CA: Morgan Kaufmann.

BASIC REFERENCES FOR SOAR

Although the papers in this volume should be accessible to cognitive scientists and computers scientists, additional reading may be required, as Soar concepts and Soar terminology are still somewhat unfamiliar. The following bibliography was recently prepared; it lists the papers that are considered by the Soar community as required reading for a *tour d'horizon* of Soar. There are many other papers that describe Soar research and there is a Soar Reference List which gives them all. That list can be obtained by sending a request by e-mail to soar-doc@cs.cmu.edu or by writing to the Soar Group, School of Computer Science, Carnegie Mellon University, 5000 Forbes Ave., Pittsburgh, Pennsylvania 15213-3890, USA.[1]

BASIC DESCRIPTION OF SOAR AS A SYSTEM

Rosenbloom, P. S., Laird, J. E., Newell, A., & McCarl, R. (1991). A preliminary analysis of the Soar architecture as a basis for general intelligence. *Artificial Intelligence, 47,* 289-325.

Laird, J. E., Newell, A., & Rosenbloom, P. S. (1987). SOAR: An architecture for general intelligence. *Artificial Intelligence, 33,* 1-64.

Laird, J. E., Congdon, C. B., Altmann, E., & Swedlow, K. (1990). *Soar user's manual: Version 5.2* (Tech. Rep. CMU-CS-90-179). Pittsburgh, PA: Carnegie Mellon University, School of Computer Science. This report is also available from the Department of Electrical Engineering and Computer Science, University of Michigan, Ann Arbor, Michigan.

Steier, D. M., Laird, J. E., Newell, A., Rosenbloom, P. S., Flynn, R. A., Golding, A., Polk, T. A., Shivers, O. G., Unruh, A., & Yost, G. R. (1987). Varieties of learning in Soar: 1987. In *Proceedings of the Fourth International Workshop on Machine Learning* (pp. 300-311). San Mateo, CA: Morgan Kaufmann.

UNIFIED THEORY OF COGNITION

Lewis, R. L., Huffman, S. B., John, B. E., Laird, J. E., Lehman, J. F., Newell, A., Rosenbloom, P. S., Simon, T., & Tessler, S. G. (1990). Soar as a unified theory of cognition: Spring 1990. In *Proceedings of the Twelfth Annual Conference of the Cognitive Science Society* (pp. 1035-1042). Hillsdale, NJ: Erlbaum.

Newell, A. (1990). *Unified theories of cognition*. Cambridge, MA: Harvard University Press.

SPECIAL TOPICS

Lehman, J. F., Lewis, R. L., & Newell, A. (1991). *Integrating knowledge sources in language comprehension.* Manuscript submitted for publication. This report is also available from the School of Computer Science, Carnegie Mellon University,.Pittsburg, Pennsylvania.

Tambe, M., Newell, A., & Rosenbloom, P. S. (1990). The problem of expensive chunks and its solution by restricting expressiveness. *Machine Learning*, *5*, 299-348.

Laird, J. E., & Rosenbloom, P. S. (1990). Integrating execution, planning, and learning in Soar for external environments. In *Proceedings of the Eight National Conference on Artificial Intelligence* (pp. 1022-1029). San Mateo, CA: Morgan Kaufmann.

Yost, G. R., & Newell, A. (1989). A problem space approach to expert system specification. In *Proceedings of the Eleventh International Joint Conference on Artificial Intelligence* (pp. 621-627). San Mateo, CA: Morgan Kaufmann.

Rosenbloom, P. S. (1989). A symbolic goal-oriented perspective on connectionism and Soar. In R. Pfeiffer, Z. Schreter, F. Fogelman-Soulié, & L. Steels (Ed.), *Connectionism in perspective* (pp. 245-263). Amsterdam: North-Holland.

Tambe, M., Kalp, D., Gupta, A., Forgy, C. L., Milnes, B. G., & Newell, A. (1988). Soar/PSM-E: Investigating match parallelism in a learning production system. In *Proceedings of the ACM/SIGPLAN Symposium on Parallel Programming: Experience with Applications, Languages, and Systems* (pp. 146-160). San Mateo, CA: Morgan Kaufmann.

Rosenbloom, P. S., & Laird, J. E. (1986). Mapping explanation-based generalization onto Soar. In *Proceedings of the Fifth National Conference on Artificial Intelligence* (pp. 561-567). San Mateo, CA: Morgan Kaufmann.

Laird, J. E. (1991). *Extending problem spaces to external environments.* Unpublished manuscript, Department of Electrical Engineering and Computer Science, University of Michigan, Ann Arbor.

NOTE

[1]The Soar system has been put into the public domain and may be obtained by anonymous FTP from the address centro.soar.cs.cmu.edu [128.2.242.245] by retrieving the file: /afs/cs.cmu.edu/project/soar/5.2/2/public/compressedSoar.5.2.2.tar.Z.

AUTHOR INDEX

SUBJECT INDEX

STUDIES IN COGNITIVE SYSTEMS

Series Editor: James H. Fetzer, *University of Minnesota, Duluth*

1. J. H. Fetzer (ed.): *Aspects of Artificial Intelligence.* 1988
   ISBN 1-55608-037-9; Pb 1-55608-038-7
2. J. Kulas, J.H. Fetzer and T.L. Rankin (eds.): *Philosophy, Language, and Artificial Intelligence.* Resources for Processing Natural Language. 1988
   ISBN 1-55608-073-5
3. D.J. Cole, J.H. Fetzer and T.L. Rankin (eds.): *Philosophy, Mind and Cognitive Inquiry.* Resources for Understanding Mental Processes. 1990
   ISBN 0-7923-0427-6
4. J.H. Fetzer: *Artificial Intelligence: Its Scope and Limits.* 1990
   ISBN 0-7923-0505-1; Pb 0-7923-0548-5
5. H.E. Kyburg, Jr., R.P. Loui and G.N. Carlson (eds.): *Knowledge Representation and Defeasible Reasoning.* 1990 ISBN 0-7923-0677-5
6. J.H. Fetzer (ed.): *Epistemology and Cognition.* 1991
   ISBN 0-7923-0892-1
7. E.C. Way: *Knowledge Representation and Metaphor.* 1991
   ISBN 0-7923-1005-5
8. J. Dinsmore: *Partitioned Representations.* A Study in Mental Representation, Language Understanding and Linguistic Structure. 1991
   ISBN 0-7923-1348-8
9. T. Horgan and J. Tienson (eds.): *Connectionism and the Philosophy of Mind.* 1991 ISBN 0-7923-1482-4
10. J.A. Michon and A. Akyürek (eds.): *Soar: A Cognitive Architecture in Perspective.* 1992 ISBN 0-7923-1660-6

KLUWER ACADEMIC PUBLISHERS – DORDRECHT / BOSTON / LONDON

MIX
Papier aus verantwortungsvollen Quellen
Paper from responsible sources
FSC® C105338
FSC
www.fsc.org

If you have any concerns about our products,
you can contact us on
ProductSafety@springernature.com

In case Publisher is established outside the EU,
the EU authorized representative is:
Springer Nature Customer Service Center GmbH
Europaplatz 3, 69115 Heidelberg, Germany

Printed by Libri Plureos GmbH
in Hamburg, Germany